Sacred Psychology

Global Philosophy

Series Editor—Mohammed Rustom,
Carleton University / Tokat Institute for Advanced Islamic Studies

Given the tremendous amount of interest in non-Western philosophy today, teachers, students, and the general public are beginning to come away with a clearer picture of what "philosophy" means in various civilizations and to large sectors of humanity beyond the Anglo-American and European worlds. This series in global philosophy seeks to further this interest by highlighting the epistemic diversity and profound insights of Africana, Buddhist, Confucian, Hindu, Islamic, Jain, Jewish, Latin American, Mesoamerican, Native American, Russian, and Taoist philosophy. To accomplish its goals, the series focuses on publishing accessible and lively books on these philosophical traditions and scholarly translations of their key works.

PUBLISHED

A Sourcebook in Global Philosophy
Edited by Mohammed Rustom

Exploring Hindu Philosophy
Ankur Barua

Exploring Islamic Philosophy
Sayeh Meisami

What Is Metaphysics? Ruminations on Principial Knowledge and Some of Its Applications
Seyyed Hossein Nasr

Sacred Psychology

A Global Perspective

SAMUEL BENDECK SOTILLOS

equinox

SHEFFIELD uk   BRISTOL ct

Published by Equinox Publishing Ltd.

UK: Office 415, The Workstation, 15 Paternoster Row, Sheffield, South Yorkshire S1 2BX

USA: ISD, 70 Enterprise Drive, Bristol, CT 06010

www.equinoxpub.com

First published 2025

British Library Cataloguing-in-Publication Data

A catalogue record for this book is available from the British Library.

ISBN-13   978 1 80050 573 5   (hardback)
            978 1 80050 574 2   (paperback)
            978 1 80050 575 9   (ePDF)
            978 1 80050 667 1   (ePub)

Library of Congress Cataloging-in-Publication Data

Names: Bendeck Sotillos, Samuel, 1972- author.
Title: Sacred psychology : a global perspective / Samuel Bendeck Sotillos.
Description: Sheffield, South Yorkshire ; Bristol, CT : Equinox Publishing Ltd, [2025] | Series: Global philosophy | Includes bibliographical references and index. | Summary: "A true "science of the soul" has existed for millennia in all the world's diverse spiritual cultures. Although a plethora of modern therapies are now available, they are hindered in their efficacy by having become entirely divorced from sacred reality. This work argues that it is necessary to restore this "science of the soul" by drawing on the perspective of non-Western wisdom traditions as understood since time immemorial. Furthermore, this book shows how non-Western philosophy can help rehabilitate an authentically healing psychology in support of promoting sound mental health in our afflicted modern culture. Sacred psychologies afford us the best opportunity to tackle the innumerable challenges that confront human beings today, such as trauma, mental illness, addiction, death, and the meaning of our lives"-- Provided by publisher.
Identifiers: LCCN 2025013399 (print) | LCCN 2025013400 (ebook) | ISBN 9781800505735 (hardback) | ISBN 9781800505742 (paperback) | ISBN 9781800505759 (pdf) | ISBN 9781800506671 (epub)
Subjects: LCSH: Psychology and religion | Psychology--Religious aspects | Psychology--Philosophy | Healing-- Religious aspects | Healing--Psychological aspects
Classification: LCC BF51 .B46 2025 (print) | LCC BF51 (ebook)
LC record available at https://lccn.loc.gov/2025013399
LC ebook record available at https://lccn.loc.gov/2025013400

Typeset by Scribe Inc.

Contents

Series Foreword

Given the tremendous amount of interest in non-Western philosophy today, teachers, students, and the general public are beginning to come away with a clearer picture of what "philosophy" means in various civilizations and to large sectors of humanity beyond the Anglo-American and European worlds. This series in global philosophy seeks to further this interest by highlighting the epistemic diversity and profound insights of Africana, Buddhist, Confucian, Hindu, Islamic, Jain, Jewish, Latin American, Mesoamerican, Native American, Russian, and Taoist philosophy. To accomplish its goals, the series focuses on publishing accessible and lively books on these philosophical traditions, as well as scholarly translations of their key works.

Mohammed Rustom
Series Editor, *Global Philosophy*
Carleton University / Tokat Institute for Advanced Islamic Studies

Acknowledgments

My deep gratitude goes to John Paraskevopoulos and Abigail Tardiff of the Radius Foundation for their thorough reading of the manuscript, as well as for their substantial editorial advice and other recommendations. Many thanks are also due to William Stoddart (1925–2023) and M. Ali Lakhani for their insightful suggestions regarding several important passages in this book. My appreciation is also extended to Huston Smith (1919–2016), Wolfgang Smith (1930–2024), Laleh Bakhtiar (1938–2020), Marty Glass (1938–2022), Mahmood Bina (1938–2025), and Seyyed Hossein Nasr for sharing their discerning insights during the course of many helpful conversations on the theme of psychology. I am very thankful to Sharon Hamrick and St. Patrick's Seminary and University, who assisted me with obtaining difficult and hard-to-find journal articles and other literature that was invaluable to the work. I am very grateful to Professor Mohammed Rustom and the staff at Equinox Publishing, who saw this book to its completion. I am also indebted to those anonymous readers who reviewed the manuscript prior to publication for their thoughtful comments.

Furthermore, my sincere thanks go to the following for their kind permission to reproduce earlier versions of the articles that appear in this publication: Martin Dojčár, editor of *Spirituality Studies* (chapters 1 and 5); M. Ali Lakhani, editor of *Sacred Web* (chapters 2 and 4); Seyed G. Safavi, editor of *Transcendent Philosophy*, and the London Academy of Iranian Studies (chapter 3); and John Carey, editor of the *Temenos Academy Review*, and the Temenos Academy (chapter 6). Their kind consent is greatly appreciated.

Introduction

THEORETICAL PRESUPPOSITIONS

Our world today is afflicted with a radical instability that is creating fissures both in society at large and within ourselves. Never before in history have there been so many people struggling with mental health problems and addictions of all types, nor have we seen so much reliance on psychotropic medications or been rocked by such an unprecedented rise in suicides. What does all this mean for our psychological well-being, and how can we ensure our psychic health in a world that has completely lost its bearings?

Some will dispute this assessment of the world today by suggesting that there was never a time when things were in a state of perfect order and that the world has always been the way that it is. Others will say that it only appears to be in greater disarray because of our access to immediate (and incessant) media coverage of events from all over the world, which we were spared from in the past. While these elements may indeed contribute to the disorder around us, they do not quite account for the acutely dysfunctional conditions in which we find ourselves right now. Many of us find that our lives are hurtling toward a destination that we feel unable to control or influence.

The dystopic narratives captured in popular novels and films—which portray a foreign and unimaginably distant future—are, in fact, unfolding now in these very times.

Although much has been written about how to avert the worst consequences of our current global mental health crisis (e.g., by using improved self-care, novel therapeutic modalities, psychotropic interventions, and other alternative approaches), none of these have proven sufficient to ameliorate our predicament.

Modern Western psychology dominates every attempt to address this global mental health crisis as if it were the only psychology available to us. It is astonishing to find that this is very much the case in practically every part of the world, and if you suggest that there is another possible worldview, you are met with bewilderment. This reaction reflects a hardened conviction that there is only one kind of psychology (the modern, Western variety) while failing to acknowledge the many other approaches we find in the diverse experiences of traditional peoples and their healing

1

arts. These ancient cultures exhibit a fully integrated psychology that is informed by a metaphysical framework rooted in the sacred—one that is capable of providing a more effective and enduring kind of wholeness.

Accordingly, this book will show how the hegemonic agenda of modern science served to spawn the desacralized form of psychology that we know today. Furthermore, it will demonstrate how this exclusive way of understanding the human psyche has been imposed on people the world over in a manner that is nothing short of totalitarian and colonialist. The word *science* comes from the Latin word *scientia*, which literally means "knowledge." Yet we may well ask what kind of knowledge is offered to us by psychology today. After all, do not the diverse cultures of traditional humanity also have their own forms of knowledge about the human psyche, which are a kind of science even if that word is not used to describe them? It is as if the modern discipline of psychology suffers from amnesia—or worse, that our profane scientific culture privileges its own knowledge claims above those of other, older civilizations that possess impressive healing lore that is, lamentably, either ignored or derided.

Modern science certainly has its place, but it must not stray beyond the confines of its epistemological competence by claiming a monopoly on knowledge to which it is not entitled. When it does trespass in this way, it becomes the ideology of "scientism," the view that the Western scientific method offers the sole means of understanding reality (that is, in purely materialist terms). This aberration has persisted since the Enlightenment project—or the "Age of Reason"—from the seventeenth to eighteenth centuries onward. It is noteworthy that, while this movement took root in the ambiance of a burgeoning modernity, it was not a natural outgrowth of Christianity but, rather, a repudiation of its sacred tenets.

Prior to this secular trajectory that took root in the West, the Christian tradition shared a common metaphysical understanding of reality with other spiritual traditions of the world. It is this sacred epistemology that provides an integrated understanding of the human being that has always connected people to the Divine. The development of modern Western psychology, as a discipline completely divorced from its more ancient forebears, stems from the desacralized reductionism inaugurated by the European Enlightenment—a pernicious legacy that persists to this day.

Paradoxically, psychology is considered the study of the psyche or soul, yet its very science denies the spiritual dimension altogether, which, in turn, vitiates its ability to serve as an authentic psychology.

In the traditional world, reason was understood to be a bridge between the realms of matter and spirit. With the modern world having lost any sense of the sacred, the "culture of therapy" has in many ways come to attempt to fill that void (effectively replacing religion altogether). With this shift, the "eye of the heart"—our means of directly knowing spiritual reality—has been supplanted by mere reason and sensorial perception. Mainstream psychology is very much limited to a truncated epistemology that cannot provide any integrated modes of healing because it has severed its kinship with transcendent reality.

If we embrace a vision of life that is enriched by the timeless wisdom found at the heart of the world's spiritual traditions—with their profound and far-reaching "science of the soul"—we may yet find the answers we are so desperately seeking. The real cause of the global mental health crisis is that we have forgotten who we are and what it truly means to be human.

There cannot be a restoration of true mental health in a world that is bereft of meaning, and it is only through a reconnection with the metaphysical dimension of existence that an abiding wholeness in our being can begin to flourish once more. The fissures of the post-Enlightenment world are not easily remedied, even with a person's full embrace of a spiritual path and its integrated therapies. In other words, there are psychological problems that may not be alleviated by therapies informed by a sacred tradition. This is not because of any inherent limitations to the "science of the soul" but, rather, the result of cosmological factors whereby some people's trials in this world require periods of instability in one's psyche. These difficulties are not without compensation, one being an increased proximity to Divine Reality (should they be receptive to this calling). So while we must recognize that there can be impediments to the application of sacred psychology in certain cases, the spiritual recompense available in these circumstances should not be overlooked.

This work comprises a collection of articles, written over several years, that have previously been published in a variety of journals devoted to these themes. They were originally written as self-contained essays and were not conceived with a book in mind. Because each essay is now a separate chapter of this work, the reader will find some repetition of certain themes. Various terms and phrases are employed synonymously with *sacred psychology* such as "science of the soul," "spiritual psychology," "traditional psychology," "salvific psychology," and "pneumatology," among other terms which need to be distinguished from modern Western psychology.

Chapter 1 ("A Wayward Beginning") provides an overview of how modern psychology has become a colonialist enterprise that ignores or belittles traditional non-Western ways of understanding the human psyche. Chapter 2 ("Birth as Theophany") explores the profound mystery of the human condition and its inherent unity with the transpersonal order, a reality that is often dismissed by secular psychotherapy. Chapter 3 ("The Metaphysics of Trauma") examines a phenomenon that has become ubiquitous in our culture and discusses its connection to a broader crisis in well-being that afflicts society today. Chapter 4 ("The Enigma of Psychosis") documents the global mental health epidemic that appears to have resisted conventional attempts to overcome it due to the desacralized forms of treatment that ignore the spiritual dimension. Chapter 5 ("Addiction and Wholeness") examines the alarming rise in addictions today and the failure of modern Western psychology to admit the connection between the loss of a sense of the sacred and, for example, substance use disorders and other forms of self-harm. Chapter 6 ("Death as Transformation") looks at what the world's religions have to say about purification, illumination, and spiritual reintegration as pathways to restore true wholeness of being.

1

A Wayward Beginning

It has become increasingly clear to many around the world that *rethinking psychiatry* is an imperative task, and yet, what is often overlooked is that *rethinking psychology* is also essential.[1] That the foundations of contemporary psychology, and its mental health systems, are now looking precarious is by no means a new insight: "Psychotherapy is today in a state of disarray, almost exactly as it was two hundred years ago."[2] Decolonizing the human psyche is needed more than ever today. The apparatus of oppression and control in modern Western psychology is inseparable from its impoverished scientistic *Weltanschauung* and has become increasingly more nuanced and subtle. It privileges its own methodology above all other modes of knowing the world and appears oblivious to its own unquestioned theoretical assumptions. This tendency first became apparent when Sigmund Freud (1856–1939) triumphantly announced, "It was no small thing to have the whole human race as one's patient."[3] He actually admitted that his role was to be a colonizer of the human psyche: "I am actually not at all a man of science, not an observer, not an experimenter, not a thinker. I am by temperament nothing but a conquistador."[4]

The field of mental health can no longer turn a blind eye to the inescapable fact that "modern Western psychology [is] a secular and largely culture-bound discipline."[5] It avows that modern science alone holds the key to knowing truth and reality, but this dogmatic arrogance prevents it from noticing its own blind spot. It must be made crystal clear that "modern science *is* not—and never *has been*—the 'disinterested quest of truth.'"[6] Many practitioners today readily acknowledge these serious limitations: "[Modern] Western psychology and medicine are incomplete both in their understanding of human nature and in their ability to promote health and well-being."[7] Although the situation is more dismal than this statement suggests, it nonetheless distills the inherent errors of the discipline as practiced today.

---

1. See Bendeck Sotillos, "Madness," 65–94.
2. Zilboorg, "Rediscovery of the Patient," 108.
3. Freud, *Character and Culture*, 261.
4. Freud, *Complete Letters*, 398.
5. Badri, *Contemplation*, 1. All emphasis in quotations throughout were present in the sources.
6. Smith, *Physics and Vertical Causation*, 61.
7. Welwood, *Awakening the Heart*, vii.

We need to completely reenvisage modern Western psychology and psychiatry in the context of addressing mental health issues. At the root of the problem is "the inherent limitation of the original epistemological premises of modern science,"[8] and the only way to overcome this is to expose the "epistemological fallacies of Occidental civilization."[9] The impasse that faces modern Western psychology and its destructive consequences are clearly laid out by Gill Edwards:

> [Modern] science has claimed a monopoly on truth, seeing the scientific method as the only valid path towards knowledge. . . . As recent products of their culture, modern psychology and psychotherapy were built upon the shifting sands of Cartesian-Newtonian assumptions—with devastating consequences . . . [, and] many therapists are still clinging to the scientific tradition . . . and refusing to open their eyes. . . . The old paradigm gave birth to a positivist, materialist psychology which values objectivity, rationality and empiricism. . . . The mechanistic, reductionist, determinist assumptions of the Cartesian-Newtonian world view are endemic in psychology and psychotherapy.[10]

Without considering the historical antecedents and their connections to the development of modern science, this plight will continue unabated. Compelling mental health professionals to work in a theoretical and clinical vacuum will only perpetuate this crisis. Modern psychology is simply not prepared to accept valuable insights that differ from its own worldview but that are sorely needed if we are to offer more integrated and holistic treatment options for individuals. It is time, therefore, to challenge the ideological tyranny of psychology as practiced today and to consider how its pernicious influence can be curtailed.

The tendency of modern science to assert itself as the sole arbiter of what we can know about the human mind negates the crucial dimension that makes it conform to a true metaphysical order as found in many of the world's sapiential traditions. This reductionism of modern psychology has rendered null and void any fuller understanding of what is still understood by many as the 'soul': "psychology, having first bargained away its soul and then gone out of its mind, seems now, as it faces an untimely end, to have lost all consciousness."[11]

That spirituality and metaphysics are deemed irrelevant by modern science is the reason for the disarray in which contemporary psychology finds itself. This claim will strike many as ludicrous because it suggests that we need to turn back the clock to the dark ages of knowledge. Yet it must be understood that the exclusion of metaphysics from science goes to the heart of modernism's deviations. As Titus Burckhardt (1908–84) presciently observed, psychology can only be authentic when it relies on metaphysics:

8. Nasr, *Knowledge and the Sacred*, 206.
9. Bateson, *Steps*, 491.
10. Edwards, "Does Psychotherapy Need a Soul?," 195, 198, 194, 199, 198–99.
11. Burt, "Concept of Consciousness," 229.

> [Sacred] psychology does not separate the soul either from the metaphysical or from the cosmic order. The connection with the metaphysical order provides spiritual psychology with qualitative criteria such as are wholly lacking in profane [modern Western] psychology, which studies only the dynamic character of phenomena of the psyche and their proximate causes.[12]

The belief that only the scientific method gives access to valid forms of knowledge is not only flawed but totalitarian, having its roots in the European Enlightenment or the so-called Age of Reason. Without question, as Boaventura de Sousa Santos rightly points out, the "understanding of the world far exceeds the Western understanding of the world."[13]

This dogmatic outlook is not science but an ideology known as *scientism*, which has nothing to do with the proper exercise of the scientific method. Renowned scholar of Islam and Sufism William Chittick underscores how dominant scientism is within modern intellectual discourse, even though many may be oblivious to its overreach: "It is very difficult to characterize the modern worldview with a single label. One word that has often been suggested is 'scientism,' the belief that the scientific method and scientific findings are the sole criterion for truth."[14] As the American psychiatrist M. Scott Peck (1936–2005) astutely noted, contemporary science is largely relegated to dealing with approximations; in doing so, it is always modifying its understanding and thus is in no position to declare what can be finally known with certainty:

> What is paraded as scientific fact is simply the current belief of some scientists. We are accustomed to regard science as Truth with a capital "T." What scientific knowledge is, in fact, is the best available approximation of truth in the judgment of the majority of scientists who work in the particular specialty involved. Truth is not something that we possess; it is a goal toward which we, hopefully, strive. . . . The current opinion of the scientific establishment is only the latest and never the last word.[15]

The hegemony of modern Western science has become so dominant and commonplace that its implications are barely discerned today. American psychologist Amedeo Giorgi points out that "the perennial crisis of . . . [modern Western] psychology is due to the fact that it does not see that the problem lies in the meaning of science it adopted."[16] If we are truly going to speak about the importance of culture and human diversity in a way that is still meaningful, other modes of knowing must be recognized as valid.[17]

---

12. Burckhardt, *Introduction to Sufi Doctrine*, 26–27.
13. De Sousa Santos, *End of the Cognitive Empire*, 181.
14. Chittick, *Science of the Cosmos*, 48.
15. Peck, *People of the Lie*, 257–58.
16. Giorgi, "Crisis of Humanistic Psychology," 19. See also Koch, *Psychology in Human Context*; and Koch and Leary, *Century of Psychology*.
17. See Bendeck Sotillos, "Self and the Other," 34–76; and Bendeck Sotillos, "Human Diversity," 121–34.

Mircea Eliade (1907–86), the Romanian historian of religion, provides a salutary caution that remains unheeded:

> Western culture will be in danger of a decline into a sterilizing provincialism if it despises or neglects the dialogue with other cultures. . . . The West is forced (one might almost say, condemned) to this encounter and confrontation with the cultural values of "the others." . . . One day the West will have to know and to understand the existential situations and the cultural universes of the non-Western peoples; moreover, the West will come to value them as integral with the history of the human spirit and will no longer regard them as immature episodes or as aberrations from an exemplary History of man—a History conceived, of course, only as that of Western man.[18]

A true postcolonial psychology, or rather "science of the soul,"[19] would be grounded in an authentic metaphysical framework that reflects the diverse religious and spiritual traditions of humanity. This approach draws on the universal principles that disclose all levels of reality and buttress all modes of knowledge. In order to be efficacious, a true psychology requires that we assent to the rights of spiritual truth: "Psychology, we must remember, is the study of the soul, therefore the discipline closest to the religious life. An authentic psychology discards none of the insights gained from spiritual disciplines."[20] Through a more integral framework, our real identity in the Divine can be realized: "The ultimate reality of metaphysics is a Supreme Identity in which the opposition of all contraries, even of being and not-being, is resolved,"[21] as "pure Being by its very nature comprises All-Possibility."[22] This traditional approach to the sacred, which is uncontaminated by modernism, includes a tripartite understanding of the human being consisting of Spirit, soul, and body.[23] Accordingly, Burckhardt remarks that "man in his integral nature . . . is not only a physical datum but, at one and the same time, body, soul, and spirit."[24]

According to sacred science, the human microcosm mirrors the macrocosm: "Man is a little cosmos, and the cosmos is like a big man."[25] In the same way, "the cosmos at large proves to be *ontologically trichotomous*: that even as man himself is made up of *corpus*, *anima*, and *spiritus*, so is the integral cosmos."[26] Without the inclusion of Spirit, soul, and body, it could not be a cross-cultural psychology, as these

---

18. Eliade, *Myths, Dreams, and Mysteries*, 8–9.
19. See Bendeck Sotillos, "Perennial Psychology," 111–20.
20. Roszak, *Where the Wasteland Ends*, 414.
21. Coomaraswamy, *Coomaraswamy*, 2:6.
22. Schuon, *Transfiguration of Man*, 69.
23. "In [modern] Western experience it is common to separate the mind from the body and spirit and the spirit from mind and body" (Duran and Duran, *Native American Postcolonial Psychology*, 15).
24. Burckhardt, *Mirror of the Intellect*, 173. "The distinction of spirit, soul, and body is moreover that which has been unanimously accepted by all the traditional doctrines of the West" (Guénon, *Great Triad*, 68). "May the God of peace Himself sanctify you wholly; and may your *spirit and soul and body* be kept sound and blameless at the coming of our Lord Jesus Christ" (1 Thessalonians 5:23).
25. Sufi adage, quoted in Ibn 'Arabī, *Wisdom of the Prophets*, 11.
26. Smith, *Physics and Vertical Causation*, iii.

ways of knowing and healing are found throughout the world's civilizations—"pure metaphysics is hidden in every religion."[27]

Metaphysics as understood in this sense has nothing to do with modern Western philosophy, as it "possesses branches and ramifications pertaining to cosmology, anthropology, art and other disciplines, but at its heart lies pure metaphysics, if this latter term is understood . . . as the science of Ultimate Reality, as a *scientia sacra* not to be confused with the subject bearing the name metaphysics in postmedieval Western philosophy."[28] Sacred science, which is found at the heart of all sapiential traditions, provides an effective, comprehensive, and valid mode of knowing that is not subject to the findings of modern Western psychology. Influential Muslim scholar Seyyed Hossein Nasr explains that "*scientia sacra* is none other than that sacred knowledge which lies at the heart of every revelation and is the center of that circle which encompasses and defines tradition."[29] It was this outlook that prevailed prior to the emergence of modernity, with its materialistic and reductionist worldview.[30] In fact, prior to the onset of the modern world, there were no secular civilizations to be found and no science divorced from its divine origin.

Eliade challenges reductionist methodologies as follows:

A religious phenomenon will only be recognized as such if it is grasped at its own level, that is to say, if it is studied *as* something religious. To try to grasp the essence of such a [religious] phenomenon by means of physiology, psychology, sociology, economics, linguistics, art or any other study is false; it misses the one unique and irreducible element in it—the element of the sacred.[31]

The Renaissance, the Scientific Revolution, and the European Enlightenment—like modernism and its postmodernist prolongation—have fomented the desacralized outlook of the present day.[32] This has given birth to the modern world, whose intellectual posture is unprecedented among human civilizations of the past:

It was the emergence of modernity that provided both the scientific concepts and the political language underlying the idea of race. Between the sixteenth and eighteenth centuries, Europe underwent a series of intellectual and social transformations that laid the basis of the modern world. It was the period in which the modern idea of the self, and the individual as a rational agent, began to develop; in which the authority of custom and tradition weakened, while the role of reason in explaining the natural and social world was vastly expanded; in which nature became regarded not as chaotic but as lawful and hence

---

27. Schuon, quoted in Casey, "Basis of Religion," 75.
28. Nasr, *Need for a Sacred Science*, 54.
29. Nasr, *Knowledge and the Sacred*, 130.
30. "Modern science not only eclipsed the religious and traditional philosophical understanding of the order of nature in the West, but it also all but destroyed the traditional sciences" (Nasr, *Religion*, 126).
31. Eliade, *Patterns in Comparative Religion*, xvii.
32. See Smith, *Physics*.

amenable to reason; and in which humans became part of the natural order, and knowledge became secularized. The culmination of this process came in the eighteenth-century Enlightenment.[33]

What is not commonly understood is that prior to the end of the Middle Ages, the West shared with the East a common mindset that was shaped by an awareness of the sacred. Since the Renaissance, Christendom has seen a decline in its fortunes. This culminated in the so-called Enlightenment, which well and truly stamped a modern mentality on the West, thus giving it its characteristic outlook. This development, in turn, gave rise to scientism and the hegemonic worldview that leveled any notion of transcendence. The "great chain of being" is a hierarchal structure encompassing all levels of reality and modes of knowing them. This interconnected whole begins with the Divine and descends to include angels, humans, animals, plants, and minerals: "The 'great chain of being' of the Western tradition . . . survived in the West until it became horizontalized."[34] This loss created the conditions for scientism to flourish. "Since the Great Chain of Being collapsed with the rise of modern science, something in scientific aims and methods must be inimical to it."[35] Through these events, the conviction that modern Western civilization was superior to all others had become entrenched.

While the eclipse of the sacred began in postmedieval Western Europe, this crisis has since spread throughout the world, and humanity is now grappling with its destructive consequences. "With the collapse of metaphysics, natural theology, and objective revelation, the West is facing for the first time as a civilization the problem of living without objectively convincing absolutes."[36] It is apt to recall the catastrophic and enduring impact that this has had upon our understanding of the human psyche as we contemplate "the culturally inherited scars from the battle of the last of the nineteenth century when psychological science won its freedom from metaphysics."[37] The abandonment of metaphysics in the modern West by scientific materialism has led to the occlusion of our noetic faculty, represented by the transcendent Intellect. This has caused a fissure in consciousness, severing the mind from its transpersonal center. This bifurcation has created a void in the human psyche that has proven to be profoundly traumatic.[38]

The seemingly endless therapies found in modern psychology today are, in essence, by-products of this truncated discipline, which has shown itself unable to provide integrated modes of healing. These ideas have become so deeply assimilated into the modernist mindset that we can truly say, "Their work is in our bloodstream."[39] At its core, the loss of a sense of the sacred has degraded not only the human psyche but also our vision of the cosmos, and it continues to have a

33. Malik, *Strange Fruit*, 73.
34. Nasr, *Knowledge and the Sacred*, 197.
35. Smith, "Introduction," xviii.
36. Smith, "Foreword," xiii.
37. May, "Origins and Significance," 8.
38. See Perry, *Mystery of Individuality*, 19–38.
39. Allport, *Person in Psychology*, 14.

devastating impact on our well-being: "Of all that has thus been forfeited, *the loss of the sacred* is beyond doubt the most tragic of all: for that proves to be the privation we cannot ultimately survive."[40] A consequence of undermining the centrality of the Spirit in our lives is the rise of imbalances in the human psyche: "Mental disorder today exists everywhere."[41] Whitall N. Perry (1920–2005) supports this view: "The loss of religion as Center in the world has left a hole which [contemporary] psychology is trying to fill."[42]

If the rehabilitation of psychology should occur, and if we are to move into a truly sacred psychology, then the foundations of modern psychology—especially those of behaviorism and psychoanalysis—need to be understood for what they are: an unbridled assault on what it means to be fully human.[43]

As influential psychologist Rollo May (1909–94) has emphasized, we cannot overlook the seminal influences of modern psychology:

> We [need to] confront directly the work of Sigmund Freud. If we try to bypass Freud we shall be guilty of a kind of suppression. For what Freud thought, wrote and performed in therapy, whether we agree with it or not, permeates our whole culture, in literature and art and in almost every other aspect of western man's self-interpretation. Freud obviously had more influence on psychology and psychiatry than any other man in the twentieth century. Unless we confront him directly, consciously and unflinchingly, our discussions of therapy will always hang in a vacuum.
>
> We cannot, furthermore, dismiss Freud simply by stating our disagreements with him.[44]

While the profound influence of psychoanalysis on the formation of modern Western psychology is readily apparent, it is important to recognize that this equally applies to behaviorism and its principal exponents, such as John B. Watson (1878–1958) and B. F. Skinner (1904–90).

Modern Western psychology—as a field of science distinct from philosophy and physiology—is thought to have officially commenced in 1879 with Wilhelm Wundt's (1832–1920) establishment of the first experimental psychology laboratory at the University of Leipzig in Germany. It is a little-known fact that across the Atlantic, William James (1842–1910) had established a similar laboratory four years prior to Wundt, in 1875, at Harvard University.[45] However, others trace its beginnings to German psychologist Franz Brentano (1838–1917), who asserted in his *Habilitation* (1866) that empiricism, not metaphysics, is the basis of modern psychology: "The true method of philosophy is none other than that of the natural sciences."[46]

40. Smith, "Finding the Hidden Key," 36. See also Nasr, *Encounter of Man and Nature*.
41. Guénon, *Miscellanea*, 124.
42. Perry, *Challenges*, 200.
43. See Bendeck Sotillos, *Behaviorism*; and Bendeck Sotillos, *Dismantling Freud*.
44. May, "Phenomenological Bases of Psychotherapy," 23.
45. See Harper, "First Psychological Laboratory," 158–61.
46. Kriegel, *Routledge Handbook of Franz Brentano*, 226.

Wundt, regarded as the "father of experimental psychology," warned of the ill-fated consequences should psychology divorce itself from philosophy in his 1913 essay "Psychology's Struggle for Existence":

> Leafing through the first section of this work, one might be inclined to view it as a provocation. But one who decides to read through to the end will be convinced that, on the contrary, the work could well be regarded as a peace offering. In the opinion of some, philosophy and psychology should divorce from each other. Now, it is well known that when a married couple seeks a divorce, both members usually are at fault. In these pages it will be shown that the same is true in this instance, and that if this matter takes the course that both parties want, philosophy will lose more than it will gain, but psychology will be damaged the most. Hence, the argument over the question of whether psychology is or is not a philosophical science is for psychology a struggle for its very existence.[47]

James, often considered the "father of American psychology," makes a curious yet troubling observation:

> When . . . we talk of "psychology as a natural science," we must not assume that that means a sort of psychology that stands at last on solid ground. It means just the reverse; it means a psychology particularly fragile, and into which the waters of metaphysical criticism leak at every joint, a psychology all of whose elementary assumptions and data must be reconsidered in wider connections and translated into other terms.[48]

In fact, he reached the following conclusion regarding the limits of his discipline: "Psychology [is] a nasty little subject—all one cares to know lies outside."[49] Although James refused to consider modern psychology as a science, properly speaking, he was nonetheless optimistic and suggested that "this is no science, it is only the hope of a science."[50] The fate of psychology would have been very different if more individuals had taken heed of Wundt's or James's wise words of caution.

That said, it has been suggested that modern psychology's inception began even earlier with John Locke (1632–1704), one of the most influential thinkers of the European Enlightenment to whom was attributed the doctrine of empiricism and the associated notion of tabula rasa ("clean or erased slate").[51]

---

47. Wundt, "Psychology's Struggle," 197.
48. James, *Psychology*, 467–68.
49. James, quoted in James, *Letters of William James*, 2:2.
50. James, *Psychology*, 468.
51. "Locke [is] the founder of modern psychology" (Guénon, *Reign of Quantity*, 92). "Our business here is not to know all things, but those which concern our conduct. If we can find out those measures whereby a rational creature, put in that state which man is in in this world, may and ought to govern his opinions and actions depending thereon, we need not be troubled that some other things escape our knowledge" (Locke, *Essay Concerning Human Understanding*, 4). See also Westaway, *Scientific Method*, 133–34.

According to American psychologist Gordon W. Allport (1897–1967), there are essentially two epistemological approaches in Western psychology: "Virtually all modern psychological theories seem oriented toward one of two polar conceptions, which, at the risk of some historical oversimplification, I shall call the Lockean and the Leibnizian traditions respectively."[52]

Locke's influence is weighed heavily and endures up to the present day. His ideas have paved the way for modern science to dissociate itself from sacred principles and from what lies beyond the limitations of the empirical ego: "Locke insisted that there can be nothing in the intellect that was not first in the senses (*nihil est in intellectu quod non fuerit in sensu*)."[53] He thus turns the transcendent Intellect on its head, inverting its function and leaving only sensorial experience as the sole means of verifying the truth of reality (but only as conceived in narrowly materialist terms).

Accordingly, we can now see that modern psychology privileges sensorial experience above the noetic faculty of the Intellect, as illustrated in an often-cited statement by Fritz Perls (1893–1970): "Lose your mind and come to your senses."[54] It is critical to distinguish the faculty of *Intellect*, and its unmediated ways of knowing, from *intellectualization*, which is a defense mechanism used to reason in such a way as to avoid uncomfortable or distressing emotions. Swedish historian and philosopher Tage Lindbom (1909–2001) remarks that, "when John Locke affirmed that a pre-rational consciousness, given by God and innate in man, does not exist, he not only denied the *intellectus*. At the same time he enclosed man in subjectivism."[55] As St. Thomas Aquinas (1225–74) maintains, it is the Intellect that is connected to metaphysical insight. As such, it pertains to a transpersonal mode of knowing that supersedes our sensory perceptions while, at the same time, fully informing them: "The activity of the body has nothing in common with the activity of [the] intellect."[56]

The overthrow of the Intellect by modern science and its psychology is due to their myopic and reductionistic vision of what constitutes a human being. This is made worse by the fact that this subversion has taken place largely unbeknownst to contemporaries. René Guénon (1886–1951) makes this clear: "Modern man has become quite impermeable to any influences other than such as impinge on his senses; not only have his faculties of comprehension become more limited, but also the field of his perception has become correspondingly restricted."[57]

Since the materialist ascendency that began with the Renaissance, the Scientific Revolution, and the so-called Enlightenment, the human psyche and its essential link to the metaphysical order have steadily lost ground in psychology. As Watson famously announced, "No one has ever touched a soul,"[58] and we "cannot find consciousness in the test-tube of . . . science."[59] References to the human soul were

52. Allport, *Becoming*, 7.
53. Allport, *Becoming*, 7.
54. Perls, *Gestalt Therapy Verbatim*, 69.
55. Lindbom, *Tares and the Good Grain*, 51.
56. Aquinas, *Of God and His Creatures*, 127.
57. Guénon, *Reign of Quantity*, 101.
58. Watson, *Behaviorism*, 3.
59. Watson, "Modern Note in Psychology," 26.

increasingly expunged and replaced with the "mind" or "consciousness." Modern Western psychology, for the most part, has not only completely abandoned its metaphysical origins—first by rejecting the Spirit and then by denying the human psyche[60]—modern psychology has, in fact, gone to the opposite extreme of undermining the role of traditional wisdom on this subject: "Metaphysics should confessedly, as it does really, rest upon psychology instead of conversely."[61]

Freud went as far as to conclude, "One could venture to explain in this way the myths of paradise and the fall of man, of God, of good and evil, of immortality, and so on, and to transform *metaphysics* into *metapsychology*."[62] It now seeks to "cure" the mind taken in isolation—it cannot see that separating the human soul from the spiritual domain is the root of the problem. "The word 'mental' is often used to indicate the domain which has been explored by [modern] Western psychologists and which is often expressed by the world 'psyche,' so as to avoid metaphysical and religious inferences suggested by the word 'soul.'"[63] This becomes clear when we consider the momentous intellectual currents that emerged during the seventeenth and eighteenth centuries, which fundamentally changed the Western outlook: The "Enlightenment, when defined as the rational acquisition of knowledge, deals with only one limited aspect of human consciousness—the mental."[64] By distorting the original meaning of the term *psyche*, modern psychology has fractured our understanding of "soul," a calamity that only a few within the discipline have begun to realize.

James appeals to the modern secular mindset when he says, "The Soul-theory is, then, a complete superfluity, so far as accounting for the actually verified facts of conscious experience goes. So far, no one can be compelled to subscribe to it for definite scientific reasons."[65] James thus defined psychology by embracing the notion of "mind" but eradicating the soul: "Psychology is the Science of Mental Life, both its phenomena and of their conditions."[66] However, the figure who first formulated the notion of a "psychology without a soul,"[67] which forged the secular foundations of modern psychology, was Friedrich Albert Lange (1828–75), a German philosopher and sociologist.

Salvific psychology is diametrically opposed to scientific materialism and the reductionistic treatment of the human psyche. Exponents of modern psychology in many cases still harbor the view that religion and spirituality are unreal, consigning them to the prescientific age of myth and superstition: "Mediaeval Tradition Has Kept Psychology From Becoming a Science. Psychology, up to very recent times, has been held so rigidly under the dominance both of traditional religion and of

---

60. "Modern psychology is eager to throw metaphysics to the winds" (Lings, *Symbol and Archetype*, 17–18). See also Balz, "Metaphysical Infidelities," 337–51; and Bendeck Sotillos, "Impasse of Modern Psychology," 60–86.
61. Hall, *Founders of Modern Psychology*, 320.
62. Freud, *Psychopathology of Everyday Life*, 330.
63. Klein, *Be Who You Are*, 94. See also Reed, *From Soul to Mind*.
64. Metzner, *Unfolding Self*, 160.
65. James, *Principles of Psychology*, 1:348.
66. James, *Principles of Psychology*, 1:1.
67. Lange, *History of Materialism*, 168.

philosophy—the two great bulwarks of mediaevalism—that it has never been able to free itself and become a natural science."[68] To reject the medieval worldview is, essentially, to discard the role of metaphysics in properly understanding science and psychology. In other words, it is to renounce the timeless wisdom of all religions and their sacred psychologies: "The kingdom of God is within you" (Luke 17:21), "I am the Self . . . seated in the heart of all beings" (Bhagavad Gītā 10:20),[69] or "Heaven and earth cannot contain Me, but the heart of My faithful servant containeth Me" (Islamic sacred tradition).

What is necessary in rehabilitating a "science of the soul" is to remember that, prior to the emergence of modernism, the vital link between the human and transpersonal orders of reality had been accepted in all times and places. Eliade states that "the man of the traditional societies [and civilizations] is admittedly a *homo religiosus*."[70] He adds that "*homo religiosus* represents the 'total man.'"[71] Modern psychology reduces the human being to *homo natura*, devoid of what transcends his empirical ego and psychophysical identity. In response to this deviation, a reawakening of what it means to be human needs to be undertaken.[72] Philip Sherrard (1922–95) writes,

> Man can be truly human only when he is mindful of his theomorphic nature. When he ignores the divine in himself and in other existences he becomes sub-human. And when this happens not merely in the case of a single individual but in the case of society as a whole, then that society disintegrates through the sheer rootlessness of its own structure or through the proliferation of psychic maladies which it is powerless to heal because it has deprived itself of the one medicine capable of healing them.[73]

A crucial distinction needs to be made between premodern or traditional science, which is sacred and is always linked to metaphysics, and modern science, which divorces itself from spiritual principles. Catholic philosopher and physicist Wolfgang Smith (1930–2024) has astutely noted that "the fact is that every *bona fide* premodern science is rooted in an integral sapiential tradition."[74] Any science that does away with metaphysics or spirituality cannot be a complete science; this does not mean that modern science cannot be beneficial in understanding the manifest order as long as it does not trespass beyond its own realm of competence. This is supported by the German American psychologist Hugo Münsterberg (1863–1916): "Psychology would learn too late that an empirical science can be really free and powerful only if it recognize[s] and respect[s] its limits."[75]

---

68. Watson, *Psychology*, 1.
69. *Bhagavad-Gītā*, 241.
70. Eliade, *Sacred and the Profane*, 15.
71. Eliade, *Quest*, 8.
72. See Bendeck Sotillos, "Human and Transpersonal Dimensions," 69–107.
73. Sherrard, *Rape of Man and Nature*, 100.
74. Smith, *Wisdom of Ancient Cosmology*, 21.
75. Münsterberg, *Psychology and Life*, 111.

Modern science and sacred science can be distinguished by the former's purely empirical method of knowing (through observation, measurement, prediction, and manipulation) and the latter's basis in sapiential knowledge (a suprasensory, direct, and unmediated apprehension of reality). The world's wisdom traditions speak of a transcendent faculty known as the "eye of the heart" or the Intellect—*Intellectus* or *Spiritus* in Latin, *Rūḥ* or *ʿAql* in Arabic, *Pneuma* or *Nous* in Greek, *Buddhi* in Sanskrit.[76] It is this intuitive way of knowing to which Meister Eckhart (1260–1328) refers: "The eye in which I see God is the same eye in which God sees me. My eye and God's eye are one eye."[77] Within the Shin Buddhist tradition, a similar principle is found: "The eye with which I see Amida [Buddha] is the same with which Amida [Buddha] sees me."[78] Another example of this can be found in a poem by the Sufi Manṣūr al-Ḥallāj (858–922): "I saw my Lord with the Eye of the Heart. I said: 'Who art thou?' He answered: 'Thou.'"[79] This spiritual organ is also taught by the religion of the First Peoples and in the Shamanic traditions. The remarkable sage of the Lakota Sioux, Hehaka Sapa or Black Elk (1863–1950), remarked as follows:

> I am blind and do not see the things of this world; but when the Light comes from Above, it enlightens my heart and I can see, for the Eye of my heart (*Chante Ista*) sees everything. The heart is a sanctuary at the center of which there is a little space, wherein the Great Spirit dwells, and this is the Eye (*Ista*). This is the Eye of the Great Spirit by which He sees all things and through which we see Him. If the heart is not pure, the Great Spirit cannot be seen, and if you should die in this ignorance, your soul cannot return immediately to the Great Spirit, but it must be purified by wandering about in the world. In order to know the center of the heart where the Great Spirit dwells you must be pure and good, and live in the manner that the Great Spirit has taught us. The man who is thus pure contains the Universe in the pocket of his heart (*Chante Ognaka*).[80]

Modern science willfully ignores the limitations of empirical verification: "We make our observations in all natural sciences by the aid of our sense organs."[81] Put more succinctly, "whatever evidence there *is* for science *is* sensory evidence."[82] This approach is evidence-based, but its truths are subject to any new findings that can lead to a revision of what was previously assumed to be true. The notion that empirical knowledge admits to little or no error, precisely because of its reliance on the senses, does not hold up. Rather, it has led to what is known as a "cult of empiricism" or the "tyranny" of evidence-based practices.[83] By contrast, principial knowledge, which is grounded in metaphysics, includes (but is not confined to) what is

76. See Bendeck Sotillos, "Recovering the Eye," 29–45.
77. Eckhart, sermon 12, *Teacher and Preacher*, 270.
78. Kanamatsu, *Naturalness*, 12–13.
79. Quoted in Lings, *What Is Sufism?*, 49.
80. Black Elk, quoted in Schuon, *Feathered Sun*, 51.
81. Watson, *Psychology*, 25.
82. Quine, *Quintessence*, 263.
83. See Toulmin and Leary, "Cult of Empiricism," 594–617.

perceivable by the five senses as it extends to what lies beyond the constraints of mere sense experience:

> The premier instruments of investigation supporting the scientific method are no one other than the five senses that on their own, or in tandem with the recently developed rarefied pieces of scientific equipment that attempt to document at the quantum level and through empirical evidence the true nature of reality. In the end, we still rely on seeing, hearing, smelling, tasting, and touching in order to declare what we believe to be an objective reality.[84]

Empiricism was known in the ancient world, but it was not held to be the most authoritative way of knowing as it is today: "Without going further back than what is called 'classical' antiquity, everything concerned with experimentation was considered by the ancients as only constituting knowledge of a very inferior degree."[85] Empiricism remains vulnerable to the charge that it rejects modes of knowledge that lie beyond the scope of its restricted techniques. Frithjof Schuon (1907–98) speaks to this misguided attitude:

> The empiricist error consists not in the belief that experiment has a certain utility, which is obvious, but in thinking that there is a common measure between principial knowledge and experiment, and in attributing to the latter an absolute value, whereas in fact it can only have a bearing on modes, never on the very principles of Intellect and of Reality; this amounts to purely and simply denying the possibility of a knowledge other than the experimental and sensory.[86]

"According to empiricists, all knowledge is derived from sensory experience."[87] It is somewhat of a paradox that modern science, although secular in outlook, has its foundations in metaphysics even though it has broken away from its roots.[88] What is paramount here is that "metaphysical evidence takes precedence over 'physical' or 'phenomenal' certainty."[89] Indian philosopher Jadunath Sinha (1892–1978) points out that Hinduism, known as the *sanātana dharma* (eternal religion), also advocates this truth: "There is no empirical psychology in India. Indian psychology is based on metaphysics."[90] Modern science and, by extension, modern psychology have not come to terms with this critique. The quandary of modern Western

---

84. Herlihy, *Wisdom of the Senses*, 1.
85. Guénon, *Miscellanea*, 107.
86. Schuon, *Stations of Wisdom*, 29.
87. Schuon, *Logic and Transcendence*, trans. Perry et al., 30.
88. "The traditional conception . . . attaches all the sciences to the principles of which they are the particular applications, and it is this attachment that the modern conception refuses to admit. For Aristotle, physics was only 'second' in its relation to metaphysic, that is to say it was dependent on metaphysic and was really only an application to the province of nature of principles that stand above nature and are reflected in its laws; and one can say the same for the cosmology of the Middle Ages" (Guénon, *Crisis of the Modern World*, 45). See also Burtt, *Metaphysical Foundations of Modern Science*.
89. Schuon, *Gnosis*, trans. Palmer, 15.
90. Sinha, *Indian Psychology*, 1:xviii.

psychology persists: "To postulate a science without metaphysic is a flagrant contradiction."[91]

To ignore traditional modes of knowledge that are of supraindividual origin is to do a grave injustice to what psychology truly is. "In metaphysics there is no empiricism: principial knowledge cannot stem from any experience, even though experiences—scientific or other—can be the occasional causes of the intellect's intuitions."[92] It is this kind of knowledge that allows us to traverse the intermediary world of the human psyche, but only when we participate in a revealed spiritual tradition that is able to restore the unity of mind and body in the Spirit.

Since its inception, modern Western psychology has never been neutral, nor can it be. On the contrary, "science . . . is based on presuppositions"—it has a definite belief system from which it arises, and it rarely questions its own assumptions.[93] Bishop Kallistos Ware (1934–2022) makes the following point: "Modern science is not value-neutral. It does not offer merely an 'objective' account of the 'facts,' but it makes a series of assumptions that have far-reaching consequences on the spiritual level."[94] It needs to be remembered that "the concept of mental health depends on our concept of the nature of man."[95] In the same way, psychopathology requires a concept of health, and without knowing what health consists of, an adequate diagnosis and treatment of psychic maladies cannot be made. As Gai Eaton (1921–2010) points out, "To diagnose the ills of the time one must possess standards of health."[96]

Rescuing the human psyche from the clutches of modern Western psychology requires challenging the widespread acceptance of *scientism*, "the belief that the scientific method and scientific findings are the sole criterion for truth."[97] Freud declared his allegiance to scientific fundamentalism as follows: "No, our science is no illusion. But an illusion it would be to suppose that what science cannot give us we can get elsewhere."[98] This overwhelmingly narrow interpretation of science is reminiscent of another well-known scientistic assertion by Bertrand Russell (1872–1970): "What science cannot discover, mankind cannot know."[99]

Science, according to Freud, represents the only legitimate means of obtaining true knowledge: "There are no sources of knowledge of the universe other than the intellectual working-over of carefully scrutinized observations—in other words, what we call research—and alongside of it no knowledge derived from revelation, intuition or divination."[100] The reason that scientism endures, as the American historian and social critic Theodore Roszak (1933–2011) points out, is that it has been adopted as the new faith of the modern world to replace religion: "Science is our religion because

91. Schuon, *Light*, 131.
92. Schuon, *Roots of the Human Condition*, vii.
93. Bateson, *Mind and Nature*, 27.
94. Ware, "Foreword," xlii.
95. Fromm, *Sane Society*, 67.
96. Eaton, *King of the Castle*, 8.
97. Chittick, *Science of the Cosmos*, 48. See also Sheldrake, *Science Delusion*.
98. Freud, *Future of an Illusion*, 71.
99. Russell, *Religion and Science*, 243.
100. Freud, *New Introductory Lectures*, 196.

we cannot, most of us, with any living conviction *see around it*."[101] What is altogether misunderstood regarding the phenomenon of scientism is that its totalitarian claims contradict its essential assertions, as the renowned scholar of comparative religion Huston Smith (1919–2016) perceptively observed: "The contention that there are no truths save those of [modern] science is not itself a scientific truth; in affirming it scientism contradicts itself."[102] Scientism thus confines the scope of psychology to what is exclusively horizontal, denying its most important facet, the vertical dimension of the Spirit: "Scientism encourages man to stop his search for inwardness at the level of psychic contents."[103] An important qualification needs to be added here: "There is no conflict between science and religion when the rightful domain of each is honored."[104]

Swiss psychiatrist Ludwig Binswanger (1881–1966) offered an acute criticism of the fragmented mentality that undergirds modern Western psychology: "The cancer of all [modern] psychology up to now [is] . . . the cancer of the doctrine of subject-object cleavage of the world."[105] A key figure responsible for this pervasive dichotomy in modern science is René Descartes (1596–1650), who put forward his own brand of mind-body dualism that continues to have an enduring influence on the development of modernity's *Weltanschauung*. Guénon speaks to how extensively this fundamental scission has permeated today's intellectual climate: "The Cartesian duality . . . has imposed itself on all modern Western thought."[106] Descartes compared the human body to a machine:

> I might consider the body of a man as kind of machine equipped with and made up of bones, nerves, muscles, veins, blood and skin in such a way that, even if there were no mind in it, it would still perform all the same movements as it now does in those cases where movement is not under the control of the will or, consequently, of the mind.[107]

Comparing the human body to a machine is assuredly not a neutral position, as modern science purports to adopt. In fact, we need to remain constantly vigilant in the face of these Promethean forces. May took very seriously "the dehumanizing dangers in our tendency in modern science to make man over into the image of the machine."[108] By equating the human body with a machine, Descartes hoped to devise "a system of medicine which is founded on infallible demonstrations."[109] He appeared to predict the future of modern science, including modern psychology, seeing as

101. Roszak, *Where the Wasteland Ends*, 134–35.
102. Smith, *Forgotten Truth*, 16.
103. Needleman, *Sense of the Cosmos*, 131.
104. Smith, *Huston Smith*, 203.
105. Ludwig Binswanger, quoted in May et al., *Existence*, 11.
106. Guénon, *Great Triad*, 68. "Cartesian bifurcation created a dualism between mind and matter which has dominated Western thought since the seventeenth century, a dualism which has led many to choose the primacy of matter over mind and to establish the view that in the beginning was matter and not consciousness" (Nasr, *Essential Seyyed Hossein Nasr*, 224).
107. Descartes, *Descartes*, 58.
108. May, "Existential Bases of Psychotherapy," 686.
109. Descartes, *Philosophical Writings of Descartes*, 3:17.

current mental health practices by and large push for treatments that are exclusively confined to empirically validated techniques. The Cartesian divide between *res extensa* (extended entities) and *res cogitans* (thinking entities) makes no allowance for overcoming this bifurcation, thus reducing all human experience to the private, subjective realm and obliterating any notion of objective reality.

This mind-body dualism lives on in modern science, especially in the fields of psychology and psychiatry, where this notion is deeply embedded in its epistemological framework. It is especially to be found in the *medical model* for the clinical diagnosis and treatment of mental illness, which separates the psychological (*psyche*) from the biological (*soma*). R. D. Laing (1927–89), the Scottish psychiatrist, acknowledged how widespread the medical model is, calling it the "set of procedures in which all doctors are trained."[110] This model remains the dominant schema within these disciplines and is thoroughly reductionist, as it views mental disorders as solely the product of physiological factors and treats them, accordingly, as physical diseases; it generally divorces itself from broader psychological and transpersonal realities and becomes fixed in a schema based only on a disease's etiology.[111]

Due to concerns about the excessively narrow outlook of the medical model, the biopsychosocial model emerged to encompass more dimensions of human reality, such as the social and cultural, with a view toward gaining a fuller understanding of illness and health. It was George L. Engel (1913–99) who popularized the biopsychosocial model when he observed a "medical crisis" that he thought was derived from the medical model—that is, an "adherence to a model of disease no longer adequate for the scientific tasks and social responsibilities of either medicine or psychiatry."[112] In this attempt to overcome mind-body dualism, he asserted that all three of the following levels need to be taken into account: "the social, psychological, and biological."[113] It was the pioneering work of influential psychiatrist Adolf Meyer (1866–1950) and American psychiatrist and neurologist Roy R. Grinker Sr. (1900–1993) that contributed to the further development of the biopsychosocial model first established by Engel.

With the limits of the medical model having been recognized, the biopsychosocial model was also found to have its limitations because it could not adequately explain the various factors that determine psychopathology.[114] Even though the biopsychosocial model is more inclusive than the biomedical one, it still falls short in failing to situate the spiritual dimension at the heart of the human condition. Some have advocated for a four-dimensional model or a biopsychosocial model that embraces spirituality, and while this is certainly more satisfactory, its assumptions are still ad hoc and are not properly integrated into the vertical dimension. What is not acknowledged here is that the spiritual domain transcends (while fully embracing) brain functioning, psychological dispositions, and social influences among other

110. Laing, *Politics of the Family*, 39.
111. See Elkins, "Medical Model in Psychotherapy," 66–84.
112. Engel, "New Medical Model," 129.
113. Engel, "New Medical Model," 133.
114. See Ghaemi, "Rise and Fall," 3–4; and Ghaemi, *Biopsychosocial Model*.

factors. This corresponds to the tripartite structure of the human being, although the Spirit alone can fully bring into balance and harmonize all these aspects of our human nature.

Nasr makes an important point about modern medicine and its reliance on a mechanistic worldview:

> The truncated understanding of the body in modern medicine [is] based on reductionism, which finally sees the human body as a complicated machine and nothing more than that . . . although the modern scientific and medical understanding of the body certainly corresponds to an aspect of its reality, it does not by any means exhaust its reality. The body, in fact, has its own intelligence and speaks its own "mind," reflecting a wisdom.[115]

Yet this misconceived division does not appear in traditional healing methods found throughout the world's religions, which include the spiritual heritage of the First Peoples and Shamanic traditions. Nasr adds, "In all traditional civilizations, medicine has been closely related to the basic principles of the tradition in question. Its origin has always been seen to be divine. . . . The psyche was seen to affect the body and the spirit the psyche."[116] For example, Guénon illuminates the essential metaphysical principles found in traditional Chinese medicine and how anything comparable is completely lacking in modern Western medicine:

> Traditional Chinese medicine in particular is based more or less entirely on the distinction between *yang* and *yin*; every illness is due to a state of disequilibrium, that is, to an excess of one of these two in relation to the other; this must then be strengthened to re-establish the equilibrium, and in this way one reaches the very cause of the illness instead of being limited to treating more or less outward and superficial symptoms, as is the profane medicine of modern Westerners.[117]

Coomaraswamy outlines the distinctions between the understanding of health in modern psychology and that found in traditional or spiritual psychology:

> The health envisaged by the [modern] empirical psychotherapy is a freedom from particular pathological conditions; that envisaged by the other [traditional or sacred psychology] is a freedom from all conditions and predicaments. . . . Furthermore, the pursuit of the greater freedom necessarily involves that attainment of the lesser; psycho-physical health being a manifestation and consequence of spiritual wellbeing.[118]

Descartes's dictum "I think, therefore I am" (*cogito ergo sum*) situates human awareness in a fully enclosed sense of self and sets this up as the criterion for existence.[119]

115. Nasr, *Religion*, 259–60.
116. Nasr, *Need for a Sacred Science*, 107.
117. Guénon, *Great Triad*, 26.
118. Coomaraswamy, *Coomaraswamy*, 2:335.
119. Descartes, *Descartes*, 68.

This is totally opposed to human identity as understood by the plenary traditions. In contrast, the transpersonal modes of knowing recognize a plurality of levels in our human nature that are rooted in a universal and timeless wisdom, which can be found around the world. According to Hindu metaphysics, as found in the ancient text *Tripurā Rahasya*, consciousness has no beginning as it is always already existent—it is not generated in the brain, as is often claimed by modern science: "Therefore you cannot escape the conclusion that there must be consciousness even to know its unawareness also. So there is no moment when consciousness is not."[120] The Sufi master 'Ayn al-Quḍāt (1098–1131) points toward a pure metaphysics that resolves and transcends the dialectics of the Cartesian mind-body dualism:

> The spirit is inside and outside the body and is inside and outside the world. The spirit is also neither inside nor outside the body, and is neither inside nor outside the world. Alas! Understand what has been spoken: the spirit is not connected to the body, but is not disconnected from it. God is not connected to the world but is not disconnected from it.[121]

Thought, being, knowledge, and reality are all interconnected and unified in traditional modes of knowing. This requires a consonance between the knower and the known; as Guénon writes, the "Knower, Known, and Knowledge are truly one only."[122] Medieval epistemology defined knowledge as "*adaequatio rei et intellectus*—the understanding of the knower must be *adequate* to the thing to be known."[123] Parmenides (515–445 BCE) emphasized something similar: "To be and to know are one and the same."[124] This is to say that, in the traditional or premodern world, there were modes of knowledge, with their corresponding levels of reality, by which one could realize the Supreme Identity. In this understanding, a distinction was always made between relative knowledge and knowledge that was absolute.

The noetic faculty of the Intellect, or the "eye of the heart" immanent within the human being, enables us to know the fullness of what can be known. Sherrard describes the quandary that modern science faces, seeing as it cannot know higher levels of reality beyond itself: "Nothing can be known except according to the mode of the knower."[125] The eighth-century sage Shankara also made this clear: "Only the Self [*Ātmā*] knows the Self [*Ātmā*]."[126] Within the Buddhist tradition, the same idea can be found: "A Buddha alone is able to understand what is in the mind of another Buddha."[127] This principle is also discernible in the Christian text *Theologia Germanica*, in which it is written, "God can be known only by God."[128] No matter how broad an

120. Chap. 18, *Tripura Rahasya*, 132.
121. 'Ayn al-Quḍāt, quoted in Rustom, *Inrushes of the Heart*, 124.
122. Guénon, *Symbolism of the Cross*, 92.
123. Quoted in Schumacher, *Guide for the Perplexed*, 39.
124. Parmenides, quoted in Coomaraswamy, *What Is Civilization?*, 35.
125. Sherrard, "Science of Consciousness," 29.
126. Shankara, quoted in Shah-Kazemi, *Paths to Transcendence*, 207. "Self realizes the Self" (chap. 21, *Tripura Rahasya*, 163).
127. Quoted in Suzuki, *Essays in Zen Buddhism*, 49.
128. Chap. 42, *Theologia Germanica*, 153. "The things of God knoweth no man, but the Spirit of God" (1 Corinthians 2:11).

outlook modern science adopts, its perspective is inevitably vitiated by a dualistic framework that tries to grasp consciousness as an object of empirical study: "The highest mode of consciousness, or consciousness in itself, is that in which there is no dualism between knower and what is to be known, observer and what is to be observed, consciousness and that of which consciousness is conscious."[129] Again, "the soul, like every other domain of reality, can only be truly known by what transcends it."[130] This is captured in the tradition of the Prophet Muhammad: "He who knoweth himself knoweth his Lord."

Duo sunt in homine ("There are two [natures] in man") was an axiom in the West that recognized an outer and inner man, at least prior to the emergence of the Renaissance.[131] "In any definition of Man, his inner and outer aspect are both to be considered."[132] Our theomorphic essence is unconditioned and unaffected by the activities of the mundane self: "Everything a man does in the lower part of active life is necessarily exterior to him, so to speak, beneath him."[133] This is articulated a little differently here: "Our Inner Man is in the world but not of it, in us but not of us, our Outer Man both in the world and of it."[134] Modern Western psychology focuses on the assessment, diagnosis, and treatment of the outer human being unaware that, by definition, its materialism excludes the possibility of an "inward man" (Romans 7:22), and thus it has no framework by which to comprehend the reality of our "two natures."[135]

The ancient wisdom found in all times and places perceived a correspondence between the unseen world and that of the visible one. The former corresponds with the notion of *essences* that connect us to the realm of Spirit that pervades the whole of reality. "The things which are seen are temporal; but the things which are not seen are eternal" (2 Corinthians 4:18). This metaphysical correspondence is also to be found in Taoism, when Lao Tzu (sixth century) remarks, "All things under heaven are born of the corporeal: The corporeal is born of the Incorporeal."[136] As a paragon of Islamic spirituality, Rūmī (1207–73) captures this idea poetically:

> Every form you see has its archetype in the Divine world, beyond space; if the form perishes what matter, since its heavenly model is indestructible? Every beautiful form you have seen, every meaningful word you have heard—be not sorrowful because all this must be lost; such is not really the case. The Divine Source is immortal and its outflowing gives water without cease; since neither the one nor the other can be stopped, wherefore do you lament? . . . From the moment that you came into the world a ladder was put before you.[137]

129. Sherrard, "Science of Consciousness," 30.
130. Burckhardt, *Mirror of the Intellect*, 47.
131. St. Thomas Aquinas, question 26, fourth article, *Summa Theologica*, 336.
132. Ibn 'Arabī, *Bezels of Wisdom*, 73.
133. Chap. 8, *Cloud of Unknowing*, 72.
134. Coomaraswamy, *Coomaraswamy*, 2:371.
135. See Bendeck Sotillos, "Inner and Outer Human Being," 9–26.
136. Lao Tzu, chap. 40, *Tao Teh Ching*, 46.
137. Rūmī, quoted in Glassé, *New Encyclopedia of Islam*, 235.

In reviving the primacy of metaphysics, sacred science and its spiritual principles of psychology can return to their transcendent roots. According to this vision,
everything observable in the phenomenal world can be traced "back to its source, to
its archetype."[138] Joseph Epes Brown (1920–2000) explains how traditional peoples
understood and perceived the Divine Unity behind the created order where no bifurcation exists:

> It is often difficult for those who look on the tradition of the American Indi-
> ans from the outside, or through the "educated" mind, to understand their
> preoccupation with the animals, and with all things in the Universe. . . . But
> for these people, as of course for all traditional peoples, every created object
> is important simply because they know the metaphysical correspondence
> between this world and the real World. No object is for them what it appears
> to be, but is simply the pale shadow of a Reality. . . . It is for this reason that
> every created object is *wakan*, holy, or has a power, according to the level of
> the spiritual reality that it reflects. Thus many objects possess power for evil
> as well as for good and every object is treated with respect, for the particular
> "power" that it possesses can be transferred into you. Of course, they know
> that everything in the Universe has its counterpart in the soul of man. . . .
> The Indian humbles himself before the whole of creation (especially when
> "lamenting") because all things were created by *Wakan-Tanka* [Great Spirit]
> before him, and deserve respect, as they are older than man. However,
> although the last of created things, man is also first and unique, since he may
> know *Wakan-Tanka*.[139]

The divided mentality of the modern West will be overcome only when it returns
to the tripartite understanding of humanity mentioned earlier (namely, Spirit, soul,
and body) along with their corresponding dimensions in the cosmic order—the
formless, subtle, and gross planes of existence. This will restore the fragmented
condition of the contemporary psyche in order "to see all things in the yet undif-
ferentiated, primordial unity,"[140] as additionally expounded in the Heart Sūtra
(*Prajñāpāramitā-hridaya-sūtra*): "Form is emptiness; emptiness is form. Emptiness is
not other than form; form is not other than emptiness."[141]

The myopic scope of modern science has proven to be incapable of delivering
itself from its erroneous theoretical foundations: "In falling under the tyranny of
a fragmentary, materialistic and quantitative outlook modern science is irremedi-
ably limited by its epistemological base."[142] Guénon comments on the limited scope
of modern psychology, which is devoid of a transpersonal dimension:

> As for modern Western psychology, it deals only with a quite restricted portion
> of the human individuality, where the mental faculty is in direct relationship

---

138. Corbin, "Question of Comparative Philosophy," 3.
139. Brown, *Spiritual Legacy*, 104–5.
140. Lao Tzu, quoted in Cooper, *Illustrated Introduction to Taoism*, 37.
141. The Heart Sūtra, quoted in Lopez, *Heart Sutra Explained*, 57.
142. Oldmeadow, *Traditionalism*, 122.

with the corporeal modality, and, given the methods it employs, it is incapable of going any further. In any case, the very objective which it sets before itself and which is exclusively the study of mental phenomena [the empirical ego], limits it strictly to the realm of the individuality, so that the state which we are now discussing [the Self (*Ātmā*)] necessarily eludes its investigations.[143]

The postcolonial challenge offers the potential to correct the historical errors of modern Western psychology by providing an integral framework for understanding the "science of the soul" as conceived by all traditional civilizations.

This universal wisdom affirms that "the ontological situation of man in the total scheme of things is forever the same,"[144] and its ways of knowing are inseparable from this transpersonal dimension. Boaventura de Sousa Santos illustrates this paramount concern with respect to the split in human knowledge and understanding, writing that there is an "abyssal invisible line that separates science, philosophy, and theology, on one side, from, on the other, knowledges rendered incommensurable and incomprehensible for meeting neither the scientific methods of truth nor their acknowledged contesters in the realm of philosophy and theology."[145] For this reason sacred science, metaphysics, and its spiritual principles remain within the "realm of incomprehensible beliefs and behaviors which in no way can be considered knowledge."[146] This attack on traditional modes of knowing and healing, coupled with the repudiation of metaphysics, has had devastating consequences: "While nineteenth century materialism closed the mind of man to what is above him, twentieth century [modern Western] psychology opened it to what is below him."[147]

It is the spiritual traditions and their corresponding sacred psychologies that can facilitate a framework for metaphysical and ontological renewal in the field of mental health. By reestablishing the principles of a universal sacred science, we may be able to recover the equilibrium that has long been lost to us. As we now see, the theoretical trajectories that have led to the emergence of modernism and postmodernism are essentially bankrupt and destructive. These movements, which have spellbound contemporary man, have failed to give us the deeper understanding of reality and consciousness that we so desperately need today.[148]

Some have gone so far as to suggest that a synthesis between modern science and the spiritual traditions can be accomplished; however, this is to miss the point. Such a synthesis is not possible, as the former is premised on an erroneous epistemological foundation and is lacking a proper ontological basis.[149] It completely overlooks the fact that modern Western psychology has emerged due to a crisis of the

143. Guénon, *Man and His Becoming*, 96.
144. Nasr, *Sufi Essays*, 93.
145. De Sousa Santos, "Beyond Abyssal Thinking," 47.
146. De Sousa Santos, "Beyond Abyssal Thinking," 51.
147. Guénon, quoted in Coomaraswamy, *Hinduism and Buddhism*, 61.
148. See Bendeck Sotillos, "Realms of Consciousness," 12–21.
149. See Bendeck Sotillos, *Psychology and the Perennial Philosophy*.

modern world, of which it itself is the flawed consequence.[150] We are reminded about the ill-fated prognosis that confronts the shaky foundations of modern psychology: "Psychoanalysis is the disease of which it pretends to be the cure."[151]

Secular science and its offspring, modern psychology, are at an impasse due to their crippled means of knowledge and the absence of an immutable foundation, as illustrated by Nasr:

> Modern philosophy, psychology, or science are simply not able to explain perception which they always reduce to one of its parts or something else because the participation of the human intellect in the Light of the Divine Intellect is simply beyond the truncated worldview within which all modern thought, whether it be philosophical, psychological, or scientific operates.[152]

While points of contact may be made between traditional forms of psychology and its benighted current manifestation, the former does not need the insights of a profane science in order to validate its truths. Beyond our corporeal and psychic dimensions, sacred psychology holds that we are able to realize multiple states of consciousness along with their corresponding modes of knowing and healing. This is evident in the work of Toshihiko Izutsu (1914–93), who stated, "Existence or Reality as 'experienced' on supra-sensible levels reveals itself as of a multistratified structure."[153] As Buddhist writer Marco Pallis (1895–1989) explains, "Man is but one of an indefinite number of states of the being."[154] What is preventing modern Western psychology from being "integrated into higher orders of knowledge" is that its science has jettisoned its metaphysical roots.[155] It needs to be clear that while this sacred science admits diverse modes of knowing, it also recognizes the corresponding levels of reality: "Each higher world contains the principles of that which lies below it and lacks nothing of the lower level of reality."[156]

Without a fully integrated framework, one cannot discern between different levels of being, such as the transmundane and the noumenal. The world both reflects and conceals the Divine. In the light of metaphysical discernment, the unseen or transpersonal order is not devoid of meaning simply because it cannot be seen, for it comprises the very plenitude (beneath a veil of seeming "emptiness") that allows the world of phenomena to arise. The Divine enfolds all of reality, allowing for a plethora of perspectives to be disclosed and understood in different ways.

---

150. "It is often suggested that . . . modern psychology . . . has developed in parallel with modern science, is working in the same direction as that pursued by traditional sages and philosophers and by the few who still seek to follow them, and that it is thus making an approach to the same goal. That is not so" (Northbourne, *Looking Back on Progress*, 17).
151. Szasz, *Karl Kraus*, 24. "Psychoanalysis is an illness that pretends to be a cure" (Perls, "Life Chronology," 8).
152. Nasr, "Reply to Wolfgang Smith," 489.
153. Izutsu, *Sufism and Taoism*, 479.
154. Pallis, *Peaks and Lamas*, 127.
155. Nasr, *Knowledge and the Sacred*, 207.
156. Nasr, *Knowledge and the Sacred*, 199.

> Any truth can in fact be understood at different levels and according to differ-
> ent conceptual dimensions, that is to say, according to an indefinite number
> of modalities that correspond to all the possible aspects, likewise indefinite in
> number, of the truth in question.[157]

Additionally, "one has to understand that there are different degrees, different points
of view, different levels of reality which have to be taken into consideration."[158] It
is the metaphysical order that allows the necessary aptitude by which these distinct
modes of reality can be recognized. Schuon writes, "Any truth can in fact be understood at different levels and according to different conceptual dimensions, that is to
say, according to an indefinite number of modalities that correspond to all the possible
aspects, likewise indefinite in number, of the truth in question."[159] This understanding
of reality goes far beyond the materialistic science of the medical or biopsychosocial
models, as it is situated on a transcendent and more inclusive foundation of reality.

It is time to acknowledge that the world's spiritual traditions have complete
therapies to offer. Sacred psychology can provide not only valid and effective but
integral healing modalities, which leave behind the pernicious fallacies of the scientism that is itself the damaged legacy of modern Western psychology and its
dehumanizing ideology.

Properly rehabilitating an adequate "science of the soul" requires it to be
unshackled from the scientific point of view that denies the very existence of the
Spirit and the human soul. What is needed is to restore our true identity back to
the earth and the Spirit, which is to say to its geomorphic and theomorphic origins.[160] This can be facilitated by reflecting the Divine Unity in our diverse societies and civilizations. What is crucial is the rediscovery of metaphysics, sacred
science, and its spiritual principles, all of which inform the fullness of any enduring "science of the soul":

> It is also crucial for creating a new understanding between religion and sci-
> ence, and, with the help of traditional metaphysics, for integrating modern
> science into a hierarchy of knowledge wherein it could function without
> claims of exclusivity and without disrupting the essential relation between
> man and the cosmos, which possesses a reality beyond the realm of pure
> quantity and even beyond the empirical and the rational.[161]

American philosopher of science Thomas S. Kuhn (1922–96) has astutely pointed
out that a new paradigm will take place not through individual conversions, here
and there, in the scientific community but rather through a developed consensus

---

157. Schuon, *Transcendent Unity of Religions*, 1. "One has to understand that there are different
    degrees, different points of view, different levels of reality which have to be taken into
    consideration" (Lings, *Enduring Utterance*, 80).
158. Lings, *Enduring Utterance*, 80.
159. Schuon, *Transcendent Unity of Religions*, 1.
160. See Bendeck Sotillos, "Eclipse of the Soul," 34–55.
161. Nasr, *Religion*, 275.

over time that establishes a new paradigm "until . . . the last holdouts have died."[162] This speaks directly to the predicament facing contemporary psychology and mental health treatment; any kind of metanoia will not be sudden, even when its errors are admitted. That we are currently experiencing the "last holdouts" is suggested by the following: "*The contemporary* Weltanschauung—*which implicitly assumes bifurcation to be a scientific fact—has been disproved.*"[163]

Some might argue that even though abundant evidence has been provided to demonstrate the fissures in the so-called scientific underpinnings of contemporary psychology, this has no direct impact on how practitioners today work with people. For example, they may point out that they are not operating from its cramped theoretical assumptions. For them, research has demonstrated the efficacy of psychotherapy regardless of the type of therapeutic modality or technique being employed. Indeed, it has been argued that the effectiveness of psychotherapy does not depend on one modality or technique being preferred over any other.[164] As clinical psychologist Bruce Wampold concludes, "Clearly, the preponderance of the benefits of psychotherapy are due to factors incidental to the particular theoretical approach administered and dwarf the effects due to theoretically derived techniques."[165]

For this reason, it has been proposed that the *human relationship* itself is what has primacy in the encounter and makes any treatment effective rather than the clinical methods used. American psychiatrist Irvin Yalom has emphasized that the single most important lesson for a novice mental health therapist to learn is that "it is the relationship that heals."[166] Elsewhere, he has stressed his own personal mantra: "It's the relationship that heals, the relationship that heals, the relationship that heals—my professional rosary."[167] At the same time, some may try to sidestep the issue by identifying an "integrative" or eclectic therapist that does not associate with a given therapeutic approach. "Integration suggests that the elements are part of one combined approach to theory and practice, as opposed to eclecticism which draws ad hoc from several approaches in the approach to a particular case."[168]

We need to note that this outlook arises due to the battle between the incompatible theoretical systems of behaviorism and psychoanalysis. Yet it is important to realize that, while these approaches suggest openness and inclusivity, they do not resolve the fundamental dilemmas at hand: "These methodological considerations produce general agreement on the rules of the game rather than general acceptance of a specific theoretical position. They produce, as it were, a *modus vivendi* without cordiality."[169] All this is yet another example as to why the field is in crisis.

162. Kuhn, *Structure of Scientific Revolutions*, 152.
163. Smith, *Physics and Vertical Causation*, 16.
164. See Smith and Glass, "Meta-Analysis of Psychotherapy Outcome Studies," 752–60; Landman and Dawes, "Psychotherapy Outcome," 504–16; Seligman, "Effectiveness of Psychotherapy," 965–74.
165. Wampold, *Great Psychotherapy Debate*, 209.
166. Yalom, *Existential Psychotherapy*, 401.
167. Yalom, *Love's Executioner*, 112.
168. Martin and Margison, "Conversation Model," 57.
169. Williams, "New Eclecticism," 115.

This impasse clearly demonstrates that the present-day paradigm of contemporary psychology is now largely dysfunctional and slowly giving way.

The situation is not as simple as it might appear, seeing as what constitutes a relationship is a much more complex and nuanced question. Furthermore, there are inherent obstacles implicit in the psychotherapeutic relationship that cannot be ignored.[170] They are that the phenomena of "transference" and "countertransference"—comprising a two-way, transactional process—are in fact unavoidable, as these are challenges implicit in the horizontal realm of the human psyche that cannot be transcended or integrated without the presence of a vertical dimension. The very means by which the empirical ego perceives the phenomenal world is itself problematic, as its very starting point is an impediment to truly understanding oneself and the other (as both are unavoidably rooted in dualism). Our identification with the ego is rooted in a fictional, if not distorted, sense of self that assumes an underlying split between the subject and object or the self and the world. The dilemma of a self divided from that which is other can only be understood within a metaphysical framework. Schuon points out that "the ego as such cannot logically seek the experience of what lies beyond egoity."[171]

Relationships, as informed by metaphysics, comprise both horizontal and vertical dimensions, yet the horizontal is always subordinate to the vertical—that is to say, "the relationship between man and the world is premised on the primary relationship between God and man."[172] An effective and fully integrated psychology requires both dimensions. Relationships encompass an indefinite number of states of consciousness and levels of reality—a sacred unity both within the created order and of what lies beyond it. The Lakota proclaim *Mitakuye oyasin* or "We are all related" (literally, "All my relatives"); similarly, the Christian tradition tells us that "We are [all] members one of another" (Ephesians 4:25 ESV). The Hindu tradition has what is known as *satsang*, or an association with truth or reality, which consists of being in the company of saints and sages; however, it also signifies our ultimate encounter with the Self or the Supreme Identity. This is never truly the human confronting the human but the Divine encountering the Divine; it only appears as the former from a relative point of view. However, from the aspect of Ultimate Reality or the Absolute, there is none other than the Divine itself. In other words, the pure Subject as the Self realizes the object within itself and its inherent oneness.

If psychology returns to its origins in metaphysics, sacred science, and spiritual principles, it can again become worthy of being called a "science of the soul." The following verse frames the predicament in which contemporary psychology finds itself: "The stone which the builders rejected has become the chief cornerstone" (Psalm 118:22 ESV). This is the primacy of the Spirit that psychology needs in order to return to its origins *in divinis*. Coomaraswamy not only urges us to adopt a framework based on humanity's ancient wisdom traditions but further adds that sacred

---

170. See Schofield, *Psychotherapy*.
171. Schuon, *Esoterism as Principle*, 32.
172. Lakhani, *Timeless Relevance*, 85.

psychology "is not a science for its own sake, and can be of no use to anybody who will not practice it."[173]

Again, without metaphysics, no psychology can be a true psychology or a "science of the soul." We need to be vigilant about therapeutic modalities that do not treat the whole personality, seeing as they cannot provide a comprehensive diagnosis or treatment in keeping with our deepest human needs; rather, they can only offer ineffectual counterfeits. Modern psychology is "an illusory medicine to cure an equally illusory disease."[174] It is only metaphysics that allows for a spiritually complete diagnosis, treatment, and cure for "the diseases which affect the soul, indicate their treatment, and point out their remedies."[175] Anything less would not be a postcolonial or, rather, a sacred psychology—without which the modern West will never recover what it has long forgotten. As the old paradigm falls apart before our very eyes, no equally impotent replacement is required; what is needed to restore a "science of the soul" is to urgently turn to the universal and timeless wisdom that has reliably guided all humanity, for millennia, in its quest for true knowledge of who we really are. We ignore this remedy at our peril.

173. Coomaraswamy, *Coomaraswamy*, 2:378.
174. Ta Hui, *Swampland Flowers*, 24.
175. Abū ʿAlī Aḥmad ibn Muḥammad Miskawayh, quoted in Nasr and Aminrazavi, *Anthology of Philosophy*, 1:325.

2

Birth as Theophany

Gazing into the boundless eyes of a newborn child can convey the feeling of transcendence, as though one is looking into the face of the Absolute. In this encounter, the separative sense of *self* and *other* may diminish or dissolve altogether. To witness a human birth itself is to understand it not merely as a biological event but as a "naturally supernatural" or "supernaturally natural" theophany.[1] The birth of a human being is itself an expression of mystery. It is something that, in the present day, is often taken for granted and insufficiently contemplated. If we do not reflect on the nature of birth and death, can we truly claim to know ourselves or to understand the meaning and purpose of life?

Whitall N. Perry (1920–2005) observes as follows about the momentous quality of birth and death:

> There are two historical moments in the life of every person on earth which are inexorably real and yet totally outside the reach of empirical consciousness: the moment of birth, and the moment of death. These two decisive events occur moreover exactly once, over the entire lifespan of the individual, and scarcely enter into his reflections at all—everything else considered.[2]

There is a part of us that is not of time—that is not born when we are born and does not die when we die. This brings into play an unescapable paradox, for what is eternal does not perish with time, yet birth and death are fundamental facets of human existence. Zhuāngzi (Chuang Tzu, ca. 369–ca. 286 BCE) acknowledges a non-dual reality beyond both birth and death that ultimately defines who we are: "Birth is not a beginning; death is not an end."[3] It is through the rare opportunity afforded by the gift of life that we can come to know ourselves and realize our full potential.

Our intrinsic connection to the sacred defines who we really are; therefore, when we ignore this dimension, our true identity becomes distorted and compromised. This happens due to the obscuration of that transpersonal faculty in us that knows our spiritual reality (the Intellect or the "eye of the heart") and is often confused with mere "reason." The Quran states, "It is not the eyes that are blind, but blind are the

---

1. Schuon, *Eye of the Heart*, 129.
2. Perry, *Challenges*, 129–30.
3. Zhuāngzi, quoted in Giles, *Musings of a Chinese Mystic*, 104.

hearts within the breasts" (22:46). Through the awakening of this inward faculty, we can abide in a state that approximates our primordial nature. We cannot forget that "there is no theophany that is not prefigured in the very constitution of the human being, made as it is 'in the image of God.'"[4] The sacred that permeates the entirety of our lives, whether we are aware of it or not, as the Spirit is the supreme gift: "Every good gift and every perfect gift is from above" (James 1:17). In fact, only the Divine knows what the human being is and will ultimately become. We are reminded, "Surely we belong to God, and to Him we return" (Quran 2:156).

According to traditional cosmology and psychology, the macrocosm and the microcosm mirror each other. This is conveyed in the Hermetic maxim, "In truth certainly and without doubt, whatever is below is like that which is above, and whatever is above is like that which is below."[5] Similarly, the Zohar states, "God . . . made this [terrestrial] world corresponding to the world above, and everything which is above has its counterpart here below . . . and yet all constitute a unity."[6] In the mirroring process between what is above and what is below, each human being is a miniature of the cosmos (or a *microcosm*). The planimetric levels of reality exist both within and without individual being and are unified in the Absolute. According to Islamic spirituality, "Man is a little cosmos, and the cosmos is like a big man."[7] This is also reflected in the following verse: "We have recounted all things in an evident prototype" (Quran 36:12). The traditions teach that the human being has a triadic constitution: of Spirit, soul, and body. Because the Divine is immanent as well as transcendent, the spiritual dimension not only surpasses the psychophysical realm but also includes the human psyche. Within the Islamic tradition, it is written, "We shall show them Our signs upon the horizons and within themselves, until it be manifest unto them that it is the truth" (Quran 41:53). The notion of the human microcosm is also central in Jewish mysticism, as recorded in the Zohar:

As man's body consists of members and parts of various ranks all acting and reacting upon each other so as to form one organism, so does the world at large consist of a hierarchy of created things, which when they properly act and react upon each together form literally one organic body.[8]

Ancient wisdom discerns a correspondence between the unseen world and the seen. The former corresponds to essences connected to the Spirit, which pervades the whole of reality. The traditional cosmologies of humanity also unite the temporal order with the eternal: "The things which are seen are temporal; but the things which are not seen are eternal" (2 Corinthians 4:18). This metaphysical correspondence is also to be found in Taoism, as expressed by the sixth-century sage Lao Tzu: "All things under heaven are born of the corporeal: The corporeal is born of the Incorporeal."[9]

4. Schuon, *Survey of Metaphysics and Esoterism*, 117.
5. Hermes Trismegistus, quoted in Burckhardt, *Alchemy*, 196.
6. Zohar 2:20a, quoted in Schaya, *Universal Aspects*, 90.
7. Sufi adage, quoted in Ibn 'Arabī, *Wisdom of the Prophets*, 11.
8. *Zohar*, 1:36.
9. Lao Tzu, chap. 40, in Wu, *Tao Teh Ching*, 46.

The whole of existence is contained in, and arises from, the Absolute: "Tao begets One: one begets two: two begets three: three begets all things. All things are backed by *yin* and faced by *yang*, and harmonized by the Immaterial Breath (*ch'i*)."[10] Unlike purely empirical ways of knowing, traditional cosmologies and epistemologies do not dismiss the unseen world but recognize that it informs the realm of the senses. This is understood in terms of the horizontal and vertical dimensions: The former is of time and contingent, whereas the latter is timeless and absolute. Modern science and psychology are confined to the horizontal dimension and cannot access that which is vertical.

A human being is born without any worldly belongings, completely innocent and utterly reliant on the Absolute for all things; eventually it dies and leaves this world the same way, as conveyed in the following: "For we brought nothing into this world, and certainly we can carry nothing out" (1 Timothy 6:7). The sacred origins of human birth are noted in the book of Jeremiah: "Before I formed thee in the belly, I knew thee; and before thou camest forth out of the womb I sanctified thee" (1:5). This nakedness before the Absolute symbolizes a human being's proximity to the primordial state, or our true identity prior to developing a separate self that entangles—and has us identify with—the world. Here, nakedness refers not only to outer clothing but to the state of purity when we abide in the Absolute. Both Adam and Eve were naked in their primordial state: "And they were both naked, the man and his wife, and were not ashamed" (Genesis 2:25). This nakedness is the Spirit's own clothing for us and is not nakedness as generally understood; rather, it is an inward state. We are reminded that our "bodies are temples of the Holy Spirit" (1 Corinthians 6:19 NIV).

Due to their fallen condition, Adam and Eve lost their capacity for direct spiritual knowing. This led to them losing their sense of the sacred and the "eye of the heart" became corrupted: "And the eyes of them both were opened, and they knew that they were naked" (Genesis 3:7). Through the profanation of their primordial state, this nakedness is no longer holy and is thus condemned. St. Paul writes, "If so be that being clothed we shall not be found naked" (2 Corinthians 5:3), meaning that, by covering our fallen condition with faith and virtue, we will remain in a proper relationship to the Divine. Anything other than spiritual nakedness implies worldly separation and division and is a veil between the human and the Divine. Metaphysically speaking, as Meister Eckhart (1260–1328) confirms, to be "naked" is to be more unified with the Absolute: "The greater the nakedness, the greater the union."[11] Likewise, St. John of the Cross (1542–91) speaks of the "nakedness of spirit."[12] It is by recovering our innate mystical nakedness that we can efface ourselves and ultimately unite with the Absolute, "as having nothing, and yet possessing all things" (2 Corinthians 6:10).

The crown of the head—the summit of the human body—is the first point to depart the womb and the first to enter the world. It also defines the upright posture of the person, which is greatly symbolic. We recall Prophet Muhammad's words: "The first thing that God created was the Intellect," or "The first thing God created was

---

10. *Tao Te Ching*, chap. 42, quoted in Perry, *Treasury of Traditional Wisdom*, 23.
11. Eckhart, *Essential Sermons*, 105.
12. St. John of the Cross, *John of the Cross*, 60.

the Spirit."[13] This conveys that the Intellect (*'Aql*) and the Spirit (*Rūḥ*) refer ultimately to the same reality. The human being is considered to be the highest of all creatures because of this transcendent faculty. The psalmist recalls that "in wisdom hast thou made them all" (104:24). It is through wisdom that we can truly live and act in this world; as Christ says, "Ye shall know the Truth and the Truth shall make you free" (John 8:32).

Fools Crow (1890–1989), a Lakota spiritual leader, shows that a human being corresponds to both the geomorphic and theomorphic dimensions:

> The Great Spirit, molded us from the ground and gave this land to us. He placed us here, and told us that it is our land. So we are part of it and one in spirit with it. That is why we seek harmony with all creation. We share the same Creator and heritage.[14]

This correspondence is also found within the Abrahamic monotheisms of Judaism, Christianity, and Islam: when God created Adam from clay, and said, "The Lord God formed man of the dust of the ground, and breathed into his nostrils the breath of life; and man became a living soul" (Genesis 2:7). Likewise, the book of Genesis affirms that we are also of the earth: "For dust thou art, and unto dust shalt thou return" (3:19). Again, our very being is anchored in the sacred, as expressed in the Quran: "But His command, when He intendeth a thing, is only that He saith unto it: Be! And it is" (36:81). We find an analogous position in the Christian tradition: "He spoke and they were made: he commanded and they were created" (Psalm 32:9 DRB).

Human birth is a theophany (*tajallī*)—a Divine disclosure—a unique phenomenon that can never be replicated; at the same time, it encompasses the whole of reality within itself. Birth understood metaphysically can be regarded as "the passage from one cosmic plane to another."[15] The manifestation of the Absolute as all-possibility is unlimited and can never be exhausted. In Jewish mysticism, the human soul is said to have preexisted in the womb of eternity from the time of creation:

> Since the day when it occurred to God to create the world, and even before it was really created, all the souls of the righteous were hidden in the divine idea, every one in its peculiar form. When He shaped the world, they were actualized and they stood before Him in their various forms in the supreme heights [still in the Sefirotic world], and only then did He place them in a treasure-house in the upper Paradise.[16]

The mystic and physician Paracelsus (1493–1541) outlines the significance of the human microcosm—consisting of Spirit, soul, and body—as applied to our sojourn in this temporal existence:

---

13. See Majlisī, *Biḥār al-anwār*.
14. Fools Crow, quoted in Mails, *Fools Crow*, 47.
15. Reichel-Dolmatoff, *Amazonian Cosmos*, 151.
16. Zohar 3:302b, quoted in Scholem, *Major Trends in Jewish Mysticism*, 242.

The soul is born in this way: when the child is conceived in the womb—that is to say, born into its seed—a word from God enters into this carnal conception, which gives the flesh its soul. Thus the soul—take good note of this—becomes the centre of man, in whom now both good and evil impulses dwell. The body is the house of the soul.[17]

To be fully human is to recognize our fundamental relationship with the Divine, which is to say that our true identity *in divinis* is the primordial nature (*fiṭra*), the "image of God" (*imago Dei*), Buddha-nature (*Buddha-dhātu*), or the Self (*Ātmā*)— hence the prophetic saying, "He who knows himself knows his Lord." Ibn 'Arabī (1165–1240), the Spanish Sufi known as "the Greatest Master" (*al-Shaykh al-Akbar*), observes, "The Man is not he who realizes his Lord. The Man is he who realizes his own entity."[18] Within the Buddhist tradition, this process is known as "seeing into your true nature."[19] It must never be forgotten that our primordial nature can never be lost or destroyed, as it contains within itself the transpersonal human archetype.

In returning to the metaphysical foundations of all religions and their "science of the soul," we can understand the preciousness of human birth and what it means for our lives in this world. We recall the Patristic formula, "God became man that man might become God,"[20] or alternatively, "The Logos became man, so that man might become Logos."[21] Similarly, the sacred psychology found in all spiritual traditions could be described in the following way: "The Self became *ego* in order that the *ego* might become Self";[22] this is to say, "In man the Spirit becomes the ego in order that the ego may become pure Spirit."[23] The same principle could also be illustrated as "*Ātmā* became *Māyā* so that *Māyā* might realize *Ātmā*."[24] The relationship between the relative and the Absolute is summarized as follows: "To know that the relative comes from the absolute and depends on It is to know that the relative is not the Absolute and disappears in the face of It."[25]

Many of the religions recognize the preciousness of human life, which enables us to return to the Divine by journeying on one of the divinely revealed spiritual paths. So the eighth-century sage Shankara states that "human birth is difficult to obtain."[26] The *Uddhava Gītā* also addresses this matter: The "human body . . . is like a . . . boat—so difficult to secure . . . the man who does not strive to cross the ocean of Samsāra [cycles of birth and death], is verily a suicide" (15:17).[27] Śrī Ānandamayī Mā (1896–1982) acknowledged the importance of being born a human: "Man is the

17. Paracelsus, *Paracelsus*, 199.
18. Ibn 'Arabī, quoted in Chittick, *Sufi Path of Knowledge*, 322.
19. Hakuin, *Essential Teachings*, 62.
20. Clement of Alexandria, quoted in Osborn, *Clement of Alexandria*, 144.
21. St. Mark the Ascetic, "Letter to Nicolas the Solitary," in Palmer et al., *Philokalia*, 1:155.
22. Schuon, *Gnosis*, trans. Palmer, 71.
23. Schuon, *Understanding Islam*, 139.
24. Schuon, *Light*, 96.
25. Schuon, *Understanding Islam*, 66–67.
26. Śaṅkarācārya, verse 2, *Vivekachudamani of Sri Sankaracharya*, 2.
27. Uddhava Gītā 15:17, *Uddhava Gita*, 221–22.

image of God. To be born in a human body is the highest type of birth."[28] For this reason, Śrī Rāmakrishna (1836–86), the Paramahamsa of Dakshineshwar, emphasizes the need to make use of this precious opportunity: "He is born in vain, who, having attained the human birth, so difficult to get, does not attempt to realise God in this very life."[29] He states, "Futile is the human birth without the awakening of spiritual consciousness."[30] According to the *Kulārṇava Tantra*, Lord Shiva asks, "After obtaining a human body, which is difficult to obtain and which serves as a ladder to liberation, who is more sinful than he who does not cross over to the Self?"[31]

The Taoist adept Chang Po-tuan (Zhang Boduan, 983–1082), who was well versed in Buddhism and Confucianism, wrote the following about human birth:

> *The newborn state—what is it like?*
> *The primordial and the temporal are one energy.*
> *No discrimination, no knowledge, not a single stain—*
> *The seed of buddhas and immortals, the lair of sages.*[32]

Padmasambhāva (eighth century), an Indian tantric master, expressed something similar: "This precious human birth . . . is difficult to obtain. . . . All the victors relied on it to go beyond. . . . Day and night, without leisure, practice the genuine dharma."[33] The Tibetan monk and teacher Gampopa (1079–1153) stated, "One free and well-endowed human life is more precious than myriads of non-human lives in any of the six states of [*saṃsāric*] existence."[34] Buddhist monk and renowned Indian philosopher Śāntideva (685–763) similarly taught, "The Lord has said that human birth is exceedingly hard to win; hard as for a turtle to pass its neck into the hole of a yoke in the ocean."[35] So, too, Patrul Rinpoche (1808–87) elaborates on Shakyamuni Buddha's metaphor of how rare and precious human life is:

> Imagine the whole cosmos of a billion universes as a vast ocean. Floating upon it is a yoke, a piece of wood with a hole in it that can be fixed around the horns of a draught oxen. This yoke, tossed hither and thither by the waves, sometimes eastward, sometimes westward, never stays in the same place even for an instant. Deep down in the depths of the ocean lives a blind turtle who rises up to the surface only once every hundred years. That the yoke and the turtle might meet is extremely unlikely. The yoke itself is inanimate; the turtle is not intentionally seeking it out. The turtle, being blind, has no eyes with which to spot the yoke. If the yoke were to stay in one place, there might be a chance of their meeting; but it is continually on the move. If the turtle were to spend its entire time swimming around the surface, it might, perhaps,

28. Ānandamayī, *Sad Vani*, 49.
29. Rāmakrishna, *Sayings of Sri Ramakrishna*, 27.
30. Rāmakrishna, *Gospel of Ramakrishna*, 844.
31. Kulārṇava Tantra 1:16–27, quoted in Feuerstein, *Tantra*, 53.
32. Chang Po-tuan, *Inner Teachings of Taoism*, 110.
33. Padmasambhāva, quoted in Dzatrul, *Guide to the Thirty-Seven Practices*, 23.
34. Gampopa, quoted in Evans-Wentz, *Tibetan Yoga and Secret Doctrines*, 90.
35. Śāntideva, *Path of Light*, 49.

cross paths with the yoke; but it surfaces only once every hundred years. The chances of the yoke and the turtle coming together are therefore extremely small. Nevertheless, by sheer chance the turtle might still just slip its neck into the yoke. But it is even more difficult than that, the sūtras say, to obtain a human existence.[36]

Each human being is unique and can never be replicated, and yet there is a perfection in the imperfection of manifestation. Ibn ʿArabī elaborates on what appears as a paradox:

> God said, "He gave everything its creation" ([Quran] 20:50) and this is identical with the perfection of that thing, so it lacks (naqs) nothing. The reason for this is that we are created on the model of Him who possesses nondelimited perfection. . . . Nothing issues from the Perfect without being in accordance with the appropriate perfection. So there is no imperfect thing in the cosmos whatsoever. Were it not for the accidents which give birth to maladies, man would enjoy himself within the form of the cosmos, just as the cosmos enjoys itself, and he would delight in it, for it is the garden of the Real (bustān al-ḥaqq). . . . So perfection is an intrinsic attribute of the things, while imperfection is an accidental affair whose essence is perfection.[37]

Every person, as Plato (429–347 BCE) confirms, is fashioned by what is perfect and beyond all change:

> Now everything that becomes or is created must of necessity be created by some cause, for without a cause nothing can be created. The work of the creator, whenever he looks to the unchangeable and fashions the form and nature of his work after an unchangeable pattern, must necessarily be made fair and perfect. . . . If the world be indeed fair and the artificer good, it is manifest that he must have looked to that which is eternal.[38]

Across the spiritual traditions, there is a common agreement, as expressed by St. Augustine (354–430), that "there can be no accidents . . . in God."[39]

From the metaphysical point of view of nonduality, to be born implies duality and an irreversible separation from the Absolute within the temporal order of manifestation. This idea is found within all spiritual traditions, including the Islamic, which views the whole of the manifestation of the cosmos as an indivisible oneness expressed in the doctrine of the Divine Unity (Tawḥīd). It is from this perspective that Rābiʿa al-ʿAdawiyya (d. 801) writes, "Thine existence is a sin with which no other sin can be compared."[40] This is because there is no separate existence or identity in the Divine Unity. In Shin Buddhism, we find a similar view: "Human life is an abyss

36. Patrul Rinpoche, Words of My Perfect Teacher, 33–34.
37. Ibn ʿArabī, quoted in Chittick, Sufi Path of Knowledge, 294.
38. Plato, Timaeus 28a, 28b, 29a, Dialogues of Plato, 2:523, 524.
39. St. Augustine, bk. 5, chap. 2, Trinity, 177.
40. Rābiʿa al-ʿAdawiyya, quoted in Lings, Sufi Saint, 125.

of sin."[41] Here, "sin" refers to the darkness of spiritual ignorance (Pāli: *avijjā*; Sanskrit: *avidyā*). The great Sufi teacher Junayd (830–910) emphasizes that Divine Unity or "Tawḥīd is the return of man to his origin, so that he will be as he was before he came [in]to being."[42] Eckhart puts this dilemma slightly differently: "If my life is God's being, then God's existence must be my existence and God's is-ness is my is-ness, neither less nor more."[43] It is often forgotten that because we exist, we have no existence except in the Absolute, as St. Augustine makes clear: "They neither altogether are, nor altogether are not, for they are, since they are from Thee, but are not, because they are not, what Thou art."[44] The Sage of Arunachala, Śrī Ramana Maharshi (1879–1950), articulates the paradox of human birth from a perspective of pure nonduality:

> You who wish to celebrate the birthday, seek first whence was your birth. One's true birthday is when he enters That which transcends birth and death—the Eternal Being. At least on one's birthday one should mourn one's entry into this world (*samsara*). To glory in it and celebrate it is like delighting in and decorating a corpse. To seek one's Self and merge in the Self: that is wisdom.[45]

This renowned Buddhist passage from the Pāli cannon (*Udāna* 7:1–3) acknowledges that the highest attainment for the human being is to transcend the cosmic process of birth and death (*samsāra*):

> There is, O monks, an unborn, an unbecome, an unmade, an uncompounded; if, O monks, there were not here this unborn, unbecome, unmade, uncompounded, there would not here be an escape from the born, the become, the made, the compounded. But because there is an unborn, an unbecome, an unmade, an uncompounded, therefore there is an escape from the born, the become, the made, the compounded.[46]

Birth in the Pure Land is called "birth [of] no-birth" because one enters unconditioned reality where dependent origination (Pāli: *paṭiccasamuppāda*; Sanskrit: *pratītyasamutpāda*) comes to an end—both birth and death, as conventionally understood, no longer exist.[47] To be "unborn" is to abide in Buddha-nature, or our primordial nature, which is grounded in the Absolute.[48] Metaphysically, this idea is expounded in the Heart Sūtra (*Prajñāpāramitā-hridaya-sūtra*), "Form is emptiness; emptiness is form," highlighting the essential identity of *samsāra* and *nirvāṇa*.[49]

The empirical ego or personality, which stands between Divine transcendence and immanence, is a veil that needs to be lifted. This is summarized by Ḥāfiẓ (ca. 1315–90):

41. Kanamatsu, *Naturalness*, 98.
42. Junayd, quoted in Affifi, *Mystical Philosophy*, 138.
43. Eckhart, *Essential Sermons*, 187.
44. St. Augustine, 7.11.17, *Confessions of Saint Augustine*, 122.
45. Ramana, *Collected Works*, 91.
46. Quoted in Pallis, *Buddhist Spectrum*, 68–69.
47. Shinran, *Essential Shinran*, 206.
48. See Yōtaku, *Unborn*.
49. The Heart Sūtra, quoted in Lopez, *Heart Sutra Explained*, 57.

"Thou art thine own veil, O Ḥāfiẓ: remove thyself."[50] It is then that the Real will disclose itself as it truly is so that the secrets of our own souls will be known to us in relationship to the Absolute. The empirical ego is fueled by a separate self that is fundamentally dualistic and fragmented, and thus the root cause of human suffering. The Sufi Manṣūr al-Ḥallāj (858–922) speaks to the wound of duality as it relates to the separate self: "Between me and You there lingers an 'it is I' which torments me."[51]

Due to the temporal cycle and our fallen or *saṃsāric* consciousness, human existence is not without "travail[s] in birth" (Galatians 4:19), reflecting God's intention to "greatly multiply thy sorrow and thy conception; in sorrow thou shalt bring forth children" (Genesis 3:16); however, no matter how challenging, deprived or traumatic our circumstances may be, we must not ignore that we are called to be "partakers of the divine nature" (2 Peter 1:4). According to the Quran, we were fundamentally "created to worship God" (51:56). This awareness will allow us to endure and even flourish despite what may occur in the world of manifestation. As the saints and sages of all traditions attest, there is no trauma from which we cannot heal and move beyond. We recall that "God burdens a soul only to its capacity" (Quran 2:286), and likewise, "God . . . will not suffer you . . . above that ye are able . . . to bear" (1 Corinthians 10:13). Detractors may argue that the epidemic of suicide in the contemporary world is the direct result of human souls being burdened beyond their "capacity." However, a counterargument could be made that when a person is grounded in their religious tradition, they are provided with the necessary spiritual support to endure traumas, and the present-day epidemic is a result of one's turning away from the sacred, no longer making these supports available.

To be defined by, or limited to, our traumas interferes with our ability to become who we were born to be. It is identification with a separate empirical ego that is the source of human suffering. The Buddha taught that human existence consists of continuous ontological dissatisfaction, known as *dukkha*, which means to suffer or be in pain. For this reason, the Buddha declared that all things are "burning,"[52] underscoring that the source of suffering is rooted in our clinging to sense experience and the inability to see beyond our fallen state. With this said, we would do well to remember that there are also advantages to living in the present day, despite its numerous challenges; for "where sin abounded, grace did much more abound" (Romans 5:20).

Seeing that this precious human birth is connected to our relationship with Ultimate Reality allows for human development to flourish: "Be ye therefore perfect, even as your Father which is in heaven is perfect" (Matthew 5:48). The Lakota holy man Hehaka Sapa, more commonly known as Black Elk (1863–1950), instructs that "we should understand well that all things are the works of the Great Spirit. . . . When we do understand all this deeply in our hearts . . . then we will be and act and live as He intends."[53] This is akin to the important *ḥadīth*, "Worship God as if you see Him, for if you do not see Him, He sees you." Integral human development requires faith and

50. Ḥāfiẓ, quoted in Nasr, *Knowledge and the Sacred*, 333.
51. Manṣūr al-Ḥallāj, quoted in Massignon, *Passion of al-Ḥallāj*, 2:169.
52. Buddha Shakyamuni, quoted in Rahula, *What the Buddha Taught*, 95.
53. Black Elk, "Foreword," xx.

adherence to one of the revealed spiritual traditions. Through our reliance on and connection to the Divine, we are able to grow spiritually and become who we truly are. "When I was a child, I spake as a child, I understood as a child, I thought as a child: but when I became a man, I put away childish things" (1 Corinthians 13:11). However, we must not lose sight of the importance of the purity and naturalness reflected in children, which is essential for the spiritual path. Christ said, "Verily I say unto you: Except ye be converted, and become as little children, ye shall not enter into the kingdom of heaven" (Matthew 18:3). Rāmakrishna expressed something similar: "So long as one does not become simple as a child, one cannot get divine illumination. Forget all the worldly knowledge that thou hast learnt and become as ignorant . . . as a child, then wilt thou get the knowledge of the True."[54] Mencius (Mengzi, 372–289 BCE) said, "The great man is he who does not lose his child's heart."[55] Black Elk makes a vital point: "Grown men may learn from very little children, for the hearts of little children are pure, and, therefore, the Great Spirit may show to them many things which older people miss."[56]

In its fullest sense, human existence reflects a great circle and consists of many circles within circles. Black Elk elucidates the meaning of the circle for human beings and its development through infancy, youth, adulthood, and old age:

> You have noticed that everything an Indian does is in a circle, and that is because the Power of the World always works in circles, and everything tries to be round. . . . The sun comes forth and goes down again in a circle. The moon does the same, and both are round. Even the seasons form a great circle in their changing, and always come back again to where they were. The life of a man is a circle from childhood to childhood, and so it is in everything where power moves.[57]

The form of the human microcosm corresponds to the cosmic cycles of the macrocosm. The human psyche is influenced according to the time and place in which it finds itself in the temporal realm. The circles that make up our lives are also informed by the ambiance of the age into which we are born.

Kathleen Raine (1908–2003) offers a poignant insight about the existential reality of this late phase of the current age: "Paradise [was] already lost long before [our] birth."[58] However, this is not cause for despair, as there are always spiritual compensations found in every age, particularly the present one, when the sense of the sacred has become diminished more than ever before.

The shadow side of this "precious human birth" is taking one's own life. This is tragic, whether understood in either a religious or secular context. There are certainly exceptions in which suicide is a selfless act in the service of truth or humanity—"that a man lay down his life" (John 15:13)—which indicates that, not only is the eternal

54. Rāmakrishna, *Sayings of Sri Ramakrishna*, 73.
55. Mencius, *Works of Mencius*, 322.
56. Black Elk, quoted in Brown, *Sacred Pipe*, 74–75.
57. Black Elk, quoted in Neihardt, *Black Elk Speaks*, 194–95.
58. Raine, *Farewell Happy Fields*, 78.

more important than temporal existence, but self-sacrifice in light of the Divine is the greatest of all offerings. With this noted, suicide often represents a fundamental confusion of what it means to be human and to sanctify life. We are exhorted to always "choose life" (Deuteronomy 30:19) and live in proximity to the Divine—"the way, the truth, and the life" (John 14:6)—regardless of our individual circumstances. The increasingly widespread incidence of suicide worldwide is truly heartbreaking and reflects a loss of the sense of the sacred on a mass scale. The belief that we have complete agency to determine our own fate overlooks the truth that this world is a test. Frithjof Schuon (1907–98) wrote,

> To this false life is opposed a true death: the death of passion; this is spiritual death, the cold and crystalline purity of the soul conscious of its immortality. To false death is opposed a true life: the life of the heart turned toward God and open to the warmth of His love. To false activity is opposed a true rest, a true peace: the repose of the soul that is simple and generous and content with God, the soul that turns aside from agitations and curiosity and ambition in order to repose in divine beauty. To false rest is opposed a true activity: the battle of the spirit against the multiple weaknesses that squander the soul—and this precious life—as in a game or dream.[59]

It is the misconception of a confused and distorted mind that believes suicide will provide an escape from human suffering. Such a person likely does not recognize their soul's longing to be healed in the sacred, yet the impulse to end their life implies (metaphysically) a wish to change the conditions of existence. From the point of view of eternity, however, what matters is that we endure our lot in this world and accept its mystery, however hard that may seem in light of the appalling suffering we see all around us. One often finds in religious texts the importance of attaining a "spiritual death" in this life, as Eckhart makes clear, stating, "Your soul must lose her being and her life,"[60] or as in the Jewish tradition, known as the "cessation or annihilation of existence" (*bittul ha-yesh*)—that is, by dying in the Absolute. This implicit teaching was made explicit in the renowned words of the Prophet of Islam: "Die before ye die" (*mūtū qabla an tamūtū*).

Our first birth is into terrestrial existence. Subsequently, we are called to embark on the spiritual path, which requires a "second birth," a death to our profane identity, in order to live in the Divine. Through this spiritual death and rebirth, we can begin to discern the deeper meaning of suffering. This will not always alleviate our immediate pain but, rather, may shift our focus to a higher life that pervades it, thus allowing us to achieve "the peace . . . which passeth all understanding" (Philippians 4:7). Accordingly, to not seek wholeness and liberation from our fallen state is itself a form of suicide in light of our creation in the "image of God" (Genesis 1:27).

If we are not aware of how influential the dominant secular narratives of what life is are and what it means to be human, we may come to forget the significance of this

---

59. Schuon, *Spiritual Perspectives and Human Facts*, 227.
60. Eckhart, sermon 5, *Complete Mystical Works*, 64.

unique opportunity known as human birth. This may cause us to live an infrahuman life of profound confusion and spiritual amnesia, making it easier to be led astray by the disintegrating forces of the zeitgeist. On the other hand, by living in remembrance of our own primordial nature and its connection to what lies beyond this life, we are sure to find guidance on a spiritual path.

Due to our fallen or *saṃsāric* consciousness, we have lost sight of the primordial state and have neglected to recognize the spiritual function of our birth in this world. This life is none other than a test to see if we can remember the "one thing . . . needful" (Luke 10:42). This is our integral connection to the Divine, throughout this ephemeral and troubling human existence. If we can embrace our human birth as a unique opportunity to restore the sacred in daily life, this will allow the outer and inner horizons of reality to open up for us. An authentic "science of the soul" must be informed by an understanding of our primordial nature; otherwise, we cut off any prospects for healing our hearts. The mystery of the created order, including human birth, is disclosed in the following well-known Islamic sacred tradition: "I was a Hidden Treasure, so I wanted to be known. Therefore, I created the world that I might be known." The most important question of all thus presents itself: *How will you make use of your own "precious human birth"?*

3

The Metaphysics of Trauma

To have experienced something so painful that words cannot describe it; to feel so wounded that we do not want to remember what happened to us, even though we cannot forget; to be trapped within the isolated confines of our own skin, as if held captive like a prisoner, yet feeling safe neither within ourselves nor in the outside world; to be all alone with the turmoil inside us, our only companion being the troubling thoughts that assail our minds; to be unable to live in the world or to focus on our immediate experience and what transcends it, so that this inability becomes itself a reminder of the pain we feel; to know that this experience has come to define us, even though we are unable to free ourselves from its all-encompassing grip (all the while yearning to be liberated from this affliction): all these ordeals offer a glimpse into the world of trauma.

As if out of nowhere, *trauma* has become a commonly used term in everyday life. Although the use of this word to signify a profound psychological wound is recent, it has long been used in the medical profession. Yet the reality of suffering goes back to time immemorial, recognized as central to human existence; and trauma may be understood as the inability to adequately integrate suffering into our lives. Many people experience traumatic events, yet not everyone becomes traumatized as a result. For this reason, it is important not to equate having lived through a potentially traumatic experience with trauma itself. What is distinctive about the present-day understanding of trauma or suffering is that it has become a problem to be ultimately resolved at a purely worldly level—in other words, that it can be eliminated from the human condition once and for all so that we may be allowed to live in a state of unfettered happiness. This is to overlook the nature of our existence in an ephemeral world that is replete with trials and tribulations. Alternatively, "we must not wish for the disappearance of any of our troubles, but grace to transform them."[1] The so-called problem of trauma or suffering is inseparable from the loss of a sense of the sacred, which is intrinsic to the condition of our fallen or *saṃsāric* state.

The fact that trauma, on a collective level, is so widely discussed today reveals not only our vulnerability but the precarious state—if not spiritual crisis—of the modern world. This raises the question: Is there something triggering about the modern world itself that is creating these conditions? Or is it just a matter of us having a

---

1. Weil, *Gravity and Grace*, 35.

heightened awareness of the different types of trauma that are prevalent today: complex trauma, historical trauma, and intergenerational trauma? There is something peculiar about this phenomenon, as just about everyone has been wounded by it, in a way that is inseparable from the larger mental health crisis in our topsy-turvy era.

On closer consideration, there appears to be a deeper dimension to the mass traumatization we see in the present day, which often goes unnoticed. This is a form of anguish due to the loss of a sense of the sacred—what we might call the *trauma of secularism*. The vacuum that has been created in the modern world due to the loss of religion is not something that should be taken lightly, yet it is often unrecognized because of the hegemonic dominance of science and its empirical epistemology that rules out alternative ways of knowing reality. However, for many people, illness, suffering, or trauma can—in themselves—impel a search for the sacred.

An important element missing in early attempts to define adverse experiences is the fragmentation that occurs within ourselves. This can occur when our transpersonal Self is lost sight of, which in turn leads people to exclusively identify who they are with their mind-sense-body complex. A traumatic event can split our identity and cause a myriad of problems. Trauma can thus be defined as "an event in the subject's life defined by its intensity, by the subject's incapacity to respond adequately to it, and by the upheaval and long-lasting effects that it brings about in the psychical organization."[2]

The founder of the "talking cure," Sigmund Freud (1856–1939), wrote,

> We apply it [trauma] to an experience which within a short period of time presents the mind with an increase of stimulus too powerful to be dealt with or worked off in the normal way, and this must result in permanent disturbances of the manner in which the energy operates.[3]

Elsewhere he wrote, "Neurosis could . . . be equated with a traumatic illness and would come about owing to inability to deal with an experience whose affective colouring was excessively powerful."[4] More recent studies have confirmed that certain shocks to the organism "can alter a person's biological, psychological, and social equilibrium to such a degree that the memory of one particular event comes to taint, and dominate, all other experiences, spoiling an appreciation of the present moment."[5]

When human beings experienced suffering—prior to the emergence of the modern world—it did not cause them to lose their faith; yet the existence of trauma today is, in many cases, the chief cause of unbelief. The argument is that if a powerful and benevolent Divine Reality exists, why do we find so much evil and suffering in the world? As the wound inflicted on our collective psyche has become more palpable in the present age, there is perhaps nothing more urgent than the need to revive a true psychology—grounded in metaphysics—or "science of the soul" that can affect the healing required to restore our spiritual health.

2. Laplanche and Pontalis, *Language of Psycho-Analysis*, 465.
3. Freud, *Introductory Lectures on Psychoanalysis*, 275.
4. Freud, *Introductory Lectures on Psychoanalysis*, 275.
5. Levine, *Trauma and Memory*, xx.

Among many spiritual traditions, illness, suffering, and trauma are viewed as a blessing because they provide an opportunity to purify and transform ourselves, thus strengthening our reliance on the Divine. As St. Teresa of Ávila (1515–82) affirms, "Suffering is to purify this soul."[6] And likewise, Śrī Ānandamayī Mā (1896–1982) discloses that "God comes to you in the disguise of suffering."[7] However, this does not necessarily happen automatically, for it often requires us to undergo the discipline of submitting to a divinely revealed therapy, as found in all spiritual traditions. There is an intimate relationship between suffering or trauma and the spiritual path. Yet we need to be careful with our terminology here because we are not equating suffering with trauma or trauma with illness, per se, but rather acknowledging that a transition through suffering or an illness is a component of healing trauma.

Through our participation in one of humanity's revealed religions, we may undergo metanoia, or a profound "change of heart," which is the true source of all healing. The "dark night of the soul," as expounded by the Spanish mystic St. John of the Cross (1542–91), conveys the experience of a total absence of divine light and hope. This necessitated a great deal of suffering for St. John, but the spiritual journey out of this abyss led him to a far-reaching transformation of his being. The Buddha taught that human existence consists of an abiding dissatisfaction, known as *dukkha* (Pāli/Sanskrit: *duḥkha*), and he became awakened to the "Four Noble Truths," which are (1) the existence of suffering, (2) the cause of suffering, (3) the end of suffering, and (4) the path leading out of suffering. Undertaking a spiritual path can thus be seen as a remedy for tackling the effects of suffering, pain, or even trauma by restoring wholeness to our psyches.

With the rise of "trauma culture" and trauma-informed therapies, it is often overlooked that the anguish of living in a world devoid of spiritual nourishment is tremendously detrimental, as this has proven to be an invaluable support for human resilience and well-being. Psychology today attempts to assess, diagnose, and treat trauma without acknowledging the anguish caused by secularism. Without understanding the historical developments that led to the rise of modernity—the fruition of the "Age of Enlightenment" of the seventeenth and eighteenth centuries—it is difficult to understand how this profane trajectory radically undermined the collective psyche. The discipline of modern psychology has unapologetically participated in this antispiritual outlook, which at the same time—paradoxically and unknowingly—has also attempted to remedy the situation. Bereft of any metaphysical foundations, psychology today remains adrift in a self-contradictory morass because it has failed to address the problem at its root.

By being born, we are subject to duality, which leads to an estrangement from the Absolute in this world. As such, entry into our temporal world of relativity inflicts a psychic wound in us. "The individual suffers because he perceives duality.... Find the One everywhere and in everything and there will be an end to pain and suffering."[8] Human beings find themselves trapped in a realm of perishable phenomena that

---

6. St. Teresa of Ávila, *Interior Castle*, 168.
7. Ānandamayī, *Essential Śrī Ānandamayī Mā*, 62.
8. Ānandamayī, *Essential Śrī Ānandamayī Mā*, 71.

expose us to separation, suffering, and death. Beyond manifestation, there is no separate self that suffers or can be traumatized. Due to their fallen condition, Adam and Eve lost their capacity for direct spiritual knowing, causing alienation from the Divine and discord between themselves. This led to the infliction of the primordial wound—a loss of the sense of the sacred and the corruption of the Intellect, or "eye of the heart," the part of us that religious traditions assert is our means of discerning spiritual reality directly.

It could be said that this wound is exacerbated by all other suffering or trauma in that it keeps us bound to our experience of this temporal reality, especially when we face adverse events. When a person has been deeply wounded and cuts themselves off from a connection to both others and to the Spirit, they are essentially abiding in a realm of consciousness that is akin to hell; yet we must not forget that "the doors of hell are locked on the *inside*."[9] To lose our intrinsic spiritual vision is to abide in a cul-de-sac of profound darkness. "The house without a window is hell," says Rūmī (1207–73), adding, "The foundation of religion . . . is to make windows!"[10]

The obscuration of our "eye of the heart" helps us understand the well-known declaration by Jean-Paul Sartre (1905–80) that "hell is other people!"[11] This outlook aptly frames the predicament of the modernist perspective, which views everything, and everyone, as a problem.

Emotionally detrimental experiences can often provoke us to view others as hellish, but it is the hell we harbor within us that we ought to be most fearful of because everything begins to mirror this overwhelming abyss that we project onto the world. This, in turn, prevents us from seeing our divine True Self, which is immanent in all people and living things. It is only by awakening the "eye of the heart" that life's conflicts can be ameliorated and lasting mental health achieved.

Mainstream therapies are unable to treat the whole person as they often just target the treatment of symptoms, not the root cause of our mental health difficulties. Rarely do we hear the question, "What is behind the symptom?"[12] If you trace this back to its source, we often find a traumatic event, which may be the "overarching rubric under which most other disorders are subordinated."[13] Yet it could be said that, at the heart of all traumas, is our fallen or *saṃsāric* state. Many therapists and researchers are finding that numerous mental health diagnostic categories overlap and are triggered by a traumatic event.[14] There is a strong connection between trauma, mental disturbance, physical illness, and addiction.[15] Yet through recourse to spiritual means, we may be better placed to access the foundations of trauma, to heal its wounds, and to restore wholeness.

---

9. Lewis, *Problem of Pain*, 130.
10. Rūmī, quoted in Chittick, *Sufi Path of Love*, 121.
11. Sartre, *No Exit*, 45.
12. Menninger with Mayman and Pruyser, *Vital Balance*, 325.
13. Higgins, *Resilient Adults*, 13.
14. See Bailey et al., "Childhood Trauma," 1111–22.
15. See Felitti et al., "Relationship of Childhood Abuse," 245–58; van der Kolk, *Body Keeps the Score*.

At the root of the crisis in modern psychology is the "Cartesian bifurcation," the dualism between mind and body (along with matter) that has plagued the mindset of the contemporary West since the seventeenth century. In this myopic and truncated outlook, human beings become separated from reality, and everything is objectified, further entrenching the psyche in a subject-object dichotomy. This perpetuates the illusion of a fragmented worldview and an isolated self, which serves to undermine our relationship to the sacred. This leads to a truncated identity that desacralizes the cosmos and traumatizes humanity. When the Intellect or "eye of the heart" is restored to its integral condition, the person no longer views reality as fragmented but rather considers each phenomenon as mirroring the unity of this created order.

Every true "science of the soul" takes into account the human psyche in light of sacred cosmology:

> In the Golden Age, all people experienced their essence, no holes. Then came the Silver Age as essence diminished and the holes began to appear; then the Bronze Age. Now we're in the Iron Age. It's the darkest, heaviest. Iron is really nothing but defense. We can sometimes feel the quality of iron in our own defenses: the hardness, the determination to protect ourselves. So this is one way of viewing the present time—all defenses against holes.[16]

Ananda Coomaraswamy (1877–1947) acknowledges the connection between human behavior and the underlying cosmic order: "The pattern of man's behavior is not to be found in any code, but in the principles of the universe, which is continually revealing to us *its own nature*."[17] Today, psychology and the field of mental health do not consider cosmic cycles and how they determine the human mind according to the time and place in which it finds itself. Nor do they account for how these changes are connected to the gradual distancing of the human psyche from the Spirit, which is essential to any assessment, diagnosis, and treatment with a view to restoring wholeness.

Across the diverse traditional cultures of humanity, this bifurcation does not exist, as it is recognized that we are composed of Spirit, soul, and body. Within each of the world's religions—Judaism, Christianity, Islam, Hinduism, Buddhism, Taoism, and the traditions of the First Peoples—there exists a corresponding psychology that is fully integrated and grounded in the sacred. To provide wholeness and healing to the human psyche requires metaphysics to restore an ontological dimension to psychology so that it can become, once again, a true "science of the soul." It is only through such a "salvific" psychology that the discipline can be rehabilitated as something that will overcome the acute limitations of its modern Western form.

The spiritual traditions all teach that human faculties, including our emotions, need to be contained within their proper sphere in order to be properly harmonized. However, emotions are not to be elevated to the level of principles that guide our thoughts and behavior; to do so would lead to an unstable psyche. Contrary to the

16. Almaas, *Elements of the Real*, 23.
17. Coomaraswamy, *Dance of Shiva*, 147.

notion that "the psyche is a self-regulating system that maintains its equilibrium just as the body does,"[18] it is, in fact, the spiritual dimension that regulates the soul and the body. The Intellect—being synonymous with Spirit—is above all the faculties, including the psychophysical order that integrates them.

The intermediary realm of the human psyche is mysterious, as has been acknowledged: "There is nothing so unknown to the soul as herself."[19] For this reason, to understand and heal the human psyche requires a spiritual "infusion" from what transcends it. If, when in a state of disequilibrium, emotions are allowed to direct our lives, then exposure to suffering and trauma will become considerably heightened. When we are feeling depressed or anxious, it does not necessarily mean that the entire world is out of balance; and likewise, if we are hurt, it should not suggest that the Divine is somehow unjust toward us. Similarly, if we encounter personal tragedy, this does not entail that the rest of creation has been harmed. We need to add a caveat here that, although the existential alienation that many feel today is a sign of a decline in the cosmic cycle, it needs to be made clear that not everything we experience in our lives is necessarily a consequence of the *Kali-Yuga* or "Dark Age." Those who have sundered themselves from religion may struggle more when experiencing suffering or may be "triggered" to a larger extent than those who adhere to a revealed religion. According to Gai Eaton (1921–2010),

> When misfortune strikes profane people they suffer on two levels and their pain is doubled. On the one hand, there is the misfortune as such and the pain they feel; on the other, there is the belief that it should never have happened and that its happening proves something very bitter and very ugly about the nature of the world (and if they bring God into it, then about the nature of God). They suffer because "something is wrong"; and then they suffer again because "everything is wrong."[20]

Because human beings are subject to the constraints of time and cannot see into the future, they cannot fully grasp why certain things happen in the world or whether there is any divine purpose behind them. In other words, the significance of such events cannot be understood *sub specie aeternitatis* ("under the aspect of eternity"). The book of Ecclesiastes declares, "That which hath been is now; and that which is to be hath already been" (3:15). The well-known Chinese allegory of the horse that ran away also comes to mind here:

> The poor old man . . . lived with his son in a ruined fort at the top of a hill. He owned a horse which strayed off one day, whereupon the neighbours came to offer sympathy at his loss. "What makes you supposed that this is misfortune?" the old man asked. Later the horse returned accompanied by several wild horses and this time the neighbours came to congratulate him on his good luck. "What makes you think this is good luck?" he enquired. Having a

18. Jung, *Collected Works*, 16:153.
19. Eckhart, *Meister Eckhart*, 5.
20. Eaton, *Islam*, 193.

number of horses now available, the son took to riding and, as a result, broke his leg. Once more the neighbours rallied round to express sympathy and once again the old man asked how they could know that this was misfortune. Then the next year war broke out and because he was lame the son was exempt from going to the war.[21]

Existence in our ephemeral world consists of both gifts and losses. Much of our well-being depends on how we view these vicissitudes. According to the Austrian psychotherapist Alfred Adler (1870–1937), "We do not suffer from the shock of [traumatic] experiences. . . . We make out of them just what suits our purposes."[22] Because of the limited purview into our existence, we are unable to readily discern what is inimical to us or in our best interests, seeing as events in life may be other than how they appear. We recall that "the Lord giveth and the Lord taketh away" (Job 1:21).

The Dhammapada of the Buddhist tradition conveys how the world we believe in becomes the world we inhabit: "Everything has mind in the lead, has mind in the forefront, is made by mind" (1:1).[23] If we see the world as unsafe and hostile, we will respond accordingly. Likewise, if we view life as a temporal reality that serves as a place of trials, this will determine how we live. Through metaphysics, we can understand that, prior to the mind becoming implicated in the temporal order, its fundamental dispositions were already—by and large—determined by our fallen or *saṃsāric* condition.

The condition known as post-traumatic stress disorder (PTSD) is well known today. It concerns the experience of terrifying events with which we cannot cope. There may also be flashbacks or vivid experiences where the person mentally relives certain aspects of a traumatic episode as if it were occurring here and now. Other symptoms may include nightmares, severe anxiety, or uncontrollable thoughts pertaining to the event. It is essential not to pathologize trauma and equate it with mental illness, as it is an event that *happened* to them; it is not who the person *is*. The same goes for a person suffering from mental illness; the diagnosis is not who they truly are. We cannot "treat" the impacts of war, rape, molestation, natural calamities, or any other horrific encounter; what has occurred cannot be undone. With that said, we can treat the imprints of trauma on the human psyche and body.

Aeschylus (ca. 525–ca. 456 BCE) alludes to the wisdom that can be conferred by trauma:

> Knowledge won through suffering. / Drop, drop—in our sleep, upon the heart / sorrow falls, memory's pain, / and to us, though against our very will, / even in our own despite, / comes wisdom / by the awful grace of God.[24]

The arising of metaphysical insight may help us see that trauma does not define us and that suffering can never touch our True Self. Furthermore, we are called to

21. Quoted in Cooper, *Taoism*, 39.
22. Alfred Adler, quoted in Ansbacher and Ansbacher, *Individual Psychology of Alfred Adler*, 208.
23. Buddha, 1:1, *Dhammapada*, trans. Cleary, 7.
24. *Three Greek Plays*, 169–70.

be receptive to what adverse experiences have to teach us, perplexing or enigmatic though they may be. The great mystical poet of Tibet, Milarepa (ca. 1052–ca. 1135), shares the transformative experience of the loss of his most prized possession, demonstrating the impermanence of all phenomena:

I once had a pot, now I do not. . . .
This clay pot so important, the whole of my wealth,
Becomes my lama [teacher] in the moment it breaks,
Teaching impermanence, how amazing![25]

Religion and spirituality are vital in supporting psychological integration and resilience. Yet when cut off from sacred traditions, people are more prone to become attached to their suffering rather than see it as an inevitable feature of a finite, transitory, and imperfect world.

There are many cases today in which the effects of a traumatic event do not dissipate on their own but rather fester and worsen: "The psychical trauma—or more precisely the memory of the trauma—acts like a foreign body which long after its entry must continue to be regarded as an agent that is still at work."[26] Thus the soul's response to trauma often becomes the problem more so than the traumatic event itself.

People will be unable to overcome traumatic events unless they acknowledge what has happened to them. Mainstream psychology often constructs a narrative to explain why a person thinks and behaves in the way they do. In the words of Freud, "While the patient lives [the trauma] through as something real and actual, we have to accomplish the therapeutic task, which consists chiefly in translating it back again into terms of the past."[27] Dating back to the earliest beginnings of the "talking cure," it has been assumed that trauma "immediately and permanently disappeared when we had succeeded in bringing clearly to light the memory of the event by which it was provoked and in arousing its accompanying affect."[28] However, this is not so easy to do, as traumatic events can transcend the limits of language and thus remain ineffable.

As trauma is preverbal, not having the language to speak about it can instill a great deal of fear and anxiety. William Shakespeare (1564–1616) writes, "O horror, horror, horror! Tongue nor heart cannot conceive nor name thee! Confusion now hath made his masterpiece!"[29] The saints and sages remind us that Ultimate Reality or the Absolute escapes all attempts to be captured in words. Although language cannot contain what transcends the psychophysical order, it can help point to the Real, if informed by traditional metaphysics.[30]

Words can be useful if we understand them in the way indicated by the Buddha—namely, as a finger pointing at the moon. In the Taoist tradition, we find

25. Jetsun Milarepa, quoted in Heruka, *Life of Milarepa*, 150.
26. Breuer and Freud, *Studies on Hysteria*, 6.
27. Freud, *Collected Papers*, 2:371.
28. Breuer and Freud, *Studies on Hysteria*, 6.
29. Shakespeare, *Macbeth* 2.3.64–66, in Shakespeare, *Works of William Shakespeare*, 11:31.
30. See Whorf, *Language, Thought, and Reality*.

the affirmation "The Way that can be told of is not an Unvarying Way."[31] The mindful use of language can be therapeutic, as Shakespeare points out: "Give sorrow words: the grief that does not speak / Whispers the o'er-fraught heart, and bids it break."[32] While mainstream talking therapies can contribute to symptom reduction or management, they are not enough to support healing and wholeness; a metaphysics with a sacred orientation is also needed to fully understand the nonverbal cues that are linked to the human ternary of Spirit, soul, and body.

As every person is fundamentally unique, we need to exercise extreme humility when entering into therapeutic relationships with those seeking help. The importance of authentic presence and empathy, including silence and the willingness to listen deeply, is essential in treating people with trauma. What is missing from mainstream approaches to psychology is the transpersonal dimension, which no longer informs the discipline's outlook.

Austrian psychiatrist Viktor Frankl (1905–97) documents how faith provided strength and resilience to those who survived the atrocities of the Holocaust: "They were able to retreat from their terrible surroundings to a life of inner riches and spiritual freedom."[33] Frankl starkly asserts that the "cure is self-transcendence" and makes the important point that "in some way[s], suffering ceases to be suffering at the moment it finds a meaning."[34] Fritz Perls (1893–1970) is correct, in principle, when he remarks that "you never overcome *anything* by resisting it. You only can overcome something by going deeper into it. . . . Whatever it is, if you go deeply enough into it, then it will disappear; it will be assimilated."[35] However, without access to a reality that transcends the human condition, there is no agency to remedy our suffering or trauma or to reintegrate the human psyche into the sacred.

It is the transpersonal dimension that guides the assessment, treatment, and healing of a person. Therefore, being a wayfarer on a spiritual path is indispensable. As St. John Cassian (ca. 360–ca. 435) writes, "The Doctor of our souls has also placed the remedy in the hidden regions of the soul."[36] According to Imam 'Alī (d. 661), "Your cure is within you, but you do not know."[37] Being an active witness to another person's suffering can be therapeutic in and of itself when framed in a spiritual context. The Sufi poet and mystic Rūmī says, "Your ears are turned entirely toward the cries of the distressed, and your eyes totally toward the weeping of those who have suffered injustice—thus you apply salve to their wounds and extend a helping hand."[38]

As the saints and sages of all traditions attest, there is no trauma that cannot be healed and from which we cannot move beyond. According to the Tao Te Ching, "He knows the pain. . . . Therefore he does not have it,"[39] whereas Rūmī puts it like this:

31. Lao Tzu, chap. 1, *Tao Te Ching*, 1.
32. Shakespeare, *Macbeth* 4.3.209–10, in Shakespeare, *Works of William Shakespeare*, 11:50.
33. Frankl, *Man's Search for Meaning*, 47.
34. Frankl, *Man's Search for Meaning*, 131; Frankl, *Man's Search for Meaning*, 117.
35. Perls, *Gestalt Therapy Verbatim*, 212.
36. St. John Cassian, "On the Eight Vices," in Palmer et al., *Philokalia*, 1:76.
37. Quoted in Chittick, *Sufism*, 104.
38. Rūmī, quoted in Chittick, *Sufi Path of Love*, 104.
39. Tao Te Ching, chap. 71, quoted in *Sacred Books of China*, 113.

"Where there is pain, the cure will come."[40] We were, after all, born whole and complete, and it is this fact that confers much-needed context. In the words of Frithjof Schuon (1907–98), trauma "has no right to be absolute; it is there to be overcome and to be assimilated in view of that which is the reason for being of our life and of our very existence."[41]

In essence, it is the way in which things are perceived (rather than events in themselves) that either supports our recovery and spiritual health or disturbs the equilibrium of the human psyche. It is said that a spiritually well person is able to endure: "The spirit of a man will sustain his infirmity, but a wounded spirit who can bear?" (Proverbs 18:14). We recall that "God burdens a soul only to its capacity" (Quran 2:286), and likewise, "God . . . will not suffer you . . . above that ye are able . . . to bear" (1 Corinthians 10:13). We must not minimize human suffering, as each person has their own unique trials in this reality; however, we must also not forget that all suffering including trauma has an underlying meaning, for "a suffering which has no possible use would be pure evil."[42]

Regarding the spiritual meaning of suffering, Śrī Rāmakrishna (1836–86) said, "You are suffering; but your illness has a deep meaning."[43] Śrī Ramana Maharshi (1879–1950) goes as far as to say, "Suffering is the way for Realisation of God."[44] From a metaphysical vantage point, this challenging insight from Angelus Silesius (1624–77) becomes intelligible: "If you only knew the worth of suffering, / You would have chosen it ahead of anything."[45] As Ānandamayī Mā stated, "By sorrow does the Lord dispel sorrow and by adversity does He destroy adversity. When this is done He sends no more suffering—this must be borne in the mind at all times."[46] Hehaka Sapa, or Black Elk (1863–1950), voices the importance of self-sacrifice in the form of intentional suffering: "I shall . . . offer my body and soul to Wakan-Tanka [Great Spirit] . . . that our people may live."[47] Meister Eckhart (1260–1328) addresses the spiritual significance of adversity:

> Everything the good man suffers for God's sake, he suffers in God, and God is suffering with him in his suffering. But if my suffering is in God and God is suffering with me, how then can suffering be sorrow to me, if suffering loses its sorrow, and my sorrow is in God, and my sorrow is God?[48]

Eckhart adds, "Since you . . . know that it is God's will . . . do not consider any pain as pain."[49]

Within the Christian tradition, the experience of suffering can unite the person with the passion of Christ and its redemptive power: "When I thought to know

40. Rūmī, quoted in Chittick, Sufi Path of Love, 208.
41. Schuon, Play of Masks, 67.
42. Weil, First and Last Notebooks, 139.
43. Rāmakrishna, Original Gospel of Rāmakrishna, 97.
44. Ramana, Talks with Sri Ramana Maharshi, 103.
45. Silesius, bk. 5, Cherubinic Wanderer, trans. Shrady, 120.
46. Ānandamayī, Essential Śrī Ānandamayī Mā, 69.
47. Black Elk, quoted in Brown, Sacred Pipe, 78, 70.
48. Eckhart, Essential Sermons, 235.
49. Eckhart, sermon 4, Teacher and Preacher, 248.

this, it was too painful for me" (Psalm 73:16), and "I am troubled; I am bowed down
greatly; I go mourning all . . . day long. For my loins are filled with a loathsome disease: and there is no soundness in my flesh" (Psalm 38:6–7). Syncletica (ca. 270–
ca. 350) equates suffering to a medicine that can heal: "In the same way that a powerful
medicine cures an illness, so illness itself is a medicine."[50] St. Maximus the Confessor
(ca. 580–662) notes,

> The person who truly wishes to be healed is he who does not refuse treatment.
> This treatment consists of the pain and distress brought on by various mis-
> fortunes. He who refuses them does not realize what they accomplish in this
> world or what he will gain from them when he departs this life.[51]

Similarly, the mystic and physician Paracelsus (1493–1541) upholds the same principle when he writes, "Decay is the beginning of all birth . . . the midwife of very great
things!"[52] Lilian Staveley (ca. 1878–1928) observes, "We have no sufferings that are
not useful to us."[53] In the Islamic tradition, there is God's extra Quranic saying that
states, "I am with those whose hearts are broken for My sake." The Buddhist philosopher Nāgārjuna (ca. 150–250) concurs with this understanding: "That which hurts but
is profitable / Is drunk by the wise like medicine. / The result, afterwards attained, /
Becomes in itself incomparable."[54]

Rūmī makes the following point about suffering (from the perspective of the
Divine): "I have wounded your heart—lay no salve on the wound I inflict!"[55] In contrast to the prevailing secular mindset, some forms of suffering or trauma require the
person to actively surrender to the Divine in order to ask for healing and thus embark
on a sacred journey to restore wholeness. Without the person knowing it, the purpose of this journey is not the healing in and of itself but to draw the person closer to
the Divine, seeing as our suffering—at its root—is caused by our separation from the
spiritual realm. Rūmī stresses the importance of the human body as a vehicle for our
lives in this temporal world and also the need to embrace our embodiment without
becoming ensnared by it:

> This body is a guest-house. . . . Every morning a new guest comes running.
> Beware! Do not say, "I am left with him on my neck," for in any case he will
> soon fly back to Nonexistence. Whatever comes from the Unseen World into
> your heart is a guest—welcome it![56]

Although our physical bodies are necessary for our existence in this reality, our
true sense of safety needs to always be anchored in what is beyond the spatiotem-
poral order. Ānandamayī Mā elucidates the need to situate our consciousness in the
eternal or transpersonal order, even as we remain a guest in the human body: "My

50. Syncletica, quoted in *Desert Fathers*, 64.
51. St. Maximus the Confessor, "Four Hundred Texts on Love," in Palmer et al., *Philokalia*, 2:96.
52. Paracelsus, *Paracelsus*, 143, 144.
53. Staveley, *Christian Woman's Secret*, 56.
54. Nāgārjuna, quoted in *Elegant Sayings*, 58.
55. Rūmī, quoted in Chittick, *Sufi Path of Love*, 293.
56. Rūmī, quoted in Chittick, *Sufi Path of Love*, 254.

consciousness has never associated itself with this temporary body. Before I came on this earth . . . I was the same. As a little girl, I was the same. I grew into womanhood; [but] still I was the same."[57] If we trace suffering back to its genesis, the true source can be recognized: "The origin is the wrong identification of the body with the Self."[58] Though unseen to the naked eye, the invisible wound of trauma leaves its imprint on the mind and body. With a metaphysically informed perspective, we can better understand the underlying meaning of the following: "How could the invisible be the source of pain?"[59]

No matter how hopeless someone may appear, they will always have an indwelling connection to the Spirit—something that can never be taken away. Each person, no matter what their circumstances, is born with an indestructible wholeness. Human beings are created in the "image of God" (Genesis 1:27), which can be distorted by sin but never eradicated. This is described by one Christian writer in the following way:

> The *nous* [Intellect or Spirit (*pneuma*)] is in effect the image of God in man. This image can be masked or soiled by sin, but it cannot be destroyed: it is the indelible mark of man's most profound being, of his veritable nature, the *logos* or constitutive principle of which cannot be altered.[60]

Eaton writes, "Man cannot . . . lose his theomorphism, his likeness to the divine image, however deeply this likeness may be covered in filth. Not even the most corrosive acid could ever destroy the divine imprint."[61] All spiritual traditions affirm that our transpersonal Self cannot be lost because we are never deprived of the Divine Presence—"Grace is always there."[62] To be confined to our traumas prevents us from becoming who we truly are. Human suffering stems from our identification with a self that is cut off from the Divine.

Salvific psychology views humans as both geomorphic (of the earth) and theomorphic (of the Spirit) beings—both temporal and eternal—who find themselves at the intersection of the horizontal and vertical dimensions of reality. *Duo sunt in homine* ("There are two [natures] in man") was an axiom in the West prior to the emergence of the Renaissance that recognized both our corporeal and spiritual natures.[63] Mainstream psychology focuses on the diagnosis and treatment of the outer human being, unaware that its materialist outlook excludes the "inward man" (Romans 7:22). All wounds in this life are limited to the surface of our being and cannot undermine our innermost Self. To be fully human is to recognize our fundamental relationship with the Spirit, which is to say that our true identity *in divinis* is the primordial state (*fiṭra*), the "image of God" (*imago Dei*), Buddha-nature (*Buddha-dhātu*), or the Self (*Ātmā*). For this reason, the universal and timeless wisdom found throughout the

---

57. Ānandamayī Mā, quoted in Yogananda, *Autobiography of a Yogi*, 524.
58. Ramana, *Talks with Sri Ramana Maharshi*, 437.
59. Nāgārjuna, quoted in *Elegant Sayings*, 16.
60. Larchet, *Mental Disorders and Spiritual Healing*, 28–29.
61. Eaton, *Islam*, 198.
62. Ramana, *Talks with Sri Ramana Maharshi*, 281.
63. St. Thomas Aquinas, question 26, fourth Article, *Summa Theologica, Part II*, 336.

world's diverse spiritual cultures teaches an essential truth: "Your natural state is one of happiness."[64]

In Buddhism, each of us is said to consist of five psychophysical aggregates or "heaps" known as *khandhas* (Pāli/Sanskrit: *skandhas*): (1) form (Pāli/Sanskrit: *rūpa*), (2) sensation or feeling (Pāli/Sanskrit: *vedanā*), (3) perception (Pāli: *saññā*; Sanskrit: *saṃjñā*), (4) mental formations (Pāli: *saṅkhāras*; Sanskrit: *saṃskāras*), and (5) consciousness (Pāli: *viññāṇa*; Sanskrit: *vijñāna*). However, the existence of these aggregates does not preclude the existence of an abiding Self (Pāli: *Attā*; Sanskrit: *Ātman*) that is not bound to birth, old age, sickness, and death. The Buddha does not take issue with the Hindu understanding of the Self as *neti, neti* ("not this, not that"), which, by means of negation, conveys an apophatic understanding that eliminates all determinate conceptions, leaving only the consciousness of that which is—the Self alone; all that is not this, can be considered "non-Self" (*anattā*).

This position is indicated in the Buddha's words, "What is not self, that is not my [true] self" (*yad anattā . . . na meso attā*; *Saṃyutta Nikāya*, iii. 45, iv. 2).[65] An awareness of *neti, neti* helps us to disidentify from the phenomena that arise in our consciousness; yet this does not mean that we become sundered from the psychophysical order, because we are still required to be fully aware of our tripartite nature as Spirit, soul, and body. In other words, we need to abide in what transcends the psychophysical order while simultaneously remaining with our bodies. By means of one of humanity's hollowed paths of return, we are able to ground ourselves in what has been described as a salvific psychology that can heal and restore our wholeness.

However challenging, deprived, or traumatic our circumstances may be, we must not ignore that we are called to be "partakers of the divine nature" (2 Peter 1:4). According to the Quran, we were fundamentally "created to worship God" (51:56). This awareness will allow us to endure—and even flourish—despite the disturbing vicissitudes of the world. Additionally, the spiritual traditions teach us that to become who we are meant to be is to take a path that is far from easy; a life devoted to the sacred will inevitably be laden with challenges and difficulties. As Mencius (Mengzi, 372–289 BCE) remarked, "Sorrow and trouble bring life, whereas ease and pleasure bring death."[66] Brother Lawrence (ca. 1611–91) articulates the ideal state of surrender to God:

> Be satisfied with the condition in which God places you. . . . Pains and sufferings would be a Paradise to me, while I should suffer with my God; and the greatest pleasures would be hell to me, if I could relish them without Him; all my consolation would be to suffer something for His sake.[67]

Ultimately, as we are taught in the Quran, "surely we belong to God, and to Him we return" (2:156). Similarly, Black Elk reminds us that "everything comes from Him,

64. Ramana, *Talks with Sri Ramana Maharshi*, 284.
65. See Horner, "Attā and Anattā," 31–35.
66. Mencius, bk. 6, *Book of Mencius*, 107.
67. Lawrence, *Practice of Presence of God*, 68–69.

and sooner or later everything returns to Him."[68] It is through participating in a valid religious tradition that our adverse experiences can be understood, healed, and utilized to strengthen our connection to the Divine: "In order to vanquish . . . traumas . . . man must avail himself not only of that sacramental grace which is Invocation, but also of his intelligence, of his will, and of prayer."[69]

It would be remiss to conclude this essay without also mentioning the existence of a very unfortunate phenomenon that has emerged in the field of trauma studies. Trauma-informed practices have, in many ways, become a much popularized, profit-generating industry, with countless experts and therapeutic programs proliferating throughout the world. This trend not only muddies the waters but, again, is a sign of the times in that it stems directly from the spiritual vacuum that distinguishes the present age.

Suffering is inherent to our lives in this world—"for it must needs be that offences come" (Matthew 18:7); however, it is not that God wants us to suffer, per se, but rather that He wants us to fully surrender our hearts and minds. In many ways, our temporal ordeals are attributable to humanity's estrangement from the Divine, which disfigures our primordial nature and obscures our supernal vision—for "their hearts were hardened" (Mark 6:52 NIV). Willingly offering our travails to the working of divine grace infuses them with spiritual value. The natural need to feel safe in body and mind is intrinsic to our psychological integrity and well-being, yet our sense of safety can often be undermined by the earthly tribulations that fuel the anguish in our lives.

St. Teresa of Ávila writes about turning ourselves toward the Divine: "Until we are there where nothing can cause pain this suffering will not be taken away."[70] In essence, the modern world has been triggered and traumatized by its disjunction from the sacred; the remedy is in returning to one of humanity's divinely revealed spiritual traditions and grounding ourselves in a saving wisdom that is of neither the East nor the West.

Islam teaches that "God alters not what is in a people until they alter what is in themselves" (Quran 13:11) and, according to a prophetic saying, "For every disease there is a cure." Commitment to a religious tradition can offer the most effective means of ensuring spiritual resilience, sound mental health, and the effective healing of traumas. If we survey the trajectory of our lives, we often find that it is through the existence of illness, suffering, and other trials that a deep-seated transformation can be catalyzed in our hearts. We conclude with a prayer from the Buddhist tradition: "May all sentient beings be free from suffering and the causes of suffering."[71]

68. Black Elk, quoted in Brown, *Sacred Pipe*, 80.
69. Schuon, *Prayer Fashions Man*, 187.
70. St. Teresa of Ávila, *Interior Castle*, 143.
71. The Four Immeasurable Thoughts, quoted in Ribur, *How to Generate Bodhicitta*, 63.

4

The Enigma of Psychosis

What if you were suddenly to experience an overwhelming sense of great emotional and psychological turmoil to the extent that the very frame of reference that aids in your ability to navigate life was utterly compromised? You would lose your orientation, and both your very existence and, indeed, the world itself might start to feel unreal. It seems that very few ever contemplate such a frightening scenario unless they have had to face it themselves.

Madness has always captivated the collective imagination, perhaps like no other phenomenon of the human condition. For many, it is a taboo subject and one that is best not broached for fear of provoking madness itself; yet without question, psychosis or extreme states of mind continue to frighten and fascinate us. Millions of people today are affected by mental illness, so much so that very few have been unscathed by its impact, whether personally or through a family member, friend, colleague, or acquaintance. The World Health Organization estimates that one in eight individuals—or almost a billion people—around the world experienced mental illness in 2019, often without access to adequate therapeutic treatment.[1]

Mental illness has become a global crisis. It appears to be ubiquitous in the modern world, and we see its ravages in popular films, music, media, and the internet. So pervasive are these depictions today that the phenomenon of madness has become a telling *sign of the times*. As contemporary life becomes ever more complex and unsustainable—and with the seeming acceleration of time—time itself becomes the scarcest commodity. People are estranged from both themselves and others, to the point where virtual spaces replace *in vivo* human contact. The planetary ecosystem and all life-forms are in states of emergency, not to mention the myriad forms of violence that are proliferating by the day. Madness appears as a coping mechanism to help us endure these radically divisive and disturbing times.

While technological utopianism embraces the rise of virtual reality and artificial intelligence to bring about what has been called the "immanentization of the eschaton" or the "counterfeit of Eternity,"[2] others view this as dystopic in that it will further fuel escapism, alienation, and dehumanization. With posthumanism starting to play out, it is difficult to determine where humanity ends and machines begin.

---

1. World Health Organization, *World Mental Health Report*.
2. Voegelin, *New Science of Politics*, 163; Burckhardt, *Introduction to Sufi Doctrine*, 38.

It appears that what it means to be an individual is not only being questioned but steadily eroding before our eyes, in anticipation of what may be called the end of the human era. The blind worship of technology is transforming humanity into what Lewis Mumford (1895–1999) called "a passive, purposeless, machine-conditioned animal."[3] Perhaps now more than ever, we need to question our so-called sanity as it appears more like insanity, just as insanity appears to be an understandable response to coping with a world plunging ever further into chaos.

From this point of view, we can make sense of the provocative observation about consensus reality offered by Scottish psychiatrist R. D. Laing (1927–89), "Socially shared hallucinations is what we call reality, and our collusive madness is what we call sanity,"[4] which is part and parcel of our "appalling state of alienation called normality."[5] Very few would disagree that we are experiencing what St. John Chrysostom (349–407) identifies as a world of inversion, one where "everything is turned upside down."[6] This disequilibrium reverberates throughout the cosmic order and within the human psyche: "When the yin and yang go awry, then heaven and earth see astounding sights."[7]

The idea of madness often looms in the background of our day-to-day lives as we relentlessly assess and question whether we are losing our grip on reality. We continuously seek to verify what others think of us for fear that our shortcomings will be exposed and made known to others. The mind can then start to doubt its own identity and question the world around it.

Beneath the threshold of our conscious awareness, certain questions continue to be asked: Have I finally lost my mind? Is what I am experiencing simply all in my head? What is going on? If the intrapsychic world of most people were to be externalized and made public, its contents would surely disturb most people and bring into question the very idea of what constitutes sanity itself. In fact, to unplug from the never-ending stimuli of contemporary life would almost immediately expose the chaos that pervades a normal mind.

We are reminded that the ordinary condition of human beings in modernity is essentially ill and fragmented:

> What we call "normal" is a product of repression, denial, splitting, projection, introjection and other forms of destructive action on experience. It is radically estranged from the structure of being. . . . The condition of alienation, of being asleep, of being unconscious, of being out of one's mind, is the condition of the normal man.[8]

The aim here is not to resolve, once and for all, what madness is but rather to explore this phenomenon in a way that goes beyond the myths and stigma.

3. Mumford, *Myth of the Machine*, 3.
4. Laing, *Politics of the Family*, 73.
5. Laing, *Politics of Experience*, 167.
6. St. John Chrysostom, quoted in Larchet, *Therapy of Spiritual Illnesses*, 1:46.
7. Zhūangzi, *Chuang Tzu*, 132.
8. Laing, *Politics of the Family*, 27, 28.

It is important not to entertain any romantic notions about mental illness, nor to suggest that such disorders are "'counterfeit' or metaphorical illnesses,"[9] even though—without question—they do present "problems in living."[10] Madness defies all reductionistic constructs and cannot be isolated to a single Procrustean bed, as certain contemporary approaches to mental health suggest. The human suffering that stems from the loss of reason, the experience of radical alienation, and the shattering emotional turmoil catalyzed by mental illness are very real and can be debilitating—not just to the individual but also to families and the community.

A curious fact is that, despite all the advances in modern science, we are still unable to formalize a comprehensive etiology of mental illness because its root causes remain largely unknown. This is conveyed in the words of William Shakespeare (1564–1616), "To define true madness, / What is't but to be nothing else but mad?,"[11] while the doctor and chaplain William Pargeter (1760–1810) stated that "the original or primary cause of madness is a mystery."[12]

By all scientific accounts, schizophrenia remains not only ill-defined but a virtual mystery. This was acknowledged in the classic monograph on schizophrenia published early in the 1900s by Swiss psychiatrist Eugen Bleuler (1857–1939), in which he admitted, "We do not know what the schizophrenic process actually is."[13] In fact, it was Bleuler who actually coined the term *schizophrenia* in 1908, juxtaposing the Greek verb *schizein* ("to split") with another Greek word, *phren* (originally "diaphragm" but later coming to mean "soul, spirit, or mind").[14] Prior to adopting this term, the Latin term *dementia praecox* was used.[15] Equally, German psychiatrist Emil Kraepelin (1856–1926), widely considered the "father of modern psychiatry," stated, "The causes of *dementia praecox* [schizophrenia] are at the present time still wrapped in impenetrable darkness."[16] Even with the passing of time, we are not any closer to discovering what it is. Madness evades all attempts to be fully understood by the methods of modern science.[17]

Research on psychosis has demonstrated that one cannot easily "distinguish insanity from sanity" in contexts where madness or extreme states of mind prevail.[18] There appears to be a rift between what mental illness is and how it presents itself. In fact, the more progress contemporary science makes, the more it paradoxically hits up against the boundary of its own presuppositions and epistemic limitations. This is because of its inability to fully embrace the spiritual dimension underlying the nature of reality and human consciousness.

---

9. Szasz, *Myth of Mental Illness*, 34.
10. Szasz, *Myth of Mental Illness*, 262.
11. Shakespeare, *Hamlet* 2.2.93–94, in Furness, *New Variorum Edition of Shakespeare*, 3:137.
12. Pargeter, *Observations on Maniacal Disorders*, 14.
13. Bleuler, *Dementia Praecox*, 466.
14. See Fusar-Poli and Politi, "Paul Eugen Bleuler," 1407.
15. See Noll, *American Madness*.
16. Kraepelin, *Dementia Praecox and Paraphrenia*, 224.
17. "Never let it be doubted that depression, in its extreme form, is madness . . . the disease of depression remains a great mystery" (Styron, *Darkness Visible*, 11, 46–47).
18. Rosenhan, "Being Sane in Insane Places," 257.

At the same time, we need to point out that the conditions of our world today are not always conducive to spiritual remedies being possible for all maladies. Various forms of recovery can be secured without necessarily overcoming every psychotic manifestation in a person. Needless to say, this arena of human life is fraught with mystery, and we do not know with certainty how the triadic constitution of the human being—Spirit, soul, and body—is affected by our birth in a desacralized world, where inevitable trauma follows in its wake. The fact remains that mental illness escapes every attempt to explain its origins and continues to be inappropriately understood: "There is not a single symptom of a single psychiatric disorder for which we fully understand its physiologic basis at a molecular, cellular, and microcircuit level."[19]

The so-called pharmacological revolution that was launched in the 1950s with the discovery of chlorpromazine (commonly known as Thorazine)—the first effective antipsychotic—is regarded by some as "one of the greatest advances in 20th century medicine and history of psychiatry."[20] With all its claims of success, it has not reduced treatment over time, but rather, it has exponentially increased the number of people receiving mental health services, thus creating a global epidemic. The pharmacological revolution triggered *deinstitutionalization*, which began in 1955. This was the policy of removing severely mentally ill individuals from asylums and closing down a number of mental hospitals. In many ways, Sigmund Freud (1856–1939) predicted the ascendency of modern psychopharmacology: "This future is still far distant, but one should study analytically every case of psychosis because this knowledge will one day guide the chemical therapy."[21]

The paradox of deinstitutionalization is that many of the mentally ill, who had been warehoused against their will and faced inhumane conditions in mental hospitals, were later incarcerated in jails and prisons. This is evidenced by the over-representation of such individuals in incarceration statistics. Chronic homelessness is also a result of what is arguably the social experiment of deinstitutionalization.[22] The transition of mental health treatment from psychiatric hospitals to community-based mental health treatment has been disastrous due to poor infrastructure and inadequate funding.

The ancient world had a very different view of madness. Socrates (ca. 470–399 BCE) conveys to Phaedrus an astonishing and almost inconceivable way of looking at this phenomenon: "The greatest blessings come by way of madness, indeed of madness that is heaven-sent."[23] This assertion casts a radically different light on what constitutes "sanity," because whereas the modern world sees madness as deviating from a normative mode of behavior, civilizations from the past consider it as our inability to apprehend transcendence. For this reason, a "salvific" psychology emphasizes, as St. Ambrose (ca. 340–97) did, that "almost everything we see, we see other than it is" because the "mind roams from phantom to phantom, each one dissolving itself into

19. Wang and Krystal, "Computational Psychiatry," 640.
20. López-Muñoz et al., "History," 113.
21. Freud, quoted in Jones, *Life and Work*, 3:449.
22. See Bendeck Sotillos, "Homelessness."
23. Plato, *Phaedrus* 244a in Hamilton and *Cairns, Collected Dialogues of Plato*, 491.

the other."[24] Rūmī (1207–73) reminds us of how we often "see things the opposite of what they are."[25] This is further confirmed in the words of the sixth-century sage Lao Tzu: "To realize that our knowledge is ignorance, / This is a noble insight. / To regard our ignorance as knowledge, / This is mental sickness."[26]

So rather than being aberrant, madness has been found—across the panoply of humanity's traditional civilizations—to be quite normative in many ways: "Most peoples have regarded even extreme, psychic manifestations not only as normal and desirable, but even as characteristic of high valued and gifted individuals."[27] Due to the nature of our fallen or saṃsāric state, our perception of reality has been radically compromised, with much of this experience consisting of illusory projections of a fragmented state. Because of this predicament, contemporary psychology is arguably a caricature of true psychology (also known as the "science of the soul") insofar as it is founded on a deformed *Weltanschauung*.

From the perspective of "Divine Madness" (as opposed to its ordinary form), the words of St. Isaac the Syrian (ca. 613–ca. 700)—"May God grant us such disorder!"— subvert the conventional assumptions of contemporary psychology and psychiatry.[28] This vision needs to be recovered in order that we may, once again, be receptive to a sense of the sacred so as to heal the split between our inner and outer selves. As far-fetched as this may sound, the soul can only be healed in the "dark" recesses of the sacred. Consider these words from *The Cloud of Unknowing*:

> Forget all created things that he [God] ever made, and the purpose behind them, so that your thought and longing do not turn or reach out to them either in general or in particular. . . . When you first begin, you find only dark-ness, and as it were a cloud of unknowing. You don't know what this means except that in your will you feel a simple steadfast intention reaching out towards God. . . . This darkness and this cloud remain between you and God, and stop you both from seeing him in the clear light of rational understand-ing, and from experiencing his loving sweetness in your affection. . . . For if you are to feel him or to see him . . . it must always be in this cloud, in this darkness. . . . The soul, when it is restored by grace, is made wholly sufficient to comprehend him [God] fully by love.[29]

The relationship between madness and the supernatural was widely recognized in the premodern era, which was rooted in the spiritual domain and infused with the numinous. Christian philosopher and theologian, Jean Borella, points out that "mental pathology has always been considered, by all human civilizations, as natu-rally dependent on the sacred."[30] This is evident in the scriptures "The Lord shall

24. St. Ambrose, quoted in Larchet, *Therapy of Spiritual Illnesses*, 1:122; John the Solitary, quoted in Larchet, *Therapy of Spiritual Illnesses*, 1:111.
25. Rūmī, discourse 5, *Discourses of Rumi*, 31.
26. Lao Tzu, chap. 71; Wu, *Tao Teh Ching*, 79.
27. Benedict, "Anthropology and the Abnormal," 60.
28. St. Isaac the Syrian, quoted in *Writings from the Philokalia*, 258.
29. Chaps. 3 and 4, *Cloud of Unknowing*, 61–62, 63.
30. Borella, *Crisis of Religious Symbolism*, 194.

smite thee with madness" (Deuteronomy 28:28) and "So that thou shalt be mad for the sight of thine eyes which thou shalt see" (Deuteronomy 28:34). Examples of how Divine Madness manifests itself can be found throughout the world's religions. The Christian tradition has the "Fools for Christ": "We are fools for Christ's sake, but ye are wise in Christ; we are weak, but ye are strong; ye are honorable, but we are despised" (1 Corinthians 4:10). In Islam, these people are known as the *malāmatiyya*,[31] and in the Hindu tradition, they are called *Avadhūta*. We also find the comparable notion of the trickster or *Heyoka* in the religion of the First Peoples and their Shamanic traditions.[32]

What is often overlooked is that the traditional cultures of the world have their own integral or salvific psychology that corresponds with certain healing modalities. However, these are played down by Western psychology, which sees itself as a secular science *without* a soul, given its rejection of metaphysics and spiritual principles. It is worth recalling Freud's antagonism toward religion and the transcendent, which he dismissed as a form of psychopathology. He claimed, "The religions of mankind must be classed among the mass-delusions."[33] Mainstream psychology has not only desacralized any "science of the soul" but has also usurped it in order to have itself replace sacred tradition. This is quite apparent in the following cryptic statement made by Carl Jung (1875–1961): "The gods have become diseases."[34] This hostility directed toward religion has in many ways continued to the present day.

The shift from the term *madness* to *mental illness* is, in large part, due to the emergence of the modern world's secular outlook. The same could be said of the term *soul* or *psyche*, which has now been replaced by *mind*. As already mentioned, the discipline of psychology was originally known as the "science of the soul"; likewise, the term *psychiatry* was coined by German physician Johann Christian Reil (1759–1813) in 1808 as the "medical treatment of the soul." These are all examples of progressive attempts to reduce the study of the human psyche to a materialistic science that relies solely on empirical validation.

"Madness is of different forms,"[35] and therefore psychosis needs to be understood through a multidimensional framework informed by metaphysics and its corresponding epistemologies. In the ancient world, there was a distinction made between Divine Madness and a pathological or ordinary madness of purely human origin. In the West, Divine Madness was called *theia mania*, and ordinary madness was considered simply as *mania*.[36] The corresponding terms in the East were *divyonmāda* and *pāglāmi*, respectively.[37]

---

31. "The People of Blame [*malāmatiyya*] are the masters and leaders of the folk of God's path. Among them is the master of the cosmos, that is, Muhammad, the Messenger of God—God bless him and give him peace!" (Ibn 'Arabī, quoted in Chittick, *Sufi Path of Knowledge*, 372). See Karamustafa, *God's Unruly Friends*.
32. See Dooling, "Wisdom of the Contrary," 54–65; Laude, "Humor, Laughter, Trickster," 142–69; and Radin, *Trickster*.
33. Freud, *Civilization and Its Discontents*, 32.
34. Jung, *Secret of the Golden Flower*, 113. See also Bendeck Sotillos, "Deification of the Psyche."
35. Rūmī, bk. 2, ver. 1384, *Mathnawī of Jalālu'ddīn Rūmī*, 2:292.
36. See Ustinova, *Divine Mania*; Dodds, *Greeks and the Irrational*, 64–101; Pieper, "*Divine Madness*."
37. See McDaniel, *Madness of the Saints*.

Divine Madness is a transpersonal state of "being-beside-oneself" that is suprara-
tional, because it transcends reason (*ratio*) through the Intellect (*Intellectus*) or "eye of
the heart." St. Paul mentions our spiritual receptivity to the Intellect in the following
passage: "He . . . heard unspeakable [secret] words, which it is not lawful for a man to
utter" (2 Corinthians 12:4). Divine Madness is neither unreason nor delirium because
it is a way of knowing that bypasses mere ratiocination.

Although *theia mania* or *divyonmāda* can take on the appearance of ordinary madness in its outward form, inwardly, it is open to a dimension of reality that transcends
the phenomenal:

> According to the views of the world, there is no one so undesirable and unwor-
> thy as he. His heart is locked with feelings, he is as gay as [a] whirligig to the
> outside world. Cleaving wholly to his own nature, he laughs or cries, dances or
> begs as he wishes. Regardless of cleanliness or impurity, good or evil, his heart
> is carved in stone; but his life is a joy. People grind their teeth at him, turn
> him away from their doorsteps when he goes begging for a handful of rice. He
> has no right to talk back as he must discard all for the sake of God, accepting
> all as part of divine caprice. A tramp of nature and a beggar at that, he lives a
> strange life, almost insane, with values of his own which are contrary to those
> of others. His home being under the tree, he moves from district to district,
> all the year round, as a dancing beggar who owns nothing in the world but a
> ragged patch-work quilt.[38]

The following is a description of Shiva based on the Purāṇic sources of the Hindu
tradition:

> He laughs, sings and dances in ecstasy, and plays on a number of musical
> instruments; he leaps, gapes and weeps and makes others weep; speaks like a
> mad man or a drunkard, as also in sweet voice. . . . He dallies with the daugh-
> ters and wives of the *ṛishis*; he has erect hair, looks obscene in his nakedness
> and has an excited look.[39]

Some spiritual traditions speak about madness as "God-intoxication"—a unitive
or ecstatic consciousness.[40] This is also found in a Buddhist text called the *Laṅkāvatāra
Sūtra*, where the following state is described: "When all lesser things and ideas are
transcended and forgotten, and there remains only a perfect state of imagelessness
where Tathagata and Tathata are merged into perfect Oneness."[41] Zhūangzi (Chuang
Tzu, ca. 369–ca. 286 BCE) alludes to the "crazy wisdom" of abiding in a reality that
transcends all language: "Words exist because of meaning; once you've got the meaning, you can forget the words. Where can I find a man who has forgotten words so I
can have a word with him?"[42] Rūmī adds, "These words are for the sake of that person

---

38. Anonymous Bāul, quoted in *Songs of the Bards*, 42–43.
39. Quoted in Rao, *Elements of Hindu Iconography*, 2:43.
40. See Donkin, *Wayfarers*.
41. Laṅkāvatāra Sūtra, chap. 7, quoted in Goddard, *Buddhist Bible*, 322.
42. Zhūangzi, *Chuang Tzu*, 140.

who is in need of words in order that he may understand. But as for the man who understands without words, what need has he of words?"[43]

Śrī Rāmakrishna (1836–86) speaks to this transpersonal absorption:

How can I explain to you what I experience in samādhi? After coming down from that state I think, sometimes, that my illness may be due to samādhi. The thing is, the thought of God makes me mad. All this is the result of my divine madness. How can I help it?[44]

According to Tibetan Buddhist teacher Chögyam Trungpa (1939–87), "total enlightenment is total madness."[45] And yet, from another point of view, he elsewhere confirms that *samsāra* itself is madness, which is to say "that which is not madness is called enlightenment."[46] Madness takes on a completely different meaning when interpreted through metaphysics. The empirical order is limited to what can be perceived through the five senses. Metaphysics extends to a wholeness beyond the empirical order, which allows for a more complete perspective on the human psyche.

From the awakened point of view, Śrī Nisargadatta Maharaj (1897–1981) comments,

Insanity is universal. Sanity is rare. Yet there is hope, because the moment we perceive our insanity, we are on the way to sanity. This is the function of the Guru—to make us see the madness of our daily living.[47]

In the Islamic tradition, there is a *hadīth* narrated by Ibn Ḥibbān, which says, "Remember God with such frequency that they say 'He is Mad!'" Hujwīrī (d. 1071) recounts the story of the famous Sufi, Shiblī (861–946), who upon entering into a bazaar was told, "This is a madman," to which he replied, "You think I am mad, and I think you are sensible: may God increase my madness and your sense!"[48] Al-Yāfi'i tells the story of 'Ali ibn 'Abdān, who "knew a madman who wandered about in the daytime and passed the night in prayer. 'How long,' he asked him, 'hast thou been mad?' 'Ever since I *knew.*'"[49]

From the perspective of Ultimate Reality or the Absolute, to identify who we really are with the empirical ego would be tantamount to delusion or madness. All the saints and sages agree that it is this identification that lies behind all human suffering. The Buddha taught that human existence consists of a continuous ontological dissatisfaction known as *dukkha* whose source is our clinging to sense experience, which prevents us from looking beyond the snares of *samsāra*. To believe we are solely the ego, or the physical body, is to come under the sway of *māyā*, or illusion. We see and experience the world as we interpret it, not as it really is. From this perspective, we can better understand the statement by Michel de Montaigne (1533–92)

43. Rūmī, discourse 6, *Discourses of Rumi*, 33.
44. Rāmakrishna, *Gospel of Ramakrishna*, 905.
45. Trungpa, *Myth of Freedom*, 124.
46. Trungpa, *Transcending Madness*, 83.
47. Dikshit, *I Am That*, 282.
48. 'Alī B. 'Uthmān Al-Jullābī Al-Hujwīrī, *Kashf al-Maḥjub*, 156.
49. Quoted in Perry, *Treasury of Traditional Wisdom*, 643.

that "man is certainly stark mad,"[50] or Blaise Pascal (1623–62), who wrote, "Men are so necessarily mad, that not to be mad would amount to another form of madness."[51]

Modern Western psychology and psychiatry, for the most part, ignore different orders of reality simply because they cannot be verified by the senses. This is not the case with a proper "science of the soul," which is found in all of humanity's sapiential traditions. Also known as *salvific psychology*, it upholds that while there are many realities, there is only one that is absolute or unconditioned. The empirical ego's attempt to fathom itself through its own limitations—while admitting no higher level of reality (or its healing potential)—lies at the heart of the crisis we find in modern Western psychology and psychiatry:

> All [mainstream] psychological therapies . . . are based on a point of view which, for *Vedanta*, is the very cause of what one might call a fundamental neurosis, a metaphysical neurosis, which is the arising of an ego believing itself to be separate. The aim . . . is to restore health and balance to this separate ego which it considers as a justified reality. . . . When we wish to be a balanced self we, in fact, wish to prolong an imbalance under the best possible conditions by appealing to energies which may reinforce, fix and establish an egotistic state which is really the basic imbalance, the source of all others. This is just as absurd as fighting the symptoms of an illness without applying oneself to the illness itself. The . . . cure is therefore not really a cure. It does not rid the sick man of his sickness, it helps him to live it, with the ego. His sickness is an imaginary one.[52]

In the same way that a Hindu proverb speaks of mistaking "a rope for a snake," human beings superimpose a separate ego onto the transpersonal Self. In Plato's (429–347 BCE) allegory of the cave, people mistake shadows for the real world. The experience of being shackled in a cave can be likened to a psychosis comprising hallucinations and delusional thinking about the ontological status of these shadows. To face the real world beyond the shadows requires entering a spiritual path that leads beyond the cave. From the point of view of Ultimate Reality, we need to discern what lies beyond the phenomenal world of fleeting appearances:

> It is like a cinema show. There is light on the screen and the shadows flitting across impress the audience as the acting of some story. Now suppose that in this film story an audience is also shown on the screen. The seer and the seen will then both be on the screen. Apply this to yourself. You are the screen, the Self has created the ego, the ego has its accretions of thoughts, which are displayed as the world, trees, plants, etc., about which you are asking. In reality all these are nothing but the Self. If you see the Self it will be found to be all, everywhere and always. Nothing but the Self exists.[53]

50. Montaigne, *Essays of Montaigne*, 2:387.
51. Pascal, *Pensées*, 110.
52. Klein, *Be Who You Are*, 46.
53. Ramana Maharshi, quoted in Osborne, *Teachings of Ramana Maharshi*, 91.

Laing makes a distinction between what he terms "ontological security" and "ontological insecurity" in order to create a framework in which to understand madness. He describes the ontologically secure person as follows:

> The individual . . . may experience his own being as real, alive, whole; as differentiated from the rest of the world in ordinary circumstances so clearly that his identity and autonomy are never in question; as a continuum in time; as having an inner consistency, substantiality, genuineness, and worth; as spatially coextensive with the body; and, usually, as having begun in or around birth and liable to extinction with death. He thus has a firm core of ontological security.[54]

The ontologically insecure person lacks these attributes and thus does not enjoy a stable human experience. Laing continues:

> [The person may feel] that his identity and autonomy are always in question. He may lack the experience of his own temporal continuity. He may not possess an over-riding sense of personal consistency or cohesiveness. He may feel more insubstantial than substantial, and unable to assume that the stuff he is made of is genuine, good, valuable.[55]

This distinction is useful, yet the experience of ontological security and insecurity exists on a spectrum within the limited realm of the empirical ego. True "ontological security" or the "centrally firm sense of his own and other people's reality and identity" depends on a reality—beyond the empirical ego—that is essentially supraindividual or transpersonal.[56] It is through participation in a spiritual tradition that we are ontologically grounded and connected to a sacred center. Our sanity and happiness in this life are predicated on our ability not only to abide in this center but to be the center, in order to stay rooted in the here and now and disidentify with the fleeting phenomena of the periphery.

From the point of view of the Absolute, the empirical ego itself is a chimera. As the Sage of Arunachala, Śrī Ramana Maharshi (1879–1950), affirms, "Reality is simply the loss of ego. Destroy the ego by seeking its identity. Because the ego is no entity it will automatically vanish and reality will shine forth by itself."[57] The more we attempt to situate human identity in the empirical ego that perceives itself to be separate from everything else, the more it evades our grasp.

We recall the story of the man who came looking for the famous Sufi Bāyazīd al-Besṭāmī (d. 874) and knocked on his door. Bāyazīd said, "Who do you want?" to which the man answered, "I am looking for Bāyazīd." Bāyazīd replied, "For thirty years Bāyazīd has been looking for Bāyazīd and has not seen him, so how will you see him?"[58] Similarly, when Bodhidharma (d. 532), the legendary exponent of Zen

---

54. Laing, *Divided Self*, 41–42.
55. Laing, *Divided Self*, 42.
56. Laing, *Divided Self*, 39.
57. Ramana, *Talks with Sri Ramana Maharshi*, 130.
58. Bāyazīd al-Besṭāmī, quoted in Ernst, *Words of Ecstasy in Sufism*, 26.

or Chan Buddhism, was asked by a disciple, "My mind has not found peace, I beg you, master, to pacify it for me," the master replied, "Bring forth your mind to me and I will pacify it for you." After a long silence, the disciple responded that he had searched for the mind but could not find it. Thereupon Bodhidharma said, "Behold, I have already pacified the mind for you!"[59] These encounters speak to the illusory nature of the empirical ego. Therefore, we must become reintegrated into our primordial nature (*fiṭra*), the "image of God" (*imago Dei*), Buddha-nature (*Buddha-dhātu*), or the Self (*Ātmā*)—our true identity *in divinis*.

No matter how hopeless someone may appear, there is always an indwelling connection to the Spirit that can never be erased. Every human being, no matter their circumstances, is born with an innate sanity. For this reason, the diverse wisdom traditions of the world teach an essential truth, which is that "your natural state is one of happiness."[60]

Psychopathology requires an integrated vision of health and wholeness, lacking which no fully effective diagnosis or treatment is possible. It needs to be remembered that "the concept of mental health depends on our concept of the nature of man."[61] Therefore, if psychopathology does not know what health consists of, an adequate diagnosis and treatment of psychic maladies will elude it. As Gai Eaton (1921–2010) rightly points out, "To diagnose the ills of the time one must possess standards of health."[62]

According to the *Diagnostic and Statistical Manual of Mental Disorders, Fifth Edition* (DSM-5), the definition of mental illness is as follows: "A mental disorder is a syndrome characterized by clinically significant disturbance in an individual's cognition, emotion regulation, or behavior that reflects a dysfunction in the psychological, biological, or developmental processes underlying mental functioning."[63] This definition provides little room for determining precise pathogenesis or for making the necessary distinctions between disorders.

The loosening of diagnostic criteria has allowed for perfectly well people to be misdiagnosed as having a mental illness. We need to be vigilant about therapeutic modalities that do not treat the *whole* human being but, instead, dispense "an illusory medicine to cure an equally illusory disease."[64] It is through a true "science of the soul" that we can actually begin to address "what is behind the symptom" in order to fathom its metaphysical roots.[65]

What does modern science tell us about the origins of madness or extreme states of mind? The Cartesian bifurcation of mind-body dualism continues to have an enduring influence on modern science, psychiatry, and psychology. Its ideology permeates modern philosophical assumptions. At the root of the problem is "the

59. Quoted in Wu, *Golden Age of Zen*, 46.
60. Ramana, *Talks with Sri Ramana Maharshi*, 284.
61. Fromm, *Sane Society*, 67.
62. Eaton, *King of the Castle*, 8.
63. American Psychiatric Association, *Manual of Mental Disorders*, 5th ed., 20.
64. Ta Hui, *Swampland Flowers*, 24.
65. Menninger with Mayman and Pruyser, *Vital Balance*, 325.

inherent limitation of the original epistemological premises of modern science,"[66] which, in turn, requires that we expose the "epistemological fallacies of Occidental civilization."[67]

This split is reflected in the dominant paradigm known as the *medical model* or a "set of procedures in which all doctors are trained,"[68] which is utilized to diagnose and treat psychopathology. Psychiatry today supports a largely biomedical form of reductionism, which upholds that all disease can be reduced to biological causes. Seeing the limitations of this approach, a *biopsychosocial model* has been developed to account for further dimensions of human nature.[69] Yet this perspective also has its drawbacks because it does not provide a framework that can be empirically tested to explain the various interactions or causal influences that determine psychopathology. Even though the biopsychosocial model is more inclusive than the biomedical one, it is still inadequate in situating the transpersonal dimension that is central to an adequate understanding of people in their full plenitude.[70]

Modern science, for the most part, upholds the chemical-imbalance or brain-disease theory of mental disorders as the genesis of psychopathology; however, this theory is now widely considered to be erroneous and has been debunked by many authorities. In his book *A History of Psychiatry*, Edward Shorter (Jason A. Hannah Chair in the History of Medicine at University of Toronto) speaks to the prevalence of this theory today, stating that the "biological approach to psychiatry—treating mental illness as a genetically influenced disorder of brain chemistry" has become the "central intellectual reality at the end of the twentieth century."[71]

In 1984, Nancy C. Andreasen—an American neuropsychiatrist—made the case in her book *The Broken Brain* that "mental illness is due to chemical imbalances in the brain and that treatment involves correcting these chemical imbalances."[72] Yet this idea's origin could be traced further back to the work of Benjamin Rush (1746–1813), regarded as the "father of American psychiatry," who, in 1812, provided one of the earliest accounts of mental illness as a brain disease. Rush writes, "The cause of madness is seated primarily in the blood-vessels of the brain."[73] Yet as Elliot S. Valenstein, professor emeritus of psychology and neuroscience at the University of Michigan, points out, "The evidence does not support any of the biochemical theories of mental illness."[74] Similarly, the US Surgeon General David Satcher—in his 1999 report *Mental Health*—confessed that "the precise causes (etiology) of most mental disorders are not known."[75] In fact, Joseph Glenmullen, an instructor of psychiatry at Harvard Medical School, informs us that "in every instance where such an imbalance was thought

66. Nasr, *Knowledge and the Sacred*, 206.
67. Bateson, *Steps*, 491.
68. Laing, *Politics of the Family*, 39. See also Elkins, *Human Elements of Psychotherapy*.
69. See Engel, "New Medical Model," 129–36.
70. See Ghaemi, "Biopsychosocial Model," 3–4.
71. Shorter, *History of Psychiatry*, vii.
72. Andreasen, *Broken Brain*, 133.
73. Rush, *Medical Inquiries*, 17.
74. Valenstein, *Blaming the Brain*, 96.
75. Satcher, quoted in US Department of Health and Human Services, *Mental Health*, 49.

to have been found, it was later proven false."[76] Furthermore, American psychiatrist Kenneth S. Kendler asserts that every attempt to prove the chemical-imbalance theory has come up short if not altogether been proven false: "We have hunted for big, simple neuropathological explanations for psychiatric disorders and have not found them."[77]

If no scientific evidence has been obtained, why then is this theory perpetuated within the discipline? And why is this not more widely known to nonspecialists outside the mental health field? This is a serious matter that raises fundamental questions about the premises of contemporary science and its ability to address today's mental health epidemic. As one commentator notes, "Notwithstanding periodic breathless proclamations to the contrary, the roots of schizophrenia or of major depression remain wrapped in mystery and confusion."[78] It appears as though we are back to square one, forcing us to admit that madness or extreme states of mind continue to be a mystery.

Hippocrates of Kos (460–377 BCE) was among the first therapists to situate madness outside a supernatural context by promulgating a medical classification that he, interestingly, called "a sacred disease":

> Men ought to know that from the brain, and from the brain only, arise our pleasures, joys, laughter and jests, as well as our sorrows, pains, griefs and fears. Through it, in particular, we think, see, hear, and distinguish the ugly from the beautiful, the bad from the good, the pleasant from the unpleasant. . . . It is the same thing which makes us mad or delirious, inspires us with dread and fear, whether by night or by day, brings sleeplessness, inopportune mistakes, aimless anxieties, absent-mindedness, and acts that are contrary to habit. These things that we suffer all come from the brain, when it is not healthy, but becomes abnormally hot, cold, moist, or dry, or suffers [from] any other unnatural affection to which it was not accustomed. Madness comes from its moistness.[79]

The emergence of the modern world—which began with the Renaissance, the Scientific Revolution, and the Enlightenment—heralded the steady decline of religion and spirituality. This brought about a psychological outlook bereft of any spiritual considerations, along with its deleterious consequences for the human psyche. According to Borella, the rise of psychopathology is directly correlated to the desacralization of the cosmos:

> The seventeenth century witnessed an increase in the number of the insane, itself resulting from the progressive disappearance of the medieval mythocosm and religion's cultural universe. The frantic and permanent exclusion of insanity, and the never-satisfied desire for a totally pure reason, are

76. Glenmullen, *Prozac Backlash*, 196.
77. Kendler, "Toward a Philosophical Structure," 434–35. See also Moncrieff et al., "Serotonin Theory of Depression," 3243–56.
78. Scull, *Madness in Civilization*, 15.
79. Hippocrates, *Hippocrates*, 2:175.

themselves only a kind of desperate wish to conjure away the threat of a "sacred madness" ever reborn at the very heart of the human spirit.[80]

The historic trajectory of how mental illness and psychopathology have been regarded is worth noting:

At the end of the seventeenth century, insanity was of little significance and was little discussed. At the end of the eighteenth century, it was perceived as probably increasing and was of some concern. At the end of the nineteenth century, it was perceived as an epidemic and was a major concern. And at the end of the twentieth century, insanity was simply accepted as part of the fabric of life.[81]

The institutionalization of the mad in asylums was a means of social engineering designed to sequester anyone who did not conform to the narrow norms of Enlightenment ideology. A historian observes as follows:

Not least, the asylum idea reflected the long-term cultural shift from religion to scientific secularism. In traditional Christendom, it was the distinction between believers and heretics, saints and sinners, which had been crucial—that between the sane and the crazy had counted for little. This changed, and the great divide, since the "age of reason," became that between the rational and the rest, demarcated and enforced at bottom by the asylum walls. The keys of St Peter had been replaced by the keys of psychiatry. The instituting of the asylum set up a cordon sanitaire delineating the "normal" from the "mad," which underlined the Otherhood of the insane and carved out a managerial milieu in which that alienness could be handled.[82]

Claims of scientific progress during the Enlightenment were not what they initially appeared to be: "The Enlightenment's many attempts to find the imagined true categories of 'mental illness' led to no useful advances in physiological explanations. The categorizers simply remolded the old theories to fit their new categories."[83]

Reductionist attempts to psychologize the saints and sages of the world's religions are simply a profanation of their rich inner lives. According to a desacralized worldview, many have supposed that holy individuals were simply victims of mental illness:

Psychiatric literature contains numerous articles and books that discuss what would be the most appropriate clinical diagnoses for many of the great figures of spiritual history. St. John of the Cross has been called "hereditary

---

80. Borella, *Crisis of Religious Symbolism*, 159.
81. Torrey and Miller, *Invisible Plague*, 5.
82. Porter, *Madness*, 122.
83. Read, "History of Madness," 16. Eminent British psychiatrist William Battie (1703–76) wrote a seminal text entitled *A Treatise on Madness* (1758). Although there were earlier works such as English physician Timothy Bright's (ca. 1549–1615) *Treatise of Melancholy* (1586) and British clergyman Robert Burton's (1577–1640) *Anatomy of Melancholy* (1621), Battie's book was the first written specifically on madness.

degenerate," St. Teresa of Avila dismissed as a severe hysterical psychotic, and [Prophet] Mohammed's mystical experiences have been attributed to epilepsy. Many other religious and spiritual personages, such as the Buddha, Jesus, Ramakrishna, and Shri Ramana Maharshi have been seen as suffering from psychoses, because of their visionary experiences and "delusions."[84]

While mystical or unitive states have been perceived as betraying a psychological imbalance, they may, in fact, exemplify a state of heightened well-being. It is apt to recall here the axiom: "By their fruits ye shall know them" (Matthew 7:20).

Nevertheless, we are beginning to see a shift in this outlook. For example, the *Diagnostic and Statistical Manual of Mental Disorders, Fourth Edition* (DSM-IV) created a new diagnostic category in 1994 entitled "Religious or Spiritual Problem." This can be briefly described as follows:

> V62.89: This category can be used when the focus of clinical attention is a religious or spiritual problem. Examples include distressing experiences that involve loss or questioning of faith, problems associated with conversion to a new faith, or questioning of other spiritual values which may not necessarily be related to an organized church or religious institution.[85]

Even though the title of this new diagnostic category does not sound complimentary toward people of faith, the nonpathologizing of religious experience was, nonetheless, an important advance.

Another positive development appeared in both the *DSM-IV* and its revised edition, the *DSM-IV-TR*. These distinguish nonpathological from pathological states, which aids in understanding the complexity of these phenomena: "Voluntarily induced experiences of depersonalization or derealization form part of meditative and trance practices that are prevalent in many religions and cultures."[86] St. John of the Cross (1542–91), for example, describes spiritual absorption as an "elevation and immersion of the mind in God, in which the soul is as though carried away and absorbed . . . entirely transformed in God, does not allow attention to any worldly thing."[87] St. Teresa of Ávila (1515–82) describes the mystical experience in this way:

> [Spiritual] union is like what we have when rain falls from the sky into a river or fount; all is water, for the rain that fell from heaven cannot be divided or separated from the water of the river. Or it is like what we have when a little stream enters the sea, there is no means of separating the two. Or, like the bright light entering a room through two different windows; although the streams of light are separate when entering the room, they become one.[88]

84. Grof, *Psychology of the Future*, 215. "Medical materialism finishes up Saint Paul by calling his vision on the road to Damascus a discharging lesion of the occipital cortex, he being an epileptic. It snuffs out Saint Teresa [of Ávila] as an hysteric, Saint Francis of Assisi as an hereditary degenerate" (James, *Varieties of Religious Experience*, 13).
85. American Psychiatric Association, *Manual of Mental Disorders*, 4th ed., 685.
86. American Psychiatric Association, *Manual of Mental Disorders*, 4th ed. Text Revision, 531.
87. St. John of the Cross, *John of the Cross*, 263.
88. St. Teresa of Ávila, *Interior Castle*, 179.

What is altogether missing from the modern diagnosis and treatment of mental illness is an understanding of time and the human psyche in light of traditional cosmology. Modern Western psychology does not recognize how human beings are related to time, which was (contrary to current notions of "evolution" and "progress") unanimously perceived as cyclical by traditional cultures. Time begins with human beings living in proximity to the sacred, but with time's passage, individuals become increasingly alienated from their source; the psychological implication of this estrangement is that we gradually become disconnected from the spiritual realm.[89]

Both the DSM and the *International Statistical Classification of Diseases and Related Health Problems* (ICD) operate on false premises that have infected their scientific outlooks based, as it is, on the materialism of the Enlightenment period, which in turn gave birth to modern psychology. According to Thomas R. Insel, former director of the National Institute of Mental Health (NIMH), "The DSM had created a common language, but much of that language had not been validated by science."[90] Modern sciences cannot effectively diagnose psychiatric disorders because the psyche they are investigating derives from a dimension beyond their grasp:

> They do not contribute anything of value whatever to our knowledge of symptomatology, diagnosis or treatment. Practically the only point on which the writers of our textbooks agree is that there is no one fundamental principle upon which a satisfactory classification can be based.[91]

Furthermore, "diagnoses reveal nothing about *the underlying events and dynamics that animate the perceptions and experiences in question.*"[92]

The *DSM* remains embroiled in controversy to this day.[93] For this reason, it has been observed that the "*Kali-Yuga* [is] the age of the wrong diagnosis,"[94] as its diagnostic methods place the cart before the horse and are unable to take into account all of the multilevel etiologies that need to be considered. We are astutely reminded that "no sickness can be cured, no remedy prescribed for those who are suffering, unless we carefully examine and investigate the cause of the disease."[95] It is by means of an integrated spiritual metaphysics that we can accurately assess, diagnose, and treat the dire conditions that we find in this crepuscular age.

According to Laing, mental illness is a healing process that could lead people to wholeness: "Madness need not be all breakdown. It may also be breakthrough. It is

89. "In the Golden Age, all people experienced their essence, no holes. Then came the Silver Age as essence diminished and the holes began to appear; then the Bronze Age. Now we're in the Iron Age. It's the darkest, heaviest. Iron is really nothing but defense. We can sometimes feel the quality of iron in our own defenses: the hardness, the determination to protect ourselves. So this is one way of viewing the present time—all defenses against holes" (Almaas, *Elements of the Real*, 23).
90. Insel, *Healing*, 130.
91. May, *Mental Diseases*, 246.
92. Maté with Maté, *Myth of Normal*, 242.
93. See Frances, *Saving Normal*.
94. Glass, *Yuga*, 323.
95. St. John Cassian, quoted in Larchet, *Therapy of Spiritual Illnesses*, 3:125.

potentially liberation and renewal as well as enslavement and existential death."[96]
Laing borrowed this idea from the English anthropologist Gregory Bateson (1904–80),
who called it "spontaneous remission,"[97] something he viewed as the natural result
of mental illness:

> It would appear that once precipitated into psychosis the patient has a course
> to run. He is, as it were, embarked upon a voyage of discovery which is only
> completed by his return to the normal world, to which he comes back with
> insights different from those of the inhabitants who never embarked on such a
> voyage. Once begun, a schizophrenic episode would appear to have as definite
> a course as an initiation ceremony a—death and rebirth—into which the nov-
> ice may have been precipitated by his family life or by adventitious circum-
> stances, but which in its course is largely steered by endogenous processes.[98]

This approach emphasizes that mental illness is not a disease but, rather, a passage
toward wholeness. By means of this process, some have suggested that the person
can emerge "weller than well."[99] Czech psychiatrist Stanislav Grof discusses the
importance of letting this potential unfold without having to suppress or control it
with pharmacological agents:

> One of the most important implications . . . is the realization that many of
> the conditions, which are currently diagnosed as psychotic and indiscrimi-
> nately treated by suppressive medication, are actually difficult stages of a
> radical personality transformation and of spiritual opening. If they are cor-
> rectly understood and supported, these psychospiritual crises can result in
> emotional and psychosomatic healing, remarkable psychological changes.[100]

From time immemorial this kind of transformation or metanoia has been found
across all religions, including those of the First Peoples and their Shamanic traditions. This is why Milarepa (ca. 1052–ca. 1135), the great mystical poet of Tibet,
proclaimed, "I am the madman who counts death happiness."[101] This pertains to an
initiatic process: "Spiritual discipline implies initiation in one form or another—that
is, the experience of ritual death and resurrection."[102] We recall Mircea Eliade's
(1907–86) definition of shamanism as the "technique of ecstasy."[103] The shaman is
often regarded as a "wounded healer" who, having undergone a spiritual ordeal and
been cured through this process, learns how to heal others. In this context, Laing
makes a further distinction between "true" sanity and "true" madness:

---

96. Laing, *Politics of Experience*, 133. "The spirits of madmen know that this spirit is the shell of
    the spirit: For the sake of this knowledge, you must pass beyond knowledge into madness"
    (Rūmī, quoted in Chittick, *Sufi Path of Love*, 227).
97. Bateson, "Introduction" to *Perceval's Narrative*, xiv.
98. Bateson, "Introduction" to *Perceval's Narrative*, xiv.
99. Menninger with Mayman and Pruyser, *Vital Balance*, 406.
100. Grof, *Psychology of the Future*, 137.
101. Milarepa, *Songs of Milarepa*, 12.
102. Eliade, *Yoga*, 272.
103. Eliade, *Shamanism*, 4.

From the alienated starting point of our pseudo-sanity, everything is equivo-
cal. Our sanity is not "true" sanity. Their madness is not "true" madness. . . .
The madness that we encounter in "patients" is a gross travesty, a mockery, a
grotesque caricature of what the natural healing of that estranged integration
we call sanity might be. True sanity entails in one way or another the dissolu-
tion of the normal ego, that false self competently adjusted to our alienated
social reality: the emergence of the "inner" archetypal mediators of divine
power, and through this death a rebirth, and the eventual re-establishment
of a new kind of ego-functioning, the ego now being the servant of the divine,
no longer its betrayer.[104]

Yet it needs to be made clear that the shaman differs from the schizophrenic in
that they are rooted in the traditional norms of their culture and religion, whereas
the schizophrenic has radically severed this connection and is without a symbolic
or spiritual framework. This mystical renewal can also be seen as a "second birth,"
which is "common to all traditional doctrines."[105] Confucius (551–479 BCE) conveys
the therapeutic implications of this psychospiritual rejuvenation when he asserts
that "to be thoroughly transformed is to have no more fixations."[106]

History is witness to a myriad of seekers who have endured a crisis in their
inner lives or what has been termed a spiritual emergence,[107] or even a mystical
psychosis,[108] consisting of a psychic opening to paranormal realms or extraordinary
states of consciousness. Such experiences can be very dangerous and destabilizing,
for which reason all sapiential traditions warn against deliberately seeking them out.
Divorced from a serious commitment to spiritual methods that are necessary to help
develop a solid foundation in a revealed tradition, mere dabbling in such practices
can be detrimental to proper growth on one's chosen path.

Mere experiences, in and of themselves, mean nothing and should not be mistaken for spiritual realization per se. While there are always exceptions, the phenomenon of spontaneous psychic openings illustrates the confusion between the psychic
and the spiritual domain and is emblematic of New Age pseudospirituality.[109] Huston
Smith (1919–2016), one of the twentieth century's most renowned doyens of comparative religion, once remarked that "religion is interested not in altered states but
in altered traits" or the total transformation of one's life.[110] Ibn ʿArabī stresses the
need to go beyond all spiritual experiences: "None of the great ones . . . ever seek
states. They only seek stations."[111] This is why emphasis is always placed on adher-

104. Laing, "Transcendental Experience," 15.
105. Guénon, Introduction, 156.
106. Confucius, quoted in Wu, Golden Age of Zen, 33.
107. See Bragdon, Call of Spiritual Emergency; St. Arnaud and Cormier, "Psychosis or Spiritual
     Emergency," 44–59.
108. See Deikman, "Bimodal Consciousness," 481–89.
109. See Guénon, Reign of Quantity, 235–40.
110. Smith, quoted in Smoley and Kinney, "Tradition and Truth," 35. See also Bendeck Sotillos,
     "Entheogens and Sacred Psychology," 41–68.
111. Quoted in Chittick, Self-Disclosure of God, 266.

ence to a valid religious form, as underscored here: "Enter houses by their doors" (Quran 2:189).

The difference between the sages of the world's religions and individuals suffering from mental illness is captured in the following metaphor: "The mystic, endowed with native talents . . . and following . . . the instruction of a master, enters the waters and finds he can swim; whereas the schizophrenic, unprepared, unguided, and ungifted, has fallen or has intentionally plunged, and is drowning."[112] In addition, "he [the schizophrenic] muddles ego with self, inner with outer, natural and supernatural."[113]

The French metaphysician René Guénon (1886–1951) identified what he called "fissures" that have appeared in the "Great Wall" (known in the Hindu tradition as the mountain of Lokāloka) that divides the cosmos (loka) from the outer darkness (aloka). These fissures have caused breaches in the protective barrier of the world, which, in turn, are reflected in a disequilibrium that afflicts the human psyche. As the temporal cycle (yuga) moves further away from the Spirit—especially during the Kali-Yuga—these subversive psychic forces act with more intensity on our cognition, feelings, and behavior.[114] An ordered balance between the human microcosm and the cosmic macrocosm is essential for the well-being of the world and its sentient beings, for, as Michel Foucault (1926–84) states, "It is man's insanity that invokes and makes necessary the world's end."[115]

In Buddhist cosmology, there are six realms that constitute life in saṃsāra (the cycle of birth and death): hell beings, hungry ghosts, animals, humans, fighting spirits, and gods. If we conceive of these worlds not only as posthumous states that we experience after death but as realms in which we can become immersed here and now, we can better understand the nature of extreme mental states. Throughout all spiritual traditions, we find examples of how both heaven and hell are present within the human psyche. The Anglican divine William Law (1686–1761) writes, "There cannot be the smallest Thing, or the smallest Quality of any Thing in this World, but what is a Quality of Heaven or Hell, discovered under a temporal Form."[116]

Metaphysically speaking, to perceive other realms does not mean that they are not real. They can be just as real as our experiences in this world, but it must be remembered that our current temporal existence is relative and not absolute. Appearances, as they arise in the manifest order, are inseparable from māyā and are thus implicated in the varied (but relative) perspectives through which we envisage the Absolute. Because of this, a certain measure of ambiguity overshadows our experience of this reality, which, ultimately, is neither real nor unreal.[117] Again, it is the interference of these extreme states in our lives that can cause severe problems and distress for those subject to them.

112. Campbell, Myths to Live By, 209.
113. Laing, "Transcendental Experience," 8.
114. See Guénon, Reign of Quantity, 172–76.
115. Foucault, Madness and Civilization, 17.
116. Law, Works, 6:116.
117. See Bendeck Sotillos, "Realms of Consciousness," 12–21.

It is essential that every true "science of the soul" be grounded in a sapiential tradition in order that we may be equipped to distinguish the Real from the unreal, the Absolute from the relative. This requires being rooted in one of the divinely revealed traditions that alone can furnish us with robust safeguards when confronted by the spiritual confusion of the present day. "Beloved, believe not every spirit, but try the spirits whether they are of God" (1 John 4:1).

Under the pretext of being value-free, modern Western psychology and psychiatry have created a Procrustean mold into which every human being's psychopathology must be fitted. This fails to appreciate the full gamut of diverse therapies that traditional civilizations have yielded to the world over. Even with the little understanding of what psychopathology is, the contemporary form of the discipline is nonetheless being exported throughout developing countries under the guise of "mental health literacy." Yet because madness has a different meaning in these diverse cultures, they are perceived to be deprived of this "literacy." This not only illustrates the cultural incompetence of modern therapies, but it does a grave injustice to the profound wisdom of these older, more integrated cultures.

With all the claims of scientific progress that we see from advocates of modern psychology and psychiatry, it is interesting to note that the recovery rates are higher in the developing countries than in the West, not to mention that the number of individuals diagnosed, in the first place, with a severe mental illness is significantly lower in the developing world.[118] There is an urgent need for the decolonization of therapy today. By returning to the universal and timeless wisdom found in humanity's spiritual cultures, we can gain insight into more effective modes of healing.

The contemporary world has rejected the realm of Spirit. If sanity or mental health is to be found in a return to a divine order of reality, we can expect to see a very different approach to mental health and illness. Likewise, if our true selves are rooted in the Divine, then healing and treatment modalities need to be grounded in this transpersonal source of human identity.

In an era that prizes the primacy of empirically verifiable evidence, it is troubling that much of what constitutes "madness remains remarkably mysterious and hard to comprehend, though that is not what the dominant ideology in psychiatry would have the rest of us believe."[119] It is unlikely that the vast majority of mental health professionals will candidly confess that the underlying principles of psychopathology are still unknown and remain elusive.

Macbeth inquired, "Canst thou not minister to a mind diseased"?[120] The same question remains today. While many may assert that the future of the mental health field appears promising, if we pause to take stock of the present reality, what becomes obvious is that psychology and psychiatry are not only at an impasse but

118. See Sartorius et al., "Cross-Cultural Differences," 102–13; Sartorius et al., "Long-Term Follow-Up," 249–58; Hopper and Wanderling, "Revisiting," 835–46; Kulhara and Chakrabarti, "Culture and Schizophrenia," 449–64; and Pescosolido et al., "Theory of Industrial Society," 783–825.
119. Scull, *Madness in Civilization*, 380.
120. Shakespeare, *Macbeth* 5.3.41, in Furness, *New Variorum Edition of Shakespeare*, 2:40.

actually caught in an acute crisis. This has been made evident by two of the most important twentieth-century historians of psychiatry, Richard Hunter (1923–81) and Ida Macalpine (1899–1974), who identified this quandary in the 1960s. The following observation, from their epochal work, remains just as relevant today:

> There is not even an objective method of describing or communicating clinical findings without subjective interpretation and no exact and uniform terminology which conveys precisely the same to all. In consequence there is wide divergence of diagnosis, even of diagnoses, a steady flow of new terms and an ever-changing nomenclature, as well as a surfeit of hypotheses which tend to be presented as fact. Furthermore, etiology remains speculative, pathogenesis largely obscure, classification predominantly symptomatic and hence arbitrary and possibly ephemeral; physical treatments are empirical and subject to fashion, and psychotherapies still only in their infancy and doctrinaire.[121]

It would be fair to say that current behavioral health systems mimic the very symptoms of mental illness that they seek to treat. What is needed now are certainly not new therapies to replace the endless innovations of previous ones, for these are simply part of the malady that needs to be overcome. The obsession with treatments that are short-lived and consequently shelved only to be replaced later by other therapeutic modalities is an indicator of how unstable such foundations are. This ad hoc process of construction and reconstruction goes on indefinitely without addressing the fundamental source of the problem: the untenable science behind modern Western psychology and psychiatry, which is materialistic, reductionistic, and dehumanizing because it excludes the spiritual dimension of the psyche. Due to this baneful and distorted worldview, the deep richness of the human mind remains an enigma to the mental health profession, especially extreme states such as psychosis. "No area of Western thought is more in need of input from the spiritual disciplines than our understanding of the psychoses. These mysterious maladies penetrate through the deepest levels of soma and psyche to the roots of the human soul."[122]

Our understanding of mental illness today remains captive to a desacralized outlook that was catalyzed by the legacy of the Enlightenment project. Thus, the onset of the so-called Age of Reason was, in many ways, the culmination of a pernicious "Age of Madness."[123] A consequence of undermining the centrality of the Spirit in our lives has been the rise of a profound disequilibrium in the human psyche: "Mental disorder today exists everywhere."[124]

Seeing as modern science has failed to adequately understand extreme states of mind, we would do well to consider how traditional wisdom might be able to illuminate this phenomenon.

Madness is an enigma because it is inherently ambiguous; on the one hand, for example, are the "Fools for Christ," and on the other, individuals with psychotic

---

121. Hunter and Macalpine, *Three Hundred Years of Psychiatry*, vii.
122. Nelson, *Healing the Split*, xv.
123. See Szasz, *Age of Madness*.
124. Guénon, *Miscellanea*, 124.

breakdowns unrelated to anything associated with the sacred. In other words, there is "Divine Madness" (*theia mania*), and there is pathological madness (*mania*) of purely human origin. The latter need not always be thought of as an illness (as is often the case in modern Western psychology and psychiatry), though we must acknowledge that what is considered ordinary madness can be a devastating condition. This is a complicated question that requires nuanced assessment, diagnosis, and treatment—something with which traditional metaphysics can assist.

If we persist with a thoroughly profane understanding of what is viewed as "insanity," there will be continued obstacles—especially for those with religious backgrounds—to seek mental health support, which may very well lead to misdiagnosis and potential harm. It is possible to view madness as a unique expression of the Spirit, albeit in a manner that may perplex or disturb us. We cannot know with complete certainty what madness is or how to resolve all forms of psychosis. Nevertheless, by restoring a sense of the sacred to our healing modalities—through the rehabilitation of the transpersonal Intellect—we will come closer to providing the integrated treatment that is necessary to realize the wholeness of body and mind.

The task now is to return to the sapiential traditions and their understanding of how our body, soul, and Spirit form an integrated whole. Without this discernment, there can be no effective healing of traumas, given such a fragmented vision of humanity. One of the great exponents of Islamic spirituality, Rūmī, asks, "Am I mad, or are you?"[125] Psychosis or madness is intimately connected to the fundamental question that we all need to ask ourselves: "Who am I?" As the well-known dictum by Socrates asserts, "The unexamined life is not worth living."[126] Yet modern psychology, since its inception, has subverted this way of looking at our lives: "The moment a man questions the meaning and value of life, he is sick, since objectively neither has any existence."[127] Perhaps we are all a little mad, to varying degrees, in this topsy-turvy age. As Rāmakrishna asks, "If you must be mad, why should you be mad for the things of the world? If you must be mad, be mad for God alone."[128] As for the state of this world, I conclude with a devotional declaration (*kirtan*) directed to the Divine Mother, Kālī: "This world, O Mother, is Thy madhouse!"[129]

125. Rūmī, quoted in Chittick, *Sufi Path of Love*, 231.
126. Socrates, quoted in Plato, *Apology* 38a, *Plato*, 133.
127. Freud, quoted in E. Freud, *Letters of Sigmund Freud*, 436.
128. Rāmakrishna, *Gospel of Ramakrishna*, 449.
129. Rāmakrishna, *Gospel of Ramakrishna*, 516.

5

Addiction and Wholeness

Modern psychology, and its mental health systems, are endemically limited in their attempts to comprehend and treat addictions.[1] It is striking that in today's "therapeutic culture," the epidemic of addiction has become so commonplace that most people have become desensitized to it—to the degree that its prevalence has been normalized and its deeper dimensions, in large part, remain undiscerned. Life in modernity is out of balance because of its totalizing worldview, which is completely desacralized, individualistic, reductionist, and materialistic. It appears to be rapidly ravaging societies around the world by inciting endless desires that can never be fulfilled and that are fundamentally destructive to the human condition. It is as if the massive rise in addictions of every sort, now also referred to as *substance use disorders*, has always been the norm. Although addictions have existed since the earliest times, the data on the human and social impact of addiction and its devastation across all cultures of the world is alarming. As such, this blight needs to be regarded not only as a public health disaster but, principally, as a spiritual crisis facing all of humanity. For this reason, it has been rightly observed that "addiction is the sacred disease of our time."[2]

Contemporary psychology is, in many ways, an attempt to fill the spiritual absence—a loss of the sense of the sacred—both in society and in the human microcosm. But without acknowledging and including the sacred, this discipline cannot provide holistic modes of treatment and healing. We must not overlook the fact that psychology also contributed to the loss of faith we find in the present day and to what we might call the trauma of secularism. A proper "science of the soul" has been replaced with a caricature of how psychology was traditionally envisioned.

This chapter surveys the origins of addiction in order to improve our understanding of this ubiquitous phenomenon. In doing so, it aims to promote a quest for healing based on holistic methods that are grounded in the traditional wisdom found among humanity's spiritual traditions. The proliferation of addictions in the modern world is not just limited to drugs and alcohol but extends to the full gamut of human preoccupations, such as gambling, shopping, smoking, pornography, sex, food, video games, mobile phones, and the internet. The roots of addiction undoubtedly betray an underlying metaphysical reality that permeates the psychospiritual dimension

---

1. See Alexander, *Globalization of Addiction*.
2. May, *Addiction and Grace*, viii.

of our being and, by extension, the human body. It should be noted that there are severe forms of substance abuse that can cause a physical dependence that may be life-threatening. Such cases almost invariably include a psychological dimension also, but these will not be the focus of this chapter.

The myriad addictions of the present day, when understood according to the framework of metaphysics, are a symptom of the pathology of fallen humanity within *saṃsāra*, which seeks to find wholeness in that which is unable to give it. The religions have understood and foretold that it is the increasing dissociation of the human psyche from the Spirit—which denies a connection acknowledged by the traditional cosmologies—that makes such attempts futile. It is through the religions and spiritual traditions that we can identify a metaphysical basis for a multidimensional understanding of addiction as well as develop methods for whole-person treatments and healing.

An integrated understanding of the human person reveals that the exclusion of metaphysics from psychology is at the very root of its current crisis. This predicament stems from psychology's inability to see that its overreliance on modern science reduces its sphere of authority merely to the empirical order—to what can be known through the five senses and the faculty of human reason. By contrast, sacred psychology is able to discern the tripartite constitution of human beings and that of the cosmos—of which we are but a mirror—consisting of Spirit, soul, and body or the spiritual, psychic, and corporeal states. This section examines the problem of addiction from the perspective of the world's religions and their mystical paths. It is through an application—to the study of psychology—of the universal wisdom found in these sacred traditions that we may resurrect a "science of the soul" that affords a more profound understanding of the human condition. This approach is also known as sacred psychology.

At the outset, it is important to begin any consideration of addiction by understanding that the phenomenon of addiction can be likened to an exaggerated condition that is common to all people. In a sense, we are all struggling with one form of addiction or another. Although not everyone will be diagnosed with a substance use disorder, there are certain dysfunctional dependencies that we can all identify within ourselves. They do not have to turn our lives upside down to be addictions; the important thing is to see the underlying process that drives them and understand how it informs our thoughts and behaviors.

Addictions were normalized by Sigmund Freud (1856–1939), who developed the psychoanalytic "talking cure" and laid the foundations for the discipline of modern psychology: "There is a general tendency of our mental apparatus. . . . It seems to find expression in the tenacity with which we hold on to the sources of pleasure at our disposal, and in the difficulty with which we renounce them."[3] The irony is that no substance or outward activity can satisfy our inner feelings of emptiness or craving for meaning. According to Craig Nakken,

3. Freud, *Collected Papers*, 4:16.

Addiction is an illness in which people believe in and seek spiritual connection through objects and behaviors that can only produce temporary sensations. These repeated, vain attempts to connect with the Divine produce hopelessness, fear, and grieving that further alienate the addict from spirituality and humanity.[4]

The nature of desire is to generate incessant needs that can never be ultimately satisfied, and Aristotle (384–322 BCE) observed that, despite the insatiable nature of craving, "most men live only for the gratification of it."[5] In our fallen *saṃsāric* state, the following prognosis of the human condition is fitting: "To be alive is to be addicted."[6] And it is fairly easy to find examples of this just about anywhere we look.

We will now turn our attention to some examples of how the world's religions comprehend human suffering and how this informs their approaches to addressing addiction. It is not the objects of our addictions that are the problem but our clinging to them. The Spanish mystic St. John of the Cross (1542–91) explained, "Since the things of the world cannot enter the soul, they are not in themselves an encumbrance or harm to it; rather, it is the will and appetite dwelling within that cause the damage when set on these things."[7]

The Buddha taught that human existence consists of continuous ontological dissatisfaction known as *dukkha* (Pāli/Sanskrit: *duḥkha*), meaning "suffering" or "pain." The term *dukkha* can also be applied in a broader sense to anything that is unsatisfactory, including both bodily and mental illnesses. Closely related to suffering is craving or desire (Pāli: *taṇhā*; Sanskrit: *tr̥ṣṇā*). At the heart of the Buddhist tradition is the teaching of *dependent origination* (Pāli: *paṭiccasamuppāda*; Sanskrit: *pratītyasamutpāda*), which describes the chain of causation that determines the causes of suffering and the conditions that lead to birth, old age, and death along with the Four Noble Truths: (1) the existence of suffering, (2) the cause of suffering, (3) the end of suffering, and (4) the path leading out of suffering. Buddhist psychology therefore aims to identify *dukkha* and eradicate it from human existence. This includes the "three poisons" of greed (*lobha*), hatred (*dosa*), and delusion (*moha*).

In Buddhist cosmology and psychology, there are six realms that constitute life in *saṃsāra* (the cycle of birth and death): hell beings, hungry ghosts, animals, humans, fighting spirits, and gods. The realm of the hungry ghost (Sanskrit: *preta*) is depicted as being populated by those who have an insatiable appetite for drugs, drink, sex, food, and material objects and are never satisfied and never feel that they have enough of these things. Hungry ghosts are traditionally portrayed as creatures with oversized, empty stomachs with minuscule mouths and thin, elongated necks that prevent them from consuming, thus keeping them in a state of perpetual hunger. Tibetan Buddhist teacher Chögyam Trungpa (1940–87) underscored how this tendency operates to varying degrees within everyone and why we struggle to obtain enduring happiness:

---

4. Nakken, *Addictive Personality*, 5.
5. Aristotle, bk. 2, chap. 7, 1267b, *Politics of Aristotle*, 46.
6. May, *Addiction and Grace*, 11.
7. St. John of the Cross, Ascent of Mount Carmel, bk. 1, chap. 4, *Collected Works*, 123.

The joy of possessing does not bring us pleasure any more once we already possess something, and we are constantly trying to look for more possessions, but it turns out to be the same process all over again; so there is constant intense hunger which is based not on a sense of poverty but on the realization that we already have everything yet we cannot enjoy it.[8]

It is the mindset of craving or desire, unable to discern what it truly wants, that causes the human being to suffer. The renowned Indian sage Śāntideva (685–763) realized that "although they do not wish to suffer / They are greatly attached to its [suffering's] causes."[9] For this reason, the Buddha taught a path beyond craving or desire: "From craving arises sorrow and from craving arises fear. If a man is free from craving, he is free from fear and sorrow."[10] Similarly, Sufi poet and mystic Rūmī (1207–73) avowed, "For all pains arise out of the fact that you desire something, and that is not attainable. When you no more desire, the pain no more remains."[11]

Thus we glean the insight that this emptiness and craving is the underlying impulse for all addiction, and as such, we search for wholeness and healing through its eradication. It is the confusion of this yearning for the sacred that leads to the many pathways of harmful behaviors. The connection between trauma exposure, addiction, mental illness, and physical health has been well established,[12] but through the secularizing trajectory of modernism and postmodernism—and the consequent loss of the sense of the sacred—great harm has been inflicted on the human psyche. With the rise of trauma-informed approaches, it is too often overlooked that the anguish of living in a world devoid of nourishing forms of religion and spirituality is tremendously detrimental, as these are invaluable supports for human resiliency and psychological well-being.

Saints and sages inform us that, if we embed our existence in the transient phenomena of this world, we will never find enduring happiness. Swami Ramdas (1884–1963) pointed out, "We may live for thousands of years and may obtain whatever we desire of the world, but we shall never be happy so long as our hunger for earthly things does not perish."[13] The emptiness that is discerned in the external world is one and the same void felt by human beings. Many people find that the endless pursuits of worldly ambitions are radically unfulfilling; indeed, they can become a serious ordeal "when you've gotten to the top of the ladder and find it's against the wrong wall."[14] The search to remedy this sense of vacancy can lead individuals either on the quest for transcendence or to pursue the gratification of endless and destructive desires. Rūmī poignantly outlined our hidden longing for wholeness in the Divine:

8. Trungpa, "Commentary," in *Tibetan Book of the Dead*, 7.
9. Śāntideva, *Guide*, 68.
10. Buddha, 16:216, *Dhammapada*, trans. Mascaró, 66.
11. Rūmī, discourse 31, *Discourses of Rumi*, 139.
12. See Felitti et al., "Relationship of Childhood Abuse," 245–58; van der Kolk, *Body Keeps the Score*.
13. Swami Ramdas, *Pathless Path*, 12.
14. Osbon, *Reflections*, 68.

The human quest consists in seeking a thing which one has not yet found; night and day a man is engaged in searching for that. But the quest where the thing has been found and the object attained, and yet there is one who is seeking for that thing—that is a strange quest indeed, surpassing the human imagination, inconceivable to man. For man's quest is for something new which he has not yet found; this quest is for something one has found already and then one seeks. This is God's quest . . . for God has found all things, and so He is the Finder. Yet for all that God most High is the Seeker. . . . O man, so long as you are engaged in the quest that is created in time, which is a human attribute, you remain far from the goal. When your quest passes away in God's quest and God's quest overrides your quest, then you become a seeker by virtue of God's quest.[15]

The Divine is therefore seeking us all the time, yet we remain oftentimes unreceptive to this call, continually distracted and forgetful of what transcends the sensory world and our involvement in it. The sapiential traditions remind us time and time again that "He is with you wherever you are" (Quran 57:4).

Jean-Claude Larchet, an authority on the Patristic traditions of the Christian East, examines the existential malady that is attributable to our fallen condition:

Man believes he can remedy this frustration by the very means which in truth is its cause: instead of recognizing that the void he senses is the absence of God in him, and that consequently only God can fill it, he wants to see therein the call to possess and delight in new sensible objects that he believes could satisfy this void. So as to avoid the pain following every pleasure, and to put an end to the deep frustration of his desire for infinite delight, fallen man perseveres in his search for new pleasures, not resting in his unbridled running after desires. He gathers and multiplies his pleasures in an attempt to reconstitute the totality, continuity and absoluteness for which he is nostalgic, believing in his delusion to find the infinite in the indefinite.[16]

For sacred psychology, it is essential to recognize that human beings were made for the Absolute and can only find peace in what transcends the psychophysical realm. Mīrābāī (ca. 1498–1547), the Hindu mystic poet, expresses her yearning for the Beloved alone in the following way: "My body is in pain, my breath burning / Come and extinguish the fire of separation / I spend the nights roving about in tears."[17] Therefore, as Rūmī adds, "the man of God realises that all these desires are the desire for God."[18] Furthermore, Fools Crow (ca. 1890–1989) points out that our longing for the Great Spirit radiates out to include the whole created order: "We seek harmony with all creation."[19]

15. Rūmī, discourse 51, *Discourses of Rumi*, 198.
16. Larchet, *Therapy of Spiritual Illnesses*, 1:81.
17. Mīrābāī, poem 96, *Devotional Poems of Mīrābāī*, 74.
18. Rūmī, discourses 9, *Discourses of Rumi*, 46.
19. Fools Crow, quoted in Mails, *Fools Crow*, 47.

This inborn desire for the Divine was powerfully asserted by Christ when he said, "Where your treasure is, there will your heart be also" (Matthew 6:21). This longing is also illustrated in the Psalms: "As a deer longs for flowing streams, so my soul longs for you, O God" (42:1 NRSV). St. Augustine (354–430) similarly affirmed that "for Thou hast made us for Thyself and our hearts are restless till they rest in Thee."[20] All attempts to seek wholeness in anything other than the Divine are bound to fail. As Julian of Norwich (ca. 1342–ca. 1416) explained, "Our soul may never have rest in anything which is beneath itself."[21] The Italian poet Dante Alighieri (1265–1321) wrote, "The desire for . . . perfection . . . is that desire which always makes every pleasure appear incomplete, for there is no joy or pleasure so great in this life that it can quench the thirst in our Soul."[22]

In a letter written to Bill Wilson (1895–1971), cofounder of Alcoholics Anonymous, Carl Jung (1875–1961) wrote about a former individual that he was treating (identified as Rowland Hazard III, 1881–1945) in a way that conveys the spiritual longing found within all human beings and how this impulse can be confused with substance abuse: "His craving for alcohol was the equivalent on a low level of the spiritual thirst of our being for wholeness, expressed in medieval language: union with God."[23] Both Jung and William James (1842–1910), the "father of American psychology," were important influences on the development of Alcoholics Anonymous.[24] James documented the connection between substance use and the search for deliverance:

> The sway of alcohol over mankind is unquestionably due to its power to stimulate the mystical faculties of human nature, usually crushed to earth by the cold facts and dry criticisms of the sober hour. Sobriety diminishes, discriminates, and says no; drunkenness expands, unites, and says yes.[25]

This is something that Omar Khayyām (1048–1131) addresses: "I drink wine . . . not for delight, / Nor unto holiness to do despite: / I do it to breathe a little, free from self."[26] The experience of intoxication as "the great exciter of the *Yes* function in man" was viewed by James as a common thread connecting the quest for inebriation with the unitive experience found in the spiritual traditions.[27] He continues,

> It brings its votary from the chill periphery of things to the radiant core. It makes him for the moment one with truth. Not through mere perversity do men run after it. To the poor and the unlettered it stands in the place of

20. St. Augustine, bk. 1, *Confessions of St. Augustine*, 3.
21. Julian of Norwich, Long Text, *Showings*, 313.
22. Dante Alighieri, 3.4.3, *Dante Alighieri, II Convito*, 119.
23. Jung, quoted in Alcoholics Anonymous, *"Pass It On,"* 384.
24. "A.A.'s indebtedness to the countless people he [Bill Wilson] felt were responsible for its creation. At the top of his [Bill Wilson] list was Carl Jung" (quoted in Alcoholics Anonymous, *"Pass It On,"* 381); "He [Bill Wilson] would later say that [William] James, though long in his grave, had been a founder of Alcoholics Anonymous" (quoted in Alcoholics Anonymous, *"Pass It On,"* 124).
25. James, *Varieties of Religious Experience*, 387.
26. Omar Khayyām, quoted in Keene, "Omar Khayyam," 30.
27. James, *Varieties of Religious Experience*, 387.

symphony concerts and of literature; and it is part of the deeper mystery and
tragedy of life that whiffs and gleams of something that we immediately recognize as excellent should be vouchsafed to so many of us only in the fleeting
earlier phases of what in its totality is so degrading a poisoning. The drunken
consciousness is one bit of the mystic consciousness, and our total opinion of
it must find its place in our opinion of that larger whole.[28]

Substance abuse, like all forms of addiction, is a substitute for the sense of the
sacred whose loss pervades the modern world. With this said, James acknowledged
the role of the spiritual dimension in recovery: "The only radical remedy I know for
dipsomania [alcoholism] is religiomania."[29] Jung observed that "alcohol in Latin is
spiritus, and you use the same word for the highest religious experience as well as for
the most depraving poison. The helpful formula therefore is: *spiritus contra spiritum*."[30]
This formula, "Spirit against the spirits," is an important insight of which contemporary psychology has yet to take into full account—namely, that the treatment of
alcoholism, or any other type of addiction, needs to consider the spiritual dimension
in the quest to restore wholeness.

The question is asked, "How could a sober man know the drunkards' intoxication?"[31]
It is through metaphysics that we can comprehend the dialectic between sobriety
and inebriation and their ultimate resolution in the Absolute. In fact, we are informed
by Rūmī that, in the essence of the Divine, both are to be found: "I am the root of
the root of sobriety and intoxication."[32] Islam recognizes itself in "sobriety" (*sahw*), as
conveyed in the Quranic verse, "O you who believe! Draw not near unto prayer when
you are drunken until you know what you are uttering" (4:43). However, within its
inner or mystical dimension of Sufism, Islam claims both realms of "sobriety" (*sahw*)
and "intoxication" (*sukr*).[33] In the mystical paths, transcendence is associated with
the former and immanence with the latter. Persian poet and mystic Rūzbihān Baqlī
(1128–1209) affirmed a unitive understanding of these concepts: "Sobriety and intoxication are one, for the lover dives into the oceans of Greatness and Might, and there
the intoxicated is not distinguished from the sober."[34]

Mystical traditions use the symbolism of "wine" for Divine Love and "intemper-
ance" for union with the Absolute. There are also cautionary reminders about not
abusing alcohol or substances: "And be not drunk with wine, wherein is excess; but
be filled with the Spirit" (Ephesians 5:18). It is an error to confuse terrestrial wine
with the celestial wine of the Spirit, which is the object of our search for transcendence. This understanding of reality differs from those who abuse alcohol or drugs,
for the celestial wine signifies union with Divine Reality, what in Hindu and Islamic

28. James, *Varieties of Religious Experience*, 387.
29. James, *Varieties of Religious Experience*, 268.
30. Jung, quoted in Alcoholics Anonymous, *"Pass It On,"* 384.
31. Rūmī, quoted in Chittick, *Sufi Path of Love*, 320.
32. Rūmī, quoted in Chittick, *Sufi Path of Love*, 266.
33. See Danner, "Intoxication and Sobriety in Sufism," 291–302.
34. Quoted in Ernst, *Words of Ecstasy in Sufism*, 49.

traditions is regarded as being-consciousness-bliss (Sanskrit: *sat-chit-ānanda*; Arabic: *wujūd-wijdān-wajd*).

Nonordinary states of consciousness may bear some semblance to the descriptions of mystical experiences found in spiritual traditions; however, there is an important difference, in that *experience* here pertains to the limits of the empirical ego rather than pure immersion in the transpersonal dimension. The saints and sages were interested not in experiences as such but in union with the Absolute. Śrī Rāmakrishna (1836–86) once remarked, "Communion with God is the true wine, the wine of ecstatic love."[35] Śrī Ānandamayī Mā (1896–1982) urged us to "become drinkers of nectar, all of you—drinkers of the wine of immortality. Tread the path of immortality, where no death exists and no disease."[36] St. Teresa of Ávila (1515–82) spoke of this state as "heavenly inebriation,"[37] and there are many other mystics who also experienced such religious ecstasy, such as St. Catherine of Alexandria (ca. 287–ca. 305), Hildegard of Bingen (ca. 1098–1179), St. Francis of Assisi (ca. 1182–1226), and St. Philip Neri (1515–95). Śrī Ramana Maharshi (1879–1950) went so far as to suggest that we are always already in a state of ecstasy (*samādhi*) and need not search for it: "Actually, one is always in *samādhi* but one does not know it. To know it all one has to do is to remove the obstacles."[38] Prior to concluding this section, it needs to also be acknowledged that the spiritual traditions equate overindulgence in alcohol with ignorance. The Japanese Pure Land Buddhist master Shinran (1173–1263) spoke of those who were "drunk with the wine of ignorance."[39]

The stopping of using substances or engaging in destructive behaviors does not resolve all the issues, for the void within still exists and will not be satiated without engaging in a profound inquiry into "Who am I?" To be fully human is to recognize our fundamental relationship with the Divine, which is to say that our true identity *in divinis* is the primordial nature (*fiṭra*), the "image of God" (*imago Dei*), Buddha-nature (*Buddha-dhātu*), or the Self (*Ātmā*). The doctrine of identity is unanimous across the traditions regarding our fundamental connection to the Divine, which is both transcendent and immanent. This is articulated in the Ashtāvakra Gītā of the Hindu tradition, "You are what you think" (1:11);[40] and in the Dhammapada of the Buddhist tradition, "All that we are is the result of what we have thought" (1:1);[41] in the Jewish tradition, "As he thinketh in his heart, so is he" (Proverbs 23:7); in the Christian tradition, "we . . . beholding . . . are changed into the same image" (2 Corinthians 3:18); and additionally in the Islamic tradition, "You are your thought."[42] Both horizontal and vertical understandings are needed to fully situate and comprehend the human psyche, yet mainstream psychology is for the most part confined to the horizontal dimension.

35. Rāmakrishna, *Gospel of Ramakrishna*, 94.
36. Ānandamayī, *Essential Śrī Ānandamayī Mā*, 79.
37. St. Teresa of Ávila, Meditations on the Song of Songs 4:4, *Collected Works of Saint Teresa*, 2:244.
38. Ramana Maharshi, quoted in Godman, *Be As You Are*, 174.
39. Shinran, *Essential Shinran*, 197.
40. Ashtāvakra Gītā 1:11, *Heart of Awareness*, 3.
41. Buddha, 1:1, *Dhammapada*, trans. Babbitt, 3.
42. Rūmī, quoted in Chittick, *Sufi Path of Love*, 96.

Abstinence from self-destructive behavior is imperative, but it is only the beginning. The notion that we are in absolute control of our lives must be reconsidered before we can acknowledge our impotence and our reliance on the Divine. Twelve-step programs such as Alcoholics Anonymous and Narcotics Anonymous have conceded the powerful and unmanageable nature of addiction pointing out the need to "quit playing God."[43] In this way, we come to see our "spiritual bankrupt[cy]" and the imperative to rely on a power greater than ourselves.[44]

At this juncture, embracing a spiritual form becomes necessary in order to not fall into the trap of substituting one addiction for another, which can often make things worse. Wholeness and healing cannot be obtained by individual effort alone; they require an agency that is not subject to the profound limitations of the ordinary self. But neither should this suggest the opposite—that we ought to remain complacent and indifferent to any effort, which is yet another trap. Due to the many misunderstandings of what religion truly is, it is necessary to recall anew that the etymological root of the English word *religion* is the Latin *religare*, meaning "to rebind" or "to bind back"—by implication, to the Divine that is at once transcendent and immanent.

As it has been expressed in the Christian tradition, "Without Me you can do nothing" (John 15:5 NKJV), but it is also said that "I can do all things through Christ which strengtheneth me" (Philippians 4:13). There is a similar Quranic verse that conveys the need to rely on the Divine: "Naught befalls us, save that which God has decreed for us" (9:51). Shin Buddhism makes the distinction between "Other-Power" (*tariki*) and "self-power" (*jiriki*), in other words, the distinction between reliance on the Primal Vow of Amida Buddha as opposed to our own efforts to attain *Nirvāṇa*. This awareness will help seekers turn to the Divine: "When My servants ask thee about Me, truly I am near. I answer the call of the caller when he calls Me" (Quran 2:186). The Divine's remembrance of us is conditional on our remembrance of the Divine: "Remember Me, and I will remember you" (Quran 2:152). The Sage of Arunachala conveyed our dependence on the transpersonal dimension: "Divine Grace is essential for Realization."[45]

Domination over oneself requires that which transcends the empirical ego or separate self. The futility of attempting to tame our desires through the ego alone was remarked by the sixty-eighth Jagadguru of Kanchi (1894–1994): "While desire fulfilled leads to further desire, desire frustrated turns into anger, like the rebound of a ball thrown at a wall."[46] It is through commitment to a spiritual form—and by adhering to its timeworn paths—that we can learn detachment. The Hindu tradition speaks of submitting ourselves completely to the Divine in order to go beyond our temporal attachments: "Only by love can men see me, and know me, and come unto me. He who works for me, who loves me, whose End Supreme I am, free from attachment to all things, and with love for all creation, he in truth comes unto me" (Bhagavad Gītā

43. Quoted in *Alcoholics Anonymous*, 62.
44. Quoted in *Alcoholics Anonymous*, 287.
45. Ramana, *Talks with Sri Ramana Maharshi*, 33.
46. Jagadguru, *Introduction to Hindu Dharma*, 138.

11:54–55)[47] and also, "When all desires that cling to the heart are surrendered, then a mortal becomes immortal" (Katha Upanishad 6:14).[48] According to Eckhart, detachment "enkindles the heart and awakens the spirit and stimulates our longings and shows us where God is."[49] Heraclitus of Ephesus (ca. 535–475 BCE) wrote powerfully about the harmful impacts of attachment: "Whatever it wants it will buy at the cost of soul."[50]

A paradoxical characteristic of those who abuse substances is that they are always, albeit unknowingly, affirming the Divine. This will at first glance seem curious and even nonsensical, for it has been said that "the worship of God is an abomination to a sinner" (Ecclesiasticus 1:32 DRB) and "surely the soul commands to evil, save whom my Lord may show mercy" (Quran 12:53). Metaphysically speaking, however, whether they realize it or not, everything affirms the Divine in every thought and act, as our entire existence is woven into the sacred. As Eckhart confirmed, "Even he who blasphemes against God praises God."[51] This statement does not, then, imply that we should continue in our excess or folly. For it has also been said, "What shall we say then? Shall we continue in sin, that grace may abound? God forbid. How shall we, that are dead to sin, live any longer therein?" (Romans 6:1–2). The Quran exhorts us, "Do not despair of God's Mercy" (39:53), as the Divine forgives all transgressions. In the Pure Land tradition of Buddhism, we find the following admonition: "It is like offering more wine before the person has become sober or urging him to take even more poison before the poison has abated. 'Here's some medicine, so drink all the poison you like'—words like these should never be said."[52]

Addiction can be understood from a metaphysical perspective as a deep-rooted form of idolatry. When anything is substituted for the Divine, it becomes an idol and an obstacle to the spiritual life. This is why it has been stated that "no man can serve two masters" (Matthew 6:24). Spiritual wayfarers are instructed to turn to the Divine by taking refuge in it: "Thou shalt have no other gods before me" (Exodus 20:3–5). It is the Divine alone that will bring peace to the human soul; therefore, we need to sacrifice our dysfunctional dependencies to the Divine itself. Śrīmad Bhāgavatam expresses this requirement with this exhortation: "Offer unto me that which is very dear to thee—which thou holdest most covetable. Infinite are the results of such an offering!" (11:5).[53]

The spiritual traditions teach that there is a part of us that is always wedded to Divine Reality. The dimension of ourselves that is caught in addictive tendencies or patterns can never compromise our primordial nature. An integral psychology informed by the wisdom traditions recognizes two distinct dimensions of human

47. *Bhagavad Gita*, trans. Mascaró, 95.
48. Katha Upanishad 6:14, *Upanishads*, trans. Mascaró, 66.
49. Eckhart, *Essential Sermons*, 294.
50. Heraclitus, fragment 51, *Heraclitus*, 58.
51. Eckhart, "Articles Condemned in the Bull of John XXII (In Agro dominico)," in *Complete Mystical Works*, 26.
52. Shinran, *Collected Works of Shinran*, 1:553.
53. Śrīmad Bhāgavatam 11:5, *Srimad Bhagavatam*, 231.

identity: one relative or horizontal, and the other absolute or vertical (while never blurring or confusing the two).[54]

> One of the most important themes in religion—*the* most important—is the confrontation between the two "selves" in man: the inner, which partakes of God's unconditional, infinite nature and is identical with his "kingdom," and the outer self, or human personality with a certain name. It is the intersection of these two dimensions that comprises the religious life. One sees man horizontally from the earthly side; the other vertically as a vehicle of divinity. The crossing point may be multiplicated both horizontally and vertically, making a cosmic web formed in one direction of layered worlds or conditions and, in the other, of the beings embodied in them—horizontal and vertical, woof and warp.[55]

Duo sunt in homine ("There are two [natures] in man") was an axiom in the West prior to the emergence of the Renaissance that recognized an outer and inner aspect to our being.[56] Ibn ʿArabī pointed out that "in any definition of Man, his inner and outer aspect are both to be considered."[57] The theomorphic essence is unconditioned and unaffected by the activities of the world: "Everything a man does in the lower part of active life is necessarily exterior to him, so to speak, beneath him."[58] This was expressed slightly differently by Ananda Coomaraswamy (1877–1947): "Our Inner Man is in the world but not of it, in us but not of us, our Outer Man both in the world and of it."[59] Mainstream psychology focuses on the diagnosis and treatment of the outer human being, unaware that its materialistic science, of necessity, excludes "inward man" (Romans 7:22) and has no framework to bridge the traditional doctrine of these two natures within us.

There are several texts in the Upanishads that speak of the "two birds who dwell on the same tree" (Muṇḍaka Upanishad 3:1:1; Shvetāshvatara Upanishad 4:6). These birds illustrate the nature of the human being: One of them eats the fruit of the tree, meaning that it engages in the world of phenomena, while the other looks on without eating—witnessing the transitory nature of all phenomena with equanimity. This describes the distinction between the corporeal and spiritual natures that exist in all of us. This same teaching can be framed as showing the inner and outer dimensions of the human being that need not be opposed to one another; rather, they are interconnected and work together when integrated into our transpersonal presence. Eckhart observed,

> In every man there are two kinds of man: One is called the outer man, which is our sensuality, with the five senses serving him, and yet the outer man works through the power of the soul. The second man is called the inner man, which is the man's inwardness. Now you should know that a spiritual man who loves God makes no use in his outer man of the soul's powers except when the five senses require

54. See Bendeck Sotillos, "Inner and Outer Human Being," 9–26.
55. Almqvist, "Every Branch in Me," 194.
56. St. Thomas Aquinas, question 26, fourth article, *Summa Theologica, Part II*, 336.
57. Ibn ʿArabī, *Bezels of Wisdom*, 73.
58. Chap. 8, *Cloud of Unknowing*, 72.
59. Coomaraswamy, *Coomaraswamy*, 2:371.

it; and his inwardness pays no heed to the five senses, except as this leads and guides them, and protects them, so that they are not employed for beastly purposes, as they are by some people who live for their carnal delight, as beasts lacking reason do. Such people deserve to be called beasts rather than men.[60]

A true "science of the soul" provides spiritual teachings and methods to integrate our outer and inner selves. Again, in our true identity as the primordial nature (*fiṭra*), the "image of God" (*imago Dei*), Buddha-nature (*Buddha-dhātu*), or the Self (*Ātmā*), we are the eternal witness that does not partake in the activities of the temporal world. No matter how many transgressions we may incur in this life, it must never be forgotten that our primordial nature can never be lost or destroyed, as it contains within itself the transpersonal human archetype. It is our essential identity in the Divine that prevents our fallen or *saṃsāric* state from becoming absolute or terminal.

We are subjected to many trials in this life, making the path to wholeness and healing difficult; yet spiritual traditions confer on us the necessary discernment to traverse these hallowed paths. It is through the hardships faced in life that we discover who we are. Grace does not always come into our lives gently and can sometimes appear contrary to what is expected. Tibetan Buddhist master Gampopa (1079–1153) went as far as to say, "One must know that misfortune, being the means of leading one to the Doctrine, is also a *guru*."[61] The Islamic tradition speaks about human beings' misunderstanding of the deeper significance of trials and tribulations on the spiritual path: "And when harm befalls man, he calls upon Us. Then, when We confer upon him a Blessing from Us, he says, 'I was only given it because of knowledge.' Nay, it is a trial, but most of them know not" (Quran 39:49).

Rūmī speaks about the importance of encountering ordeals in life and how they can catalyze the search for a spiritual path: "It is pain that guides a man in every enterprise. Until there is an ache within him, a passion and a yearning for that thing arising within him, he will never strive to attain it."[62] Again, without facing obstacles and ordeals, many people would not find their way to religion. Christian monk and ascetic Evagrius Ponticus (345–99) went as far as to suggest, "Take away temptations and no-one will be saved."[63] St. Anthony the Great (251–356) expressed something similar: "Whoever has not experienced temptation cannot enter into the Kingdom of Heaven."[64] It is through a correct understanding of trials that we can come to understand that, not only are we seeking the Divine, but the Divine also seeks us.

A way of overcoming our lower impulses has been known since the earliest times in the world's valid traditions—namely, spiritual warfare. Ultimately, we are faced with a real conflict that is waged in the human heart and symbolized in the battlefield of terrestrial existence. For example, the Buddha himself confirms the following in the Dhammapada: "If a man should conquer in battle a thousand and a thousand more, and another man should conquer himself, his would be the greater victory,

60. Eckhart, *Essential Sermons*, 290.
61. Gampopa, quoted in Evans-Wentz, *Tibetan Yoga and Secret Doctrines*, 71.
62. Rūmī, discourse 5, *Discourses of Rumi*, 33.
63. Evagrius Ponticus, quoted in *Sayings of the Desert Fathers*, 54.
64. St. Anthony the Great, quoted in *Sayings of the Desert Fathers*, 2.

because the greatest of victories is the victory over oneself" (8:103–6).[65] Within Christianity, this notion is expressed by St. Paul: "For we wrestle not against flesh and
blood, but against principalities, against powers, against the rulers of darkness of
this world, against spiritual wickedness in high places" (Ephesians 6:12). This is also
explicitly found in the Islamic tradition when the Prophet Muhammad refers to the
"lesser holy war" (al-jihād al-asghar), which seeks to protect the lovers of God through
social or military efforts, and the second and "greater holy war" (al-jihād al-akbar),
which was considered to be the highest form of spiritual warfare—one that takes place
in ourselves. The notion of spiritual warfare has also been used in the Shamanic or
primordial religion of the First Peoples. Medicine man and Sun Dance Chief Thomas
Yellowtail (1903–93) explained,

> The sun dancer and the Sun Dance itself will bless all of the tribe and all creation
> through the inner, spiritual warfare. . . . The warrior fights an enemy who is
> on the outside; the sun dancer wages a war on an enemy within himself. Each
> of us must fight a continuing battle to keep to the spiritual values that repre-
> sent our traditional heritage. If we fail to be continually alert in our prayers
> and our attitudes and to use good sense in all that we do, then we will fail in
> our interior war. In olden days, this interior warfare had the support of the
> whole tribe, and our life itself helped to guide us in our personal struggle.
> Nowadays, we must follow the Sun Dance way all the more carefully, because
> it contains the key to our sacred warfare.[66]

The conflict between human beings and the world is, in reality, a spiritual battle
between the higher and lower nature of a person; animality seeks the world of form
by gravitating to the sensory, while our theomorphic identity seeks transcendence
and gravitates to the Divine. The antidote for this spiritual warfare is exemplified
by St. Paul's exhortation (although its equivalent is found in all spiritual traditions):
"Pray without ceasing" (1 Thessalonians 5:17).

When we realize that addictions lead to a dead end and that alcohol or substance
abuse will not fill our inner emptiness, we can then begin to take steps through
a spiritual path to immerse ourselves in its teachings and practices. According to
twelve-step programs, many individuals need to "hit bottom" before they are able
to recognize the extent of their problem and to seek help.[67] It is in reaching this
nadir through excess that the following insight by William Blake (1757–1827) can be
understood: "If the fool would persist in his folly he would become wise."[68] A willingness to engage in reformative changes is only the beginning. Spiritual traditions talk
about what is traditionally known as "the descent into Hell" or when one "falls into
abysmal darkness,"[69] for it is only through fully fathoming our desperate plight that

65. Buddha, 8:103–6, Dhammapada, trans. Mascaró, 50.
66. Fitzgerald, Yellowtail, 139–40.
67. Quoted in Alcoholics Anonymous, 187.
68. Blake, Marriage of Heaven and Hell, 14.
69. See Perry, Treasury of Traditional Wisdom, 366–78. Śrīmad Bhāgavatam 11:3, Srimad Bhagav-
    atam, 215.

"the lower possibilities of the soul are revealed."[70] For the bystander, change is logical and necessary; however, for the individual in the throes of addiction, change can be very frightening and painful, a hell-like experience. In the face of so much suffering and perplexity, we are all in a sense—like Job—crying out, "Where is God my maker, who giveth songs in the night?" (35:10). Some have compared this process with entering a "dark night of the soul" as taught by St. John of the Cross:

> The shadow of death and the pains and torments of hell are most acutely felt, that is, the sense of being without God . . . a fearful apprehension has come upon [the soul] that thus it will be with it for ever. . . . It sees itself in the midst of the opposite evils, miserable imperfections and aridities, emptiness of the understanding, and abandonment of the spirit in darkness.[71]

An essential facet of the world's religions is principally affirmed in the injunction of *dying before dying*, illustrating the importance of attaining a "spiritual death" in this life. As Eckhart made clear, "A truly perfect man should be accustomed to regard himself as dead,"[72] or, as found in the Jewish tradition, one should aspire to the "cessation or annihilation of existence" (*bittul ha-yesh*)—by implication in the Absolute. This teaching was made explicit in the renowned words of the Prophet of Islam: "Die before ye die" (*mūtū qabla an tamūtū*). Joseph Epes Brown (1920–2000), renowned scholar of Native American traditions and world religions, outlined the three stages of this metanoia or integral transformative process, which appear throughout all sapiential traditions:

> All true spiritual progress involves three stages, which are not successfully experienced and left behind, but rather each in turn is realized and then integrated within the next stage, so that ultimately they become one in the individual who attains the ultimate goal. Different terms may be used for these stages, but essentially they constitute purification, perfection or expansion, and union.[73]

Across the diverse religious and spiritual traditions of the world, these transformative stages are present in distinct forms:

> Despite the many differences of technique and approach in various paths of spiritual realization, there is in every process of realization the three grand stages of purification, expansion, and union. Something in man must die, something must expand, and only then the essence of man is able to achieve that union.[74]

If transpersonal union with Ultimate Reality or the Absolute is the final goal of all spiritual disciplines, then it is necessary that the impure not be rejoined with what is pure. For this reason, a process of purification is needed.

---

70. Lings, *Shakespeare's Window into the Soul*, 80.
71. St. John of the Cross, *Dark Night of the Soul*, 84–85, 86.
72. Eckhart, German Works, *Essential Sermons*, 216.
73. Brown, *Spiritual Legacy*, 34.
74. Nasr, *Knowledge and the Sacred*, 330.

The necessity for a core transformation that can release us from addictive tendencies was noted by Thomas à Kempis (ca. 1380–1471):

> The man who is not yet wholly dead to self, is soon tempted, and is overcome in small and trifling matters. It is hard for him who is weak in spirit, and still in part carnal and inclined to the pleasures of sense, to withdraw himself altogether from earthly desires. And therefore, when he withdraweth himself from these, he is often sad, and easily angered too if any oppose his will.[75]

What secular psychology often overlooks is that individuals tend to be confused about the meaning of their lives and do not know what they need or what is best for them. This is due, in large part, to the emergence of modernism and the secular worldview that has attempted to replace sacred epistemologies with profane culture. Sacred psychology, by contrast, directly tackles this confusion. For example, this predicament is clearly acknowledged in the Islamic tradition: "It may be that you hate a thing though it be good for you, and it may be that you love a thing though it be evil for you. God knows, and you know not" (Quran 2:216). It is by traveling the spiritual path that we can obtain divine guidance, as Abba Poemen (ca. 340–450) observed: "Vigilance, self-knowledge and discernment; these are the guides of the soul."[76] At the same time, every human being is responsible for their own actions: "No soul does evil, save against itself, and none shall bear the burden of another" (Quran 6:164). Ultimately, it is we who must bear the cost of our wrongdoings: "And whoever commits a sin, commits it only against his own soul" (Quran 4:111).

As the saints and sages of all traditions attest, there is no addiction or trauma that cannot be healed and from which we cannot move beyond. We were, after all, born whole and complete, and it is this understanding that brings a sense of context that is very much needed. In the words of St. Francis de Sales (1567–1622): "Do not lose your inward peace for anything whatsoever, even if your whole world seems upset."[77] According to the traditional "science of the soul," it is the way in which things are perceived that either supports our recovery and spiritual health or disturbs the equilibrium of the human psyche rather than events in themselves. The Stoic philosopher Epictetus (ca. 50–ca. 130) observed, "It is not possible that that which is by nature free should be disturbed or thwarted by anything but itself. But it is a man's own judgements [thoughts] that disturb him."[78] We recall that "God burdens a soul only to its capacity" (Quran 2:286), and likewise, "God . . . will not suffer you . . . above that ye are able . . . to bear" (1 Corinthians 10:13). According to the sacred psychology of Islam, "God alters not what is in a people until they alter what is in themselves" (Quran 13:11), and according to a prophetic saying, "For every disease there is a cure." Nāgārjuna (ca. 150–250) equates healing with restoring our Buddha-nature: "All desires should be abandoned; / But if you are unable to do so, / Let your desire be for salvation. /

75. Thomas à Kempis, *Imitation of Christ*, 10.
76. Abba Poemen, quoted in *Sayings of the Desert Fathers*, 145.
77. St. Francis de Sales, *Selection from the Spiritual Letters*, 228.
78. Epictetus, *Discourses*, 1:131.

Thus will be found the cure."[79] Commitment to a spiritual tradition has been regarded as one of the most effective means of protecting and ensuring resilience and mental health. Although hardships occur, even traumatic events, it is through religion that one can receive steadfast support to gain perspective and persevere.

The need has been observed in twelve-step programs for those struggling with addiction to associate with others to ensure recovery: "Practical experience shows that nothing will so much insure immunity from drinking as intensive work with other alcoholics."[80] Whether we are struggling with our addictions or mental health, we require supportive relationships to help us through the recovery process and to maintain and enhance our psychological well-being. We need one another, as no one is saved alone: "We are [all] members one of another" (Ephesians 4:25 ESV). Shinran reminds us that "sentient beings, without exception, have been our parents and brothers and sisters in the course of countless lives in [the] many states of existence. On attaining Buddhahood after this present life, we can save every one of them."[81]

Relationships encompass an indefinite number of states of consciousness and levels of reality—a sacred unity both within the created order and in what lies beyond it, as this Lakota saying reveals: *Mitakuye oyasin*—"We are all related." The Hindu tradition has what is known as *satsang*, or an association with truth or reality, which consists of being in the company of saints and sages; however, it also signifies an ultimate encounter with our primordial nature or the Self.

The Buddha considered that "the entire holy life . . . is, good friendship, good companionship, good comradeship."[82] Additionally, Confucius (551–479 BCE) stressed that the person who "associates with those that possess the Way . . . thereby corrects his own faults."[83] To quote Seneca (ca. 4–65), "Associate with those who will make a better man of you. Welcome those whom you yourself can improve."[84] It is through intimate forms of spiritual fellowship that we can embark on a way of life that adheres to the middle path between extremes. This idea is found in the Gospel of Matthew: "Strait is the gate, and narrow is the way, which leadeth unto life, and few there be that find it" (7:14). St. John Cassian (ca. 360–ca. 435) wrote, "For, as the fathers have said, all extremes are equally harmful."[85] In the Islamic tradition, this is known as following the "straight path" (*al-ṣirāṭ al-mustaqīm*), and for this reason, the fellowship of Muslims (*ummah*) is described as a "middle community" (Quran 2:143). As Buddha taught, the way of "avoiding . . . extremes, the Tathāgata has realized the Middle Path: it gives vision, it gives knowledge, and it leads to calm, to insight, to enlightenment, to Nibbāna."[86] Confucius also alluded to the middle way: "To go too far is as bad as not to go far enough."[87]

---

79. Nāgārjuna, quoted in *Elegant Sayings*, 44.
80. Quoted in *Alcoholics Anonymous*, 89.
81. Shinran, *Collected Works of Shinran*, 1:664.
82. Buddha, *Connected Discourses of the Buddha*, 1524.
83. Confucius, 1:14, *Analects of Confucius*, 87.
84. Seneca, Moral Epistles 7.8, *Ad Lucilium Epistulae Morales*, 1:35.
85. St. John Cassian, "On the Holy Fathers of Sketis and on Discrimination," in Palmer et al., *Philokalia*, 1:107–8.
86. Buddha Shakyamuni, quoted in Rahula, *What the Buddha Taught*, 92.
87. Confucius, 11:15, *Analects of Confucius*, 156.

Akin to the twelve-step programs' adage of living "one day at a time,"[88] we find that all the spiritual traditions teach us to live in the present moment, as life can only be truly experienced in the here and now. "Now is the accepted time; behold, now is the day of salvation" (2 Corinthians 6:2). The present moment contains the whole of time, both past and future. This is why it is often referred to in traditions as the "eternal now." The present moment is ultimately all that exists, as the past is no longer and the future has yet to arrive. To be mindful of the here and now is to enter the contemplative state of the Real, which is none other than this timeless present. Metaphysically, the whole of time, past and future, is contained in the "eternal now," as Ānandamayī Mā teaches: "In that supreme moment, all moments are contained."[89] Nicholas of Cusa (1401–64) conveyed a similar teaching: "All time is comprised in the present or 'now.'"[90] Within Islamic spirituality, there is a well-known saying that "the Sufi is the son of the moment" (al-ṣufī ibn al-waqt).

Psychology today attempts to assess, diagnose, and treat addiction without acknowledging what we have termed the *trauma of secularism*. Without understanding the historical developments that led to the world of modernity—the fruition of the "Age of Enlightenment" of the seventeenth and eighteenth centuries—it is difficult to understand how this profane trajectory radically undermined the collective psyche. The discipline of modern psychology has unapologetically participated in this antispiritual outlook, which, paradoxically and unknowingly, it has also attempted to remedy since its inception. Deprived of metaphysics, conventional psychology remains in a hopeless, self-contradictory predicament because it cannot be called what it alleges itself to be—namely, a "science of the soul."

In an addictive state of mind, we are unable to get enough of what we do not need, and for this reason, we remain unsatisfied even when we obtain the thing desired. Similarly, we cannot get enough of what we truly need due to an inability to properly understand the underlying source of our addiction. What is forgotten or confused is that we are ultimately seeking transcendence and healing from our fallen or *saṃsāric* condition, as unambiguously taught in the world's religions. To be human is to be called to the sacred, and our souls will not rest until they return home, a journey supported by adhering to one of humanity's divinely revealed sapiential traditions. It is through metaphysics that a multidimensional model for understanding the spiritual roots of substance abuse can emerge. Informed by the diverse epistemologies of the world's cultures, we can better understand the underlying motives of addiction and the means to facilitate wholeness. To become what we are entails restoring our spiritual dimension, the "science of the soul," for "the way of healing is one of integration; resolution of the psychomachy [battle for the soul]; making peace with one's Self."[91]

88. Quoted in *Alcoholics Anonymous*, 293.
89. Ānandamayī, *Essential Śrī Ānandamayī Mā*, 91.
90. Nicholas Cusanus, bk. 2, chap. 3, *Of Learned Ignorance*, 76.
91. Moore and Coomaraswamy, *Selected Letters*, 231.

6

Death as Transformation

Perhaps the most effective way to prepare for death is to simply recognize that we are, in fact, going to die. Although we cannot deny this fact, we can often defer thinking about our mortality; yet the indubitable nature of death is always there side by side with life itself.[1] Despite this reality, "man was created alone and he dies alone."[2] Since the most remote times, there has been a practice of continuously living with the awareness of death in one's consciousness. The words of the adage *Memento mori*—Latin for "Remember that you are mortal"—encapsulate this practice. All of humanity's saints and sages speak, unanimously, of suffering as being grounded in a false identification with the empirical ego or separate self. Śrī Rāmakrishna (1836–86) expressed the need for us to die to our lower nature: "When 'I' is dead, all troubles cease."[3]

An essential element in the world's religions is the injunction that finds expression, for instance, in the well-known words of the Prophet of Islam: "Die before ye die" (*mūtū qabla an tamūtū*). In the Hindu tradition, there is the concept of being "twice-born" (*dvija*): Our initial entry into terrestrial existence is one type of birth, whereas the second is an initiation into the spiritual path. This alchemical and transformative psychospiritual process of "dying before dying" appears in a myriad of forms throughout the spiritual traditions and their sacred psychologies, yet points of convergence can readily be discerned.

Just how universal this transformative process is has been underscored by the philosopher Frithjof Schuon (1907–98): "Every complete tradition postulates in the final analysis the 'extinction' of the ego for the sake of the divine 'I.'"[4] The French metaphysician René Guénon (1886–1951) also confirms the universal nature of the doctrine of mystical death and resurrection: "The idea of a 'second birth,' understood in a purely spiritual sense, is indeed common to all spiritual doctrines."[5]

At the heart of every integral psychology or "science of the soul" is the recognition of a psychospiritual transformation or metanoia, which is inseparable from a metaphysical vision grounded in the sacred. This can be seen as a "salvific" psychology, rooted in metaphysics that speaks of a horizontal dimension comprising the

1. See Becker, *Denial of Death*.
2. Schuon, *Light*, 119.
3. Rāmakrishna, *Original Gospel of Rāmakrishna*, 19.
4. Schuon, *Gnosis*, trans. Perry et al., 63.
5. Guénon, *Introduction*, 156.

empirical ego and a vertical dimension that pertains to the transpersonal Self. Yet it is important to note that the vertical dimension provides the basis for the horizontal, which it transcends: "To deny the spiritual is to deny the human."[6] In what follows, we will explore the meaning behind mystical death and resurrection, as found in the universal and timeless wisdom traditions of the world.

Questions concerning our final ends have always weighed on human beings: What does it mean to be born, to live, and to die? And who is it that is born, lives, and dies? Such questions, though posed since time immemorial, hold as much importance today as they did in the past. They also remain just as perplexing because they confront us with the mystery of existence and the limits of human knowledge. Whitall N. Perry (1920–2005) writes,

> There are two historical moments in the life of every person on earth which are inexorably real and yet totally outside the reach of empirical consciousness: the moment of birth, and the moment of death. These two decisive events occur moreover exactly once, over the entire lifespan of the individual, and scarcely enter into his reflections at all—everything else considered.[7]

At the intersection of the horizontal and vertical dimensions, time and the temporal are juxtaposed with the timeless and eternal.[8] Through a deep study of traditional metaphysics, we can begin to make sense of the strange and enigmatic logic of death and to grasp something of its transformative potential.

While birth and death occur at opposite ends of a human lifespan, they are inextricably connected to the transcendent. Zhuāngzi (Chuang Tzu, ca. 369–ca. 286 BCE) makes a thought-provoking observation about the phenomenon of birth and death, alluding to what is beyond them both: "Birth is not a beginning; death is not an end."[9] Lord Northbourne (1896–1982) asserted that "from the 'point of view of eternity' birth and death are one."[10] The intimate relationship between birth and death has always been recognized in cultures not vitiated by secular materialism: "Life and death, then, are considered not as two separate stages of completing mankind's temporal and post-earthly existence, but as complementary phases in an ever-recurring cycle."[11]

For this reason, the well-known teacher of Zen Buddhism Shunryū Suzuki (1904–71) stated, "Our life and death are the same thing. When we realize this fact we have no fear of death anymore, and we have no actual difficulty in our life."[12] Roshi Philip Kapleau (1912–2004) makes a similar point: "Living is thus dying, and dying living. In fact, with every inhalation you are being reborn and with each exhalation you are dying."[13] Seen in the light of Ultimate Reality, both birth and death are

6. Schuon, *Eye of the Heart*, 55.
7. Perry, *Challenges*, 129–30.
8. "Eternity can no more enter into time than the Absolute can enter into contingency" (Schuon, *Face of the Absolute*, 52).
9. Zhuāngzi, quoted in Giles, *Musings of a Chinese Mystic*, 104.
10. Northbourne, *Looking Back on Progress*, 114.
11. Waters, *Book of the Hopi*, 192.
12. Suzuki, *Zen Mind, Beginner's Mind*, 94.
13. Kapleau, *Zen*, 67.

unreal, and their dichotomy needs to be transcended. The Tibetan Buddhist tradition maintains that "ultimately, there is nothing that dies, since neither self nor mind have true existence."[14] This is exemplified in the Heart Sūtra (*Prajñāpāramitā-hridaya-sūtra*): "Form is emptiness; emptiness is form. Emptiness is not other than form; form is not other than emptiness."[15] The interconnectedness of all phenomena applies not only to the world of appearances in *saṃsāra* but also to the dependence of *saṃsāra* on *nirvāṇa*—akin to the Taoist notion of *yin-yang*, where all apparent duality is fully integrated.

We soon come to see, therefore, that there are different facets to death.[16] For this reason, "one has to understand that there are different degrees, different points of view, different levels of reality which have to be taken into consideration."[17] The dying that we are considering here plays a crucial role in spiritual initiation rites found the world over, for "the essence and aim of initiation is always and everywhere the same, only its modalities differing as a result of adaptation to different times and places."[18]

As Guénon states, "Initiation is essentially the transmission of a spiritual influence" in order to actualize a "state which is the ultimate goal of all initiation . . . precisely what must be understood by the 'Supreme Identity.'"[19]

The injunction of the Prophet Muhammad—"Die before you die"—is a call for self-effacement before the Divine. As Rūmī asserts, "Sacrifice your self, and become nothing."[20] The spiritual path requires detachment from worldliness and sentimentality: "In order to 'live' inwardly one must 'die' outwardly."[21] The Japanese Zen master Bunan Zenji (1603–76) captures this principle succinctly as "While living / Be a dead man."[22] By dying to our outer limitations, we enter a dimension that is unlimited and transpersonal: "The Divine requires both a ritual and moral preparation whereby the aspirant learns to 'die' spiritually."[23] The process of dying and the disidentification with all that we cling to in this earthly existence can serve to liberate us from the crushing limitations of the mundane and the conventional.

> The experience of death is rather like that of a man who has lived all his life in a dark room and suddenly finds himself transported to a mountain top; there his gaze would embrace all the wide landscape; the works of men would seem insignificant to him. It is thus that the soul torn from the earth and from the body perceives the inexhaustible diversity of things and the incommensurable abysses of the worlds which contain them; for the first time it sees itself in

14. Jamgön, *Great Path of Awakening*, 26.
15. The Heart Sūtra, quoted in Lopez, *Heart Sutra Explained*, 57.
16. "There are different ways of dying and different degrees of death" (Schuon, *Logic and Transcendence*, trans. Perry et al., 47).
17. Lings, *Enduring Utterance*, 80.
18. Guénon, *Perspectives on Initiation*, 4.
19. Guénon, *Perspectives on Initiation*, 48, 210.
20. Rūmī, discourse 6, *Discourses of Rumi*, 37.
21. Schuon, *Logic and Transcendence*, trans. Perry et al., 190.
22. Bunan Zenji, quoted in Suzuki, *Zen and Japanese Culture*, 102.
23. Perry, *Mystery of Individuality*, 248.

its universal context, in an inexorable concatenation and in a network of mul-
titudinous and unsuspected relationships, and takes account of the fact that
life has been but an "instant," but a "play." Projected into the absolute nature
of things, man will be inescapably aware of what he is in reality; he will know
himself, ontologically and without any deforming perspective, in the light of
the normative proportions of the Universe.[24]

In this way, our attachment to the world of appearances gradually loosens its hold
so that we are not caught unawares at the critical moment of our passing:

Think often of death with attention, bringing to mind everything which
must then happen. If you do this, that hour will not catch you unawares. . . .
Men of this world flee from the thought and memory of death, so as not to
interrupt the pleasures and enjoyments of their senses, which are incompatible with memory of death. This makes their attachment to the blessings of
the world continually grow and strengthen more and more, since they meet
nothing opposed to it. But when the time comes to part with life and all the
pleasures and things they love, they are cast into excessive turmoil, terror
and torment.[25]

Our earthly sojourn is certainly to be valued and should not be squandered, for
behind the passing hourglass of time lies the Eternal:

It is very remarkable, that God who giveth plenteously to all creatures . . . hath
scattered the firmament with stars . . . yet in the distribution of our time God
seems to be straight-handed, and gives it to us, not as nature gives us riv-
ers, enough to drown us, but drop by drop, minute after minute, so that we
never can have two minutes together, but He takes away one when He gives
us another. This should teach us to value our time; since God so values it.[26]

The phenomena of death and the afterlife have had profound implications for the
world's religious traditions. Numerous sacred texts attest to this, such as the *Per-t
Em Hru* (Book of going forth by day), also known as the Egyptian *Book of the Dead*; the
Bardo Thödol (Liberation through hearing during the intermediate state), or *The Tibetan
Book of the Dead*; and the European genre of the *ars moriendi* (art of dying). There are
similar sacred texts also to be found in Hinduism and Islam and among the First Peoples. They are intended to provide guidance to human beings in order that they may
secure a more favorable spiritual state in the afterlife.

These texts teach the importance of learning the art of dying while we are healthy
and well and not postponing these lessons: "Against his will he dieth that hath not
learned to die. Learn to die and thou shalt [learn] to live, for there shall none [learn]
to live that hath not learned to die."[27] Furthermore, we read, "My Lord, it is a great

24. Schuon, *Understanding Islam*, 92.
25. Scupoli, *Unseen Warfare*, 252.
26. Taylor, *Rule and Exercises*, 39.
27. Quoted in Comper, *Book of the Craft*, 127.

art to die well, and to be learnt by men in health."[28] The posthumous states also have a correspondence with this life, for the highest reality is contained in all time and is never absent from the present. As the influential Muslim scholar Seyyed Hossein Nasr writes, "From this point of view the posthumous becoming of man is no more than a continuation of the journey on this earth to another level of existence, one which, moreover, can already be undertaken here and now."[29]

The notion of *bardo* found in Tibetan Buddhism is useful for understanding human existence as the traversing of states, not just beyond the grave, but also in this life:

> *Bar* means in between, and *do* means island or mark; a sort of landmark which stands between two things. It is rather like an island in the midst of a lake. The concept of bardo is based on the period between sanity and insanity, or the period between confusion and the confusion just about to be transformed into wisdom; and of course it could be said of the experience which stands between death and birth.[30]

The most archaic examples of understanding "mystical" death and resurrection are found among the aboriginal religions. It is through initiations that the consciousness of the Shamanic apprentice is transfigured in such a way that a psychospiritual restructuring occurs. This process elicits a new ontological orientation, allowing a rebirth to take place: "To be dead while alive, and alive while dead, is one of the primary feats of the . . . spiritual traveler."[31] Black Elk (1863–1950) elaborates on this teaching as follows:

> Men die but live again in the real world of *Wakan-Tanka* [Great Spirit], where there is nothing but the spirits of all things; and this true life we may know here on earth if we purify our bodies and minds, thus coming closer to *Wakan-Tanka*, who is all-purity.[32]

Fools Crow (ca. 1890–1989) provides the following insight:

> Death . . . is not a bad thing, since . . . we go to be with *Wakan-Tanka* [Great Spirit] forever. In fact, this is what we are born for . . . born to die, for death is really the beginning of the great life that He has in store for us.[33]

And according to the Osage Indians, "you shall have a body that is free from all causes of death."[34]

Joseph Epes Brown (1920–2000), renowned scholar of Native American traditions, outlines the three stages of this transformative process, which appear throughout all sapiential traditions:

28. Taylor, *Rule and Exercises*, vi.
29. Nasr, *Sufi Essays*, 47.
30. Trungpa, "Commentary," in *Tibetan Book of the Dead*, 10–11.
31. Tompkins, *Tree Grows Out of Hell*, 19.
32. Black Elk, quoted in Brown, *Sacred Pipe*, 32.
33. Fools Crow, quoted in Mails, *Fools Crow*, 136.
34. Osage Indians, quoted in Brown, *Sacred Pipe*, 21.

All true spiritual progress involves three stages, which are not successfully experienced and left behind, but rather each in turn is realized and then integrated within the next stage, so that ultimately they become one in the individual who attains the ultimate goal. Different terms may be used for these stages, but essentially they constitute purification, perfection or expansion, and union.[35]

Across the religious and spiritual traditions of the world, these transformative stages are present in various forms:

Despite the many differences of technique and approach in various paths of spiritual realization, there is in every process of realization the three grand stages of purification, expansion, and union. Something in man must die, something must expand, and only then the essence of man is able to achieve that union.[36]

In the ancient West, philosophy was considered the art of dying properly. A remarkable example of this is found in Plato's (429–347 BCE) dialogue *Phaedo*, in which Socrates (ca. 470–399 BCE) is awaiting his execution. In this record of his final moments of life, a discussion takes place that focuses on the question of death and its implications for living:

It may be that the rest of mankind are not aware that those who apply themselves correctly to the pursuit of philosophy are in fact practicing nothing more nor less than dying and death. If this is so, it would indeed be strange that men who had throughout their lives sought precisely this, should grumble when it came—the very thing which they had, for so long, desired and rehearsed.[37]

In his widely acclaimed *Essays*, Michel de Montaigne (1533–92) wrote a treatise entitled "To Philosophize Is to Learn How to Die" that extends Plato's notion further. He states, "To practice death is to practice freedom. A man who has learned how to die has unlearned how to be a slave,"[38] before declaring, "Death is the origin of another life."[39] One sees a similar approach taken by the Stoic philosopher Seneca (ca. 4–65), who observed, "One must spend an entire lifetime in learning how to live, and, which may surprise you more, an entire lifetime in learning how to die."[40]

---

35. Brown, *Spiritual Legacy*, 34.
36. Nasr, *Knowledge and the Sacred*, 330. These stages are consistent with the three phases contained in the diverse rites of passage as put forward by ethnographer Arnold van Gennep: "preliminal rites (rites of separation), liminal rites (rites of transition), and postliminal rites (rites of incorporation)" (van Gennep, *Rites of Passage*, 11). William E. Paden describes these states in the following way: "The common ritual structure is that of (1) some ritual 'death' to the old status, (2) a transitional period of preparation or 'incubation,' where identity between the old and new states is in process of change, and (3) incorporation into the new status, with attendant acknowledgment by the group" (Paden, *Religious Worlds*, 115).
37. Plato, *Phaedo* 64a, *Dialogues of Plato*, 72.
38. Montaigne, *Essays*, 24.
39. Montaigne, *Essays*, 30.
40. Seneca, *Dialogues and Essays*, 146.

Many of the "mystery" traditions—such as those of ancient Egypt and Greece, especially the Eleusinian, Dionysian, and Orphic mysteries—participated in the process of initiatory death and rebirth in order to be transfigured into a divine mode of being. Enigmatic wording is used to allude to this second birth: "I have the power to be born a second time."[41] One was considered extremely privileged to be allowed initiation into the ceremonies of these mystery religions:

> The rite of initiation into the Mysteries, often referred to as a second birth, is nothing other than the grafting of this chain of spiritual succession onto the psychic substance of the new initiate, thereby replacing the profane natal heredity which must not be allowed to reassert itself.[42]

The following lengthy passage cited by Stobaeus (fifth century)—thought to be from Plutarch (ca. 45–120)—is important here as it underscores the transformative process that occurs when an individual participates in the mysteries and provides a unique glimpse into this enigmatic world:

> Thus we say that the soul that has passed thither is dead (olôlenai), having regard to its complete (eis to holon) change and conversion. In this world it is without knowledge, except when it is already at the point of death; but when that time comes, it has an experience like that of men who are undergoing initiation into great mysteries; and so the verbs teleutân (die) and teleisthai (be initiated), and the actions they denote, have a similarity. In the beginning there is straying and wandering, the weariness of running this way and that, and nervous journeys through darkness that reach no goal, and then immediately before the consummation every possible terror, shivering and trembling and sweating and amazement. But after this a marvelous light meets the wanderer, and open country and meadow lands welcome him; and in that place there are voices and dancing and the solemn majesty of sacred music and holy visions. And amidst these, he walks at large in new freedom, now perfect and fully initiated, celebrating the sacred rites, a garland upon his head, and converses with pure and holy men; he surveys the uninitiated, unpurified mob here on earth, the mob of living men who, herded together in mirk and deep mire, trample one another down and in their fear of death cling to their ills, since they disbelieve in the blessing of the other world. For the soul's entanglement with the body and confinement in it are against nature, as you may discern from this.[43]

This passage makes a valuable connection between the verb phrases "to die" and "to be initiated." The Platonic philosopher Lucius Apuleius (ca. 124–70) describes his initiation into the mysteries in a similar manner: "I approached the confines of death: and having trodden on the threshold of Proserpina [Persephone] returned, having been carried through all the elements. In the depths of midnight I saw the

41. Chap. 64, *Book of the Dead*, 218.
42. Lings and Minnaar, *Underlying Religion*, x.
43. Plutarch, Fragment 178, *Moralia*, 15:317.

sun glittering with a splendid light, *together with the infernal and supernal gods*: and to these divinities approaching near, I paid the tribute of devout adoration."[44] It is through this transmutation that the human soul can be purified and restored to its original state *in divinis*, as Plotinus (ca. 205–70) reveals in this passage from his essay *On Beauty*:

> Therefore we must ascend again towards the Good, the desired of every Soul. Anyone that has seen This, knows what I intend when I say that it is beautiful. Even the desire of it is to be desired as a Good. To attain it is for those that will take the upward path, who will set all their forces towards it, who will divest themselves of all that we have put on in our descent: so, to those that approach the Holy Celebrations of the Mysteries, there are appointed purifications and the laying aside of the garments worn before, and the entry in nakedness—until, passing, on the upward way, all that is other than the God, each in the solitude of himself shall behold that solitary-dwelling Existence, the Apart, the Unmingled, the Pure, that from Which all things depend, for Which all look and live and act and know, the Source of Life and of Intellection and of Being.[45]

According to Aristotle (384–322 BCE), "those who are being initiated into the mysteries are to be expected not to learn anything but to suffer some change, to be put into a certain condition, i.e. to be fitted for some purpose."[46]

Here is a well-known account from the *Homeric Hymn to Demeter* praising the mysteries: "Happy is he among men upon earth who has seen these mysteries; but he who is uninitiate and who has no part in them, never has lot of like good things once he is dead, down in the darkness and gloom."[47] The ancient Greek playwright Sophocles (ca. 496–406 BCE) exclaims, "Thrice fortunate are those among mortals who have seen these rites before going to Hades; for they alone have life there, while others have every kind of misery."[48] Further testimonies likewise signify that, as a result of having experienced the mysteries, the soul of the initiate will be content and at peace after death. For example, the orator and philosopher Cicero (106–43 BCE) asserted that the Eleusinian mysteries disclosed how "to live happily, but also to die with a better hope."[49] What is important to note here is that these initiates do appear to be referring not to a physical death but, rather, to their disidentification with the empirical ego.

In Hinduism, the yogi attains deliverance (*mokṣa* or *mukti*) akin to a "death in life" and thus becomes one who is liberated in this very existence (*jīvan-mukta*), having realized the Self (*Ātman*). Śrī Nisargadatta Maharaj (1897–1981) confirms this: "The

44. Lucius Apuleius, Metamorphoses 11.23, quoted in Taylor, *Eleusinian and Bacchic Mysteries*, 102.
45. Plotinus, Enneads 1.6.7, *Heart of Plotinus*, 73.
46. Attributed to Aristotle by Synesius, quoted in Aristotle, *Works of Aristotle*, 12:87.
47. Hesiod, Homeric Hymn to Demeter 480–82, *Homeric Hymns and Homerica*, 323.
48. Sophocles, Fragment 837, *Fragments*, 368–69.
49. Cicero, De legibus II.xiv.36, *On the Republic*, 415.

[*jñānī*] has died before his death."[50] In this way, the yogi dies and is reborn into a new mode of being. In the summer of 1896, at the age of seventeen, Ramana Maharshi had a spontaneous experience in which he was overwhelmed by a violent fear of death that led to the recognition that "the body dies but the Spirit that transcends it cannot be touched by death. That means I am the deathless Spirit."[51] Elsewhere he puts it more directly: "Your glory lies where you cease to exist."[52]

This transformative process is also found in Buddhism, even though its early tradition was largely reticent regarding metaphysical questions. The Buddha sought to teach the truth of our existence and how to overcome the suffering caused by its limitations through the attainment of *Nirvāṇa*. Ananda Coomaraswamy (1877–1947) states that "Nirvāṇa is a kind of death, but like every death a rebirth to something other than what had been."[53] A renowned Mahāyāna text asserts that "all beings are from all eternity ever abiding in Nirvāṇa,"[54] and according to the Shin Buddhist priest Kenryo Kanamatsu (1915–86), this reality "is the absolute dying to the self, which is at once the absolute *rebirth* of the self in the Universal Self."[55]

In the Theravāda Buddhist tradition, there is a practice whereby one meditates on the human body, visualizing it as a decaying corpse in order to realize the three marks of all conditioned phenomena: impermanence (*aniccā*), unsatisfactoriness or suffering (*dukkha*), and no-self (*anattā*). Hence the body of the meditator and that of the corpse experience one and the same fate:

> Again, bhikkus, as though he were to see a corpse thrown aside in a charnel ground, one, two, or three days dead, bloated, livid, and oozing matter . . . devoured by crows, hawks, vultures, dogs, jackals, or various kinds of worms . . . a skeleton with flesh and blood, held together with sinews . . . a skeleton without flesh and blood . . . disconnected bones scattered in all directions—here a hand-bone, there a foot-bone, here a shin-bone, there a thigh-bone, here a hip-bone, there a back-bone, here a rib-bone, there a breast-bone, here an arm-bone, there a shoulder-bone, here a neck-bone, there a jaw-bone, here a tooth, there the skull . . . bleached white, the colour of shells . . . bones heaped up . . . more than a year old, rotted and crumbled to dust, a bhikku compares this same body with it thus: "This body too is of the same nature, it will be like that, it is not exempt from that fate."[56]

Buddhaghosa, a fifth-century Indian Theravāda Buddhist commentator and scholar, also taught that mindfulness of death was one of the great virtues of the spiritual path.

50. Dikshit, *I Am That*, 139.
51. Quoted in Osborne, *Teachings of Ramana Maharshi*, 9–10.
52. Quoted in Osborne, *Teachings of Ramana Maharshi*, 100.
53. Coomaraswamy, *Hinduism and Buddhism*, 64.
54. Quoted in *Awakening of Faith*, 74.
55. Kanamatsu, *Naturalness*, 10.
56. Buddha, *Middle Length Discourses*, 952.

Now when a man is truly wise,
His constant task will surely be
This recollection about death.[57]

The revered Zen master Dōgen (1200–1253) urges us to transcend dualistic interpretations and to realize that nothing is separate from spiritual realization itself:
"Just understand that birth-and-death itself is nirvana, and you will neither hate
one as being birth-and-death, nor cherish the other as being nirvana. Only then can
you be free of birth-and-death."[58] Another master has stated, "If you are really desir-
ous of mastering Zen, it is necessary for you once to give up your life and to plunge
right into the pit of death."[59] Jitoku-Eki (d. 1083) once observed that "after the root
of life has been eradicated, one is reborn variously in accordance with one's intrinsic
capacity."[60] Having already died to the profane condition, the rest follows: "One thing
is certain. If you understand Zen, you will not be afraid to die."[61] The great mystical
poet of Tibet, Milarepa (ca. 1052–ca. 1135), advises us to "meditate continually upon
the uncertainty of the hour of death."[62] The renowned Tibetan scholar Tsong-Kha-Pa
(1357–1419) avows that the traveler on the spiritual path needs to "meditate again
and again [on death] until you have turned your mind away from the activities of
this life, which are like adorning yourself while being led to the execution ground."[63]

The Zen master Hakuin (1686–1769) discusses what he calls a "death" *koan* in
order to better understand the mystery of human existence:

If you should have the desire to study Zen under a teacher and see into your
own nature, you should first investigate the word *shi* [death]. If you want to
know how to investigate this word, then at all times while walking, stand-
ing, sitting, or reclining, without despising activity, without being caught up
in quietude, merely investigate the koan: "After you are dead and cremated,
where has the main character gone?" ... Among all the teachings and instruc-
tions, the word death has the most unpleasant and disgusting connotations.
Yet if you once suddenly penetrate this "death" koan, [you will find that]
there is no more felicitous teaching than this instruction that serves as the
key to the realm in which birth and death are transcended, where the place in
which you stand is the Diamond indestructible, and where you have become
a divine immortal, unaging and undying. The word death is the vital essential
that the warrior must first determine for himself.[64]

Zen Buddhism discerns the concept of the "Great Death" as Zen scholar Masao Abe
(1915–2006) explains it: "Breaking through this antinomy [of life and death] is called,

57. Buddhaghosa, *Path of Purification*, 235.
58. Dōgen, *Heart of Dōgen's Shōbōgenzō*, 106.
59. Yekiwo, quoted in Suzuki, *Zen and Japanese Culture*, 78.
60. Jitoku-Eki, quoted in Izutsu and Izutsu, *Theory of Beauty*, 124.
61. Quoted in *Zen Flesh, Zen Bones*, 21.
62. Milarepa, *Songs of Milarepa*, 45.
63. Tsong-Kha-Pa, *Great Treatise*, 1:160.
64. Hakuin, *Zen Master Hakuin*, 219.

particularly in Zen, the 'Great Death' because it is the total negation of life-and-death and is beyond a realization of death as distinguished from life."[65] Therefore, what is known as the "Great Death" is connected to the vertical domain of existence, while the horizontal domain is a realm pertaining to "little deaths."

The leading expert on Sufism, Annemarie Schimmel (1922–2003), discusses a corresponding phenomenon within Islamic spirituality:

> "Die before you die," for every act of shedding off a lowly quality is a small death; every sacrifice for the sake of others is another small death whereby the individual gains new spiritual value; thus, in a series of deaths, the soul rises to immortality or to a level of spiritualization that it has never dreamed of.[66]

Within the Jewish tradition, especially in its mystical dimensions, there is a similar notion of "dying before dying" known as "cessation or annihilation of existence" (*bittul ha-yesh*). For example, great importance is placed by the Hasids on the preparation for death, which is central to the meaning and purpose of human existence:

> Hasid eschatology taught the Hasid the importance of dying in full possession of his consciousness. . . . Viewed in eschatological terms, the moment of death becomes the event of initiation. . . . Thus, death is the goal orientation of life, but only if death means union with the *Eyn Sof* ["the Infinite"].[67]

The human quest in Jewish mysticism is to become reintegrated into the Divine by dying to our fragmented self and returning to God alone:

> For man to find again his universal and divine wholeness, immanent in the midst of "fragments," he had to purify and spiritualize his body and his soul, by submitting them and making them accord with the supreme will and wisdom, and finally, by freeing himself from all his earthly bonds, from all his fragmentary or individual states. Henceforth, to be one with the One and again to become infinite in the infinite, a human being had to be separated from the separate and die to what is mortal, to what is finite.[68]

The following dialogue between Nicodemus and Jesus speaks to the heart of this transformation as found in Christianity:

> Jesus answered and said unto him, "Verily, verily, I say unto thee, Except a man be born again, he cannot see the kingdom of God." Nicodemus saith unto him, "How can a man be born when he is old? Can he enter the second time into his mother's womb, and be born?" Jesus answered, "Verily, verily, I say unto thee, Except a man be born of water and of the Spirit, he cannot enter into the kingdom of God. That which is born of the flesh is flesh; and that which is born of the Spirit is spirit. Marvel not that I said unto thee, 'Ye must

65. Abe, *Zen and Western Thought*, 131.
66. Schimmel, *I Am Wind*, 157–58.
67. Zalman Meshullam Schachter-Shalomi, *Spiritual Intimacy*, 38, 39, 40.
68. Schaya, *Universal Meaning of the Kabbalah*, 134–35.

be born again.' The wind bloweth where it listeth, and thou hearest the sound thereof, but canst not tell whence it cometh, and whither it goeth: so is every one that is born of the Spirit." (John 3:3 8)

By turning away from the things of the world, the wayfarer can return to life in the Spirit: "If ye live *after the flesh*, ye shall die; but if ye through the Spirit do mortify the deeds of the body, ye shall live" (Romans 8:13). This mystical death and resurrection is also found in the words "I live; yet not I, but Christ liveth in me" (Galatians 2:20). To be born again from above, in the Spirit, is to be recast in his image and likeness: "Verily, verily, I say unto you, Except *a corn of wheat* fall into the ground and *die*, it abideth alone: but if it die, it bringeth forth much fruit" (John 12:24). St. John of the Cross (1542–91) articulates this transformative process as being a "death to one's natural self through denudation and annihilation."[69] Similarly, St. Anthony the Great (251–356) writes, "Death, when understood by men, is deathlessness; but, when not understood by the foolish, it is death."[70] We also recall the following words of St. Simeon the New Theologian (949–1022): "A man who has attained the final degree of perfection is dead and yet not dead, but infinitely more alive in God with Whom he lives for he no longer lives by himself."[71] Meister Eckhart (1260–1328) encapsulates this idea with "The kingdom of God is for none but the thoroughly dead."[72]

The great Persian Sufi martyr ʿAyn al-Quḍāt Hamadhānī (1098–1131) asserts that human beings do not realize that they are not truly living but, rather, already buried in their tombs:

> Don't you realize that [corporeal] death is not real death? True death is annihilation (*fanāʾ*). Whoever does not realize this [real] death has no life. Do you understand what I say? I say that as long as "you" are "you" and caught up in your "self," you do not really exist. When "you" cease to be "you" then you [truly] become yourself. Alas! What do you hear? According to us, death is that an individual die from everything except the Beloved, so that he finds life through and in the Beloved. Then you will realize, within yourself, how death occurs.[73]

We recall the saying attributed to the Prophet, "People are asleep, but when they die, they wake up." Each human being is tasked with making sense of the world, which is primarily done through sense perception, and yet we assume that we apprehend things as they are. How can we be confident of this? As a result of this predicament, Euripides (ca. 480–406 BCE) puts forth a key question: "Who knows if life be not death and death life."[74] Perhaps what is commonly perceived to be life is in reality a kind of death and vice versa. The saints and sages suggest that human existence is akin

69. St. John of the Cross, *John of the Cross*, 96.
70. St. Anthony the Great, "On the Character of Men and on the Virtuous Life: One Hundred and Seventy Texts," in Palmer et al., *Philokalia*, 1:336.
71. St. Simeon the New Theologian, "Practical and Theological Precepts," in *Writings from the Philokalia*, 132.
72. Eckhart, sayings 11, *Meister Eckhart*, 419.
73. ʿAyn al-Quḍāt Hamadhānī, quoted in Lewisohn, *Heritage of Sufism*, 1:329.
74. Attributed to Euripides by Plato, *Gorgias* 492e, *Gorgias and Timaeus*, 74.

to a dream or an illusion and that the spiritual path allows the spiritual wayfarer to awaken to that which is abidingly real. It is through the vantage point of metaphysics that we can glean the deeper significance of the words "And surely the Abode of the Hereafter is life indeed, if they but knew" (Quran 29:64).

Sufi metaphysics employs the terms *fanā'* ("extinction" or "annihilation") and *baqā'* ("permanence" or "subsistence") to describe two contrasting states or levels on the spiritual path. These are exemplified in the following verses of the Quran: "Everything is perishing except His Face [or Essence]" (28:88), and "Everything that is thereon is passing away; and there subsisteth but the Face of thy Lord, possessor of Glory and Bounty" (55:26–27). Human beings can attain higher states of realization once the ego is resolved into its transpersonal source, which requires both "annihilation" (*fanā'*) and "subsistence" (*baqā'*).

As only Divine Reality truly exists, dying to our profane condition is essential, as Titus Burckhardt (1908–84) explains: "The Supreme Unity . . . is not the object of any distinctive knowledge, and . . . is therefore not accessible to the creature as such. Only God Himself knows himself in His Unity."[75] Ibn 'Arabī cites a saying by one of the early Sufis claiming that "annihilation" (*fanā'*) is "the annihilation of him who was not," whereas "subsistence" (*baqā'*) is "the subsistence of Him who has always been."[76] In the Hindu and Buddhist traditions, *Nirvāṇa* corresponds to *fanā'* and *Parinirvāṇa* to *fanā' al-fanā'* ("extinction of the extinction").

One of the great philosophers and theologians of the Islamic tradition, al-Ghazālī (d. 1111), instructs the faithful to go to sleep with a mindfulness of our ultimate ends:

> When you want to go to sleep, lay out your bed pointing to Mecca, and sleep on your right side, the side on which the corpse reclines in the tomb. Sleep is the similitude of death and waking of the resurrection. . . . Remember that in like manner you will lie in the tomb, completely alone; only your works will be with you, only the effort you have made will be rewarded. . . . As you go to sleep say: "In Thy name, Lord . . . I live and die; and with Thee, O God, do I take refuge."[77]

Guénon describes the necessity of initiation on the spiritual path in order to die before dying and why it is so misunderstood today:

> Of course the word "death" must here be taken in its most general sense, according to which we may say that every change of state whatsoever is at once a death and a birth, depending on whether it is considered from one side or from the other: death with respect to the antecedent state, birth with respect to the consequent state. Initiation is generally described as a "second birth," which indeed it is; but this "second birth" necessarily implies a death to the profane world and follows so to speak as an immediate sequel to it, since these are strictly speaking only the two faces of one and the same change of state.[78]

75. Burckhardt, *Introduction to Sufi Doctrine*, 103.
76. Quoted in Chittick, *Self-Disclosure of God*, 84.
77. Al-Ghazālī, *Faith and Practice*, 127–28.
78. Guénon, *Perspectives on Initiation*, 172–73.

The reality of spiritual death and rebirth in the Spirit, of "dying before dying," is largely ignored in contemporary psychology and the field of mental health. This is unfortunate in view of the fact that what dies in this spiritual transfiguration is the ego, and it is precisely the ego—defined as a condition of fixated self-reference based on an illusion of its own creation—that contributes to the imbalance and illness of the psyche. This is to say that we "mistakenly identify ourselves with the mutable psycho-physical tabernacles that our Self assumes."[79]

Through spiritual death and rebirth, human beings can overcome suffering and achieve "the peace . . . which passeth all understanding" (Philippians 4:7). This requires giving primacy to the Spirit in psychology so that the disciple can become rooted, once again, in its spiritual foundations.

The theme of mystical death and resurrection, as found across the religions and their mystical dimensions, is enigmatic and paradoxical. While they differ in their descriptions, these varied perspectives also point to a common ground that discloses what is universal and timeless across all of them. The human quest is a lifelong preparation for death. The paradox is that, in order to truly live, we are required to "die," yet this is not a corporeal death; it is, rather, to relinquish all that we presume to know and think—our mistaken identity and the relationships with all that we erroneously consider to be real.

Only when we cease to exist—when we "die before dying"—can the Divine be known: "When God seems to germinate in the soul, it is in reality the soul that dies in God."[80] Through this transformative process, we can know what it truly means to be human and to live fully. Life can be trying and difficult—sometimes even unbearable—as is evidenced by the lives of the saints and sages. Yet "men must endure / Their going hence, even as their coming hither. / Ripeness is all."[81] In fact, we are reminded time and time again that "God burdens a soul only to its capacity" (Quran 2:286) and likewise that "God . . . will not suffer you . . . above that ye are able . . . to bear" (1 Corinthians 10:13).

Our preparation for death in life is itself a form of dying, allowing transcendent reality to become known to us: "There is one great certainty in life, and this is death; whoever really understands this certainty is already dead in this life."[82] Humanity's diverse religious traditions all teach us that, as death is inseparable from life, we need to surmount the duality of both so that we may always be prepared for the encounter with our Creator: "Prepare yourself to meet death, to enter the world beyond that we cannot see."[83] We conclude with the incisive words of Angelus Silesius (1624–77) on this psychospiritual transfiguration, which has been a hallmark of all spiritual paths throughout the ages: "Die thou before thou die, that so thou shalt not die."[84]

79. Coomaraswamy, *Time and Eternity*, 86.
80. Schuon, *Gnosis*, trans. Palmer, 120.
81. Shakespeare, *King Lear* 5.2.9–11, in Shakespeare, *King Lear*, 106.
82. Schuon, *Spiritual Perspectives and Human Facts*, 226.
83. Thomas Yellowtail, quoted in Fitzgerald, *Yellowtail*, 190.
84. Silesius, *Cherubinic Wanderer*, trans. Trask, 56.

Conclusion

REHABILITATING PSYCHOLOGY

As we have aimed to demonstrate, a serious crisis confronts contemporary psychology, mental health treatment, and the systems that attempt to deliver these therapeutic services. This problem has become more apparent now than ever before—not only to the specialist practitioner but also to the public at large. Everywhere you look, there is an ongoing discussion about the all-pervasive mental health pandemic in our midst. This problem has arisen from the crippled vision that now informs our understanding of mental health, which has led to an inordinate focus on illness. This has served to limit the effectiveness of widely used psychotherapeutic models and to undermine psychiatry's ability to assist the vast majority of people who need help.

This book has endeavored to disclose what lies at the heart of this crisis. Modern Western psychology, having become severed from its metaphysical roots, can no longer offer an authentic "science of the soul"—one that resonates with the unanimous testimony of traditional cultures regarding the true nature of human beings.

By purging itself of any spiritual dimension, the modern discipline has shifted its focus from the soul (or psyche) to the mind alone. This reductionist deviation has repudiated the sacred and deformed psychology, which now finds itself at a loss to explain the phenomenon of consciousness, including the mind-body problem and the question of what lies beyond the psychophysical order.

Psychology as it is practiced today does not have an objective method for presenting clinical findings without relying on merely subjective interpretations. It lacks a common lexicon by which to precisely communicate the same conclusions to all. Each practitioner interprets symptoms through their own idiosyncratic lens, and diagnostic criteria are determined solely within a social context. These factors yield a broad divergence in diagnoses, a constantly changing nomenclature, and a surplus of hypotheses that are presented as fact. Additionally, modern psychology lacks an agreed-upon vision as to what composes mental health and so remains imbalanced in its excessive focus on psychopathology. As a result, its understanding of the origins of mental illness continues to be speculative, as is its grasp of pathogenesis. Accordingly, any clinical classifications to which its methods give rise can only be suggestive, arbitrary, and ephemeral.

While the modern concept of psychology is roughly five hundred years old, the psyche as a subject of study and practice has a much older history. This can readily be seen when we consider the worldview of ancient peoples who were able to integrate a rich understanding of human consciousness and behavior into their various forms of traditional knowledge.

What is absent from discussions that seek to address our burgeoning mental health crisis is acknowledgment of the need to transform our consciousness by means of metanoia and to admit that by desacralizing the foundations of psychology, its seemingly endless array of therapeutic treatments have become divested of their proper foundation and thus been rendered nugatory. As noted in this work, the fracturing of the discipline occurred long before the onset of these critical developments, which simply bear the marks of the Enlightenment period with its largely profane outlook.

A comprehensive understanding of mental health will remain elusive if we fail to incorporate diverse cultural understandings—including the profound psychologies found among the world's religions, along with the far-reaching spiritual epistemologies that underpin them. We hope that a compelling case has been made in support of the crucial insight that "there is no technique used in Western therapy that is not also found in other cultures" and that the way forward is to restore psychology to its sacred roots, which were its natural patrimony prior to the aberrations ushered in by the secularizing totalitarianism of modernity.[1]

So what are we to do in order to inject these urgently needed perspectives into a broader discussion on mental health? To begin with, we must deepen our understanding of the world's religions (including our own spiritual tradition if we have one). We should also become familiar with the development of modern Western psychology and its first two "forces" (behaviorism and psychoanalysis). In doing so, it will become abundantly clear that the modern discipline is still plagued by these aberrations that, if left unchallenged, will continue to exacerbate our current mental health crisis. What is required now are not novel therapies but a return to the sapiential treasury that lies at the heart of humanity's spiritual traditions. Some will object that such solutions are unrealistic, but the fact is that an unprecedented number of resources are now available that point the way to a full restitution of the sacred in treating disorders of the psyche.

It is in restoring sacred metaphysics to mental health treatment that psychology can again become a true "science of the soul" (mirroring the "science of the cosmos"). This alone can tackle the present-day maladies that afflict the psyche of humanity.

---

1. Torrey, *Mind Game*, 56.

Bibliography

Abe, Masao. *Zen and Western Thought*. Edited by William R. LaFleur. London: Macmillan, 1985.

Abhedānanda, Swāmī, ed. *The Sayings of Sri Ramakrishna*. Mylapore: Sri Ramakrishna Math, 1916.

Abhedānanda, Swāmī, and Joseph A. Fitzgerald, eds. *The Original Gospel of Rāmakrishna: Based on M.'s English Text, Abridged*. Bloomington, IN: World Wisdom, 2011.

Affifi, A. E. *The Mystical Philosophy of Muḥyid Dīn-Ibnul 'Arabī*. Cambridge: Cambridge University Press, 1939.

Alcoholics Anonymous. *Alcoholics Anonymous*. 4th ed. New York: Alcoholics Anonymous World Services, 2001.

Alcoholics Anonymous. *"Pass It On": The Story of Bill Wilson and How the A.A. Message Reached the World*. New York: Alcoholics Anonymous World Services, 1984.

Alexander, Bruce K. *The Globalization of Addiction: A Study in Poverty of the Spirit*. Oxford: Oxford University Press, 2010.

Alighieri, Dante. *Dante Alighieri, Il Convito: The Banquet of Dante Alighieri*. Translated by Elizabeth Price Sayer. London: George Routledge and Sons, 1887.

Allport, Gordon W. *Becoming: Basic Considerations for a Psychology of Personality*. New Haven, CT: Yale University Press, 1969.

Allport, Gordon W. *The Person in Psychology: Selected Essays*. Boston: Beacon, 1968.

Almaas, A. H. *Elements of the Real in Man*. Bk. 1, Diamond Heart. Berkeley, CA: Diamond, 1987.

Almqvist, Kurt. "Every Branch in Me." *Studies in Comparative Religion* 15, nos. 3–4 (Summer/Autumn 1983): 194–96.

American Psychiatric Association. *Diagnostic and Statistical Manual of Mental Disorders*. 4th ed. Washington, DC: American Psychiatric Press, 1994.

American Psychiatric Association. *Diagnostic and Statistical Manual of Mental Disorders*. 4th ed., *Text Revision*. Washington, DC: American Psychiatric Press, 2000.

American Psychiatric Association. *Diagnostic and Statistical Manual of Mental Disorders*. 5th ed. Washington, DC: American Psychiatric Association, 2013.

Ānandamayī Mā. *The Essential Śrī Ānandamayī Mā: Life and Teachings of a 20th Century Indian Saint*. Translated by Ātmānanda. Edited by Joseph A. Fitzgerald. Bloomington, IN: World Wisdom, 2007.

Ānandamayī Mā. *Sad Vani: A Collection of the Teaching of Sri Anandamayi Ma*. Translated by Ātmānanda. Edited by Bhaiji. Bhadaini: Shree Shree Anandamayee Sangha, 1973.

Andreasen, Nancy C. *The Broken Brain: The Biological Revolution in Psychiatry*. New York: Harper & Row, 1985.

Ansbacher, Heinz L., and Rowena R. Ansbacher, eds. *The Individual Psychology of Alfred Adler*. New York: Harper & Row, 1967.

Aquinas, Thomas. *Of God and His Creatures: An Annotated Translation (with Some Abridgement) of the Summa Contra Gentiles of Saint Thomas*. Translated by Joseph Rickaby. London: Burns & Oates, 1905.

Aquinas, Thomas. *Summa Theologica, Part II (Second Part), First Number, QQ. I—XLVI*. Translated by Fathers of the English Dominican Province. London: R. & T. Washbourne, 1917.

Aristotle. *The Politics of Aristotle*. Translated by Benjamin Jowett. Oxford: Clarendon, 1885.

Aristotle. *The Works of Aristotle*. Vol. 12, *Selected Fragments*. Translated by Sir David Ross. Oxford: Oxford University Press, 1952.

Augustine, Aurelius. *The Confessions of Saint Augustine*. Translated by Edward B. Pusey. Oxford: John Henry Parker, 1840.

Augustine, Aurelius. *The Confessions of St. Augustine*. Translated by F. J. Sheed. New York: Sheed & Ward, 1959.

Augustine, Aurelius. *The Trinity*. Translated by Stephen McKenna. Washington, DC: Catholic University of America Press, 2010.

The Awakening of Faith: The Classic Exposition of Mahayana Buddhism. Translated by Teitaro Suzuki. Mineola, NY: Dover Publications, 2003.

Badri, Malik. *Contemplation: An Islamic Psychospiritual Study*. Translated by Abdul-Wahid Lu'lu'a. London: International Institute of Islamic Thought, 2018.

Bailey, Thomas, Mario Alvarez-Jimenez, Ana M. Garcia-Sanchez, Carol Hulbert, Emma Barlow, and Sarah Bendall. "Childhood Trauma Is Associated with Severity of Hallucinations and Delusions in Psychotic Disorders: A Systematic Review and Meta-Analysis." *Schizophrenia Bulletin* 44, no. 5 (August 2018): 1111–22.

Balz, Albert G. A. "The Metaphysical Infidelities of Modern Psychology." *Journal of Philosophy* 33, no. 13 (June 1936): 337–51.

Bateson, Gregory. *Mind and Nature: A Necessary Unity*. New York: Bantam, 1980.

Bateson, Gregory, ed. *Perceval's Narrative: A Patient's Account of His Psychosis, 1830-1832*. New York: William Morrow, 1974.

Bateson, Gregory. *Steps to an Ecology of Mind*. Chicago: University of Chicago Press, 2000.

Becker, Ernest. *The Denial of Death*. London: Souvenir Press, 2020.

Bendeck Sotillos, Samuel. *Behaviorism: The Quandary of a Psychology Without a Soul*. Chicago: Institute of Traditional Psychology, 2017.

Bendeck Sotillos, Samuel. "The Deification of the Psyche: Carl Jung and the Spiritual Crisis of the Modern World." *Sacred Web: A Journal of Tradition and Modernity* 51 (2025).

Bendeck Sotillos, Samuel. *Dismantling Freud: Fake Therapy and the Psychoanalytic Worldview*. Brooklyn, NY: Angelico Press, 2020.

Bendeck Sotillos, Samuel. "The Eclipse of the Soul and the Rise of the Ecological Crisis." *Spirituality Studies* 8, no. 2 (Fall 2022): 34–55.

Bendeck Sotillos, Samuel. "Entheogens and Sacred Psychology." *Spirituality Studies* 10, no. 1 (Spring 2024): 41–68.

Bendeck Sotillos, Samuel. "Homelessness: A Rupture of Belonging." *Sacred Web: A Journal of Tradition and Modernity* 52 (2025).

Bendeck Sotillos, Samuel. "The Human and Transpersonal Dimensions of Personality." *Sacred Web: A Journal of Tradition and Modernity* 35 (Summer 2015): 69–107.

Bendeck Sotillos, Samuel. "Human Diversity in the Mirror of Religious Pluralism." *Religions: A Scholarly Journal* 9 (2016): 121–34.

Bendeck Sotillos, Samuel. "The Impasse of Modern Psychology: Behaviorism, Psychoanalysis, Humanistic, and Transpersonal Psychology in the Light of the Perennial Philosophy." In *Psychology and the Perennial Philosophy: Studies in Comparative Religion.* Edited by Samuel Bendeck Sotillos. Bloomington, IN: World Wisdom, 2013.

Bendeck Sotillos, Samuel. "The Inner and Outer Human Being." *Mountain Path* 60, no. 2 (April/June 2023): 9–26.

Bendeck Sotillos, Samuel. "Madness and Its Enigmatic Origins." *Sacred Web: A Journal of Tradition and Modernity* 44 (Winter 2019): 65–94.

Bendeck Sotillos, Samuel. "Modern Psychology and the Loss of Transcendence." *Journal of Comparative Literature and Aesthetics* 47, no. 4 (Winter 2024): 23–31.

Bendeck Sotillos, Samuel. "The Perennial Psychology and the Search for a Common Lexicon." *Sacred Web: A Journal of Tradition and Modernity* 32 (Winter 2013): 111–20.

Bendeck Sotillos, Samuel, ed. *Psychology and the Perennial Philosophy: Studies in Comparative Religion.* Bloomington, IN: World Wisdom, 2013.

Bendeck Sotillos, Samuel. "Realms of Consciousness and the Real." *Spirituality Studies* 9, no. 1 (Spring 2023): 12–21.

Bendeck Sotillos, Samuel. "Recovering the Eye of the Heart." *Mountain Path* 59, no. 3 (2022): 29–45.

Bendeck Sotillos, Samuel. "The Self and the Other in the Light of the One: The Metaphysics of Human Diversity." *Sacred Web: A Journal of Tradition and Modernity* 41 (Summer 2018): 34–76.

Benedict, Ruth. "Anthropology and the Abnormal." *Journal of General Psychology* 10, no. 1 (1934): 59–82.

The Bhagavad Gita. Translated by Juan Mascaró. Middlesex, UK: Penguin, 1975.

The Bhagavad-Gītā with the Commentary of Śrī Śankarachāryā. Translated by Alladi Mahadeva Sastri. Madras: V. Ramaswamy Sastrulu & Sons, 1961.

Black Elk. "Foreword." In *The Sacred Pipe: Black Elk's Account of the Seven Rites of the Oglala Sioux.* By Joseph Epes Brown. Norman: University of Oklahoma Press, 1989.

Blake, William. *The Marriage of Heaven and Hell.* Boston: John W. Luce, 1906.

Bleuler, Eugen. *Dementia Praecox or the Group of Schizophrenias.* Translated by Joseph Zinkin. New York: International Universities Press, 1950.

Bloom, Alfred, ed. *The Essential Shinran: A Buddhist Path of True Entrusting.* Bloomington, IN: World Wisdom, 2007.

The Book of the Dead. Translated by E. A. Wallis Budge. Chicago: Open Court, 1901.

Borella, Jean. *The Crisis of Religious Symbolism and Symbolism & Reality.* Translated by G. John Champoux. Kettering, OH: Angelico Press/Sophia Perennis, 2016.

Borella, Jean, and Wolfgang Smith. *Rediscovering the Integral Cosmos: Physics, Metaphysics, and Vertical Causality*. Brooklyn, NY: Angelico, 2018.

Bragdon, Emma. *The Call of Spiritual Emergency: From Personal Crisis to Personal Transformation*. New York: Harper & Row, 1990.

Breuer, Josef, and Sigmund Freud. *Studies on Hysteria*. Translated and edited by James Strachey. New York: Basic Books, 2000.

Brown, Joseph Epes. *The Sacred Pipe: Black Elk's Account of the Seven Rites of the Oglala Sioux*. Norman: University of Oklahoma Press, 1989.

Brown, Joseph Epes. *The Spiritual Legacy of the American Indian: Commemorative Edition with Letters While Living with Black Elk*. Edited by Marina Brown Weatherly, Elenita Brown, and Michael Oren Fitzgerald. Bloomington, IN: World Wisdom, 2007.

Buddha Shakyamuni. *The Connected Discourses of the Buddha: A New Translation of the Saṃyukta Nikāya*. Translated by Bhikkhu Bodhi. Boston: Wisdom, 2000.

Buddha Shakyamuni. *The Dhammapada*. Translated by Irving Babbitt. New York: New Directions, 1965.

Buddha Shakyamuni. *The Dhammapada: The Path of Perfection*. Translated by Juan Mascaró. London: Penguin, 1973.

Buddha Shakyamuni. *The Dhammapada: Sayings of Buddha*. Translated by Thomas Cleary. New York: Bantam, 1995.

Buddha Shakyamuni. *The Middle Length Discourses of the Buddha: A Translation of the Majjhima Nikaya*. Translated by Bhikkhu Ñāṇamoli and Bhikkhu Bodhi. Somerville, MA: Wisdom, 2015.

Buddhaghosa, Bhadantācariya. *The Path of Purification (Visuddhimagga)*. Translated by Bhikkhu Ñāṇamoli. Onalaska, WA: BPS Pariyatti, 1999.

Burckhardt, Titus. *Alchemy: Science of the Cosmos, Science of the Soul*. Translated by William Stoddart. Longmead, UK: Element Books, 1986.

Burckhardt, Titus. *Introduction to Sufi Doctrine*. Translated by D. M. Matheson. Bloomington, IN: World Wisdom, 2008.

Burckhardt, Titus. *Mirror of the Intellect: Essays on Traditional Science and Sacred Art*. Translated and edited by William Stoddart. Albany: State University of New York Press, 1987.

Burt, Cyril. "The Concept of Consciousness." *British Journal of Psychology* 53, no. 3 (August 1962): 229–42.

Burtt, E. A. *The Metaphysical Foundations of Modern Science*. Mineola, NY: Dover Publications, 2003.

Campbell, Joseph. *Myths to Live By*. New York: Penguin, 1993.

Casey, Deborah. "The Basis of Religion and Metaphysics: An Interview with Frithjof Schuon." *Quest* 9, no. 2 (1996): 74–84.

Chittick, William C., ed. *The Essential Seyyed Hossein Nasr*. Bloomington, IN: World Wisdom, 2007.

Chittick, William C. *Science of the Cosmos, Science of the Soul: The Pertinence of Islamic Cosmology in the Modern World*. Oxford: Oneworld, 2009.

Chittick, William C. *The Self-Disclosure of God: Principles of Ibn al-'Arabī's Cosmology*. Albany: State University of New York Press, 1998.

Chittick, William C. *The Sufi Path of Knowledge: Ibn al-'Arabī's Metaphysics of Imagination*. Albany: State University of New York Press, 1989.

Chittick, William C. *The Sufi Path of Love: The Spiritual Teachings of Rumi*. Albany: State University of New York Press, 1983.

Chittick, William C. *Sufism: A Beginner's Guide*. Oxford: Oneworld, 2008.

Cicero. *On the Republic, On the Laws*. Translated by Clinton W. Keys. Cambridge, MA: Harvard University Press, 2000.

The Cloud of Unknowing and Other Works. Translated by Clifton Wolters. New York: Penguin, 1978.

Comper, Frances M. M., ed. *The Book of the Craft of Dying*. London: Longmans, Green, 1917.

Confucius. *The Analects of Confucius*. Translated by Arthur Waley. New York: Vintage, 1938.

Coomaraswamy, Ananda K. *Coomaraswamy*. Vol. 2, *Selected Papers: Metaphysics*. Edited by Roger Lipsey. Princeton, NJ: Princeton University Press, 1978.

Coomaraswamy, Ananda K. *The Dance of Shiva: Fourteen Indian Essays*. New York: Noonday, 1957.

Coomaraswamy, Ananda K. *Hinduism and Buddhism*. New York: Philosophical Library, 1943.

Coomaraswamy, Ananda K. *Time and Eternity*. New Delhi: Indira Gandhi National Centre for the Arts, 1990.

Coomaraswamy, Ananda K. *What Is Civilization?* Ipswich, UK: Golgonooza, 1989.

Cooper, Jean C. *An Illustrated Introduction to Taoism: The Wisdom of the Sages*. Edited by Joseph A. Fitzgerald. Bloomington, IN: World Wisdom, 2010.

Cooper, Jean C. *Taoism: The Way of the Mystic*. London: Mandala, 1991.

Corbin, Henry. "The Question of Comparative Philosophy: Convergences in Iranian and European Thought." Translated by Jane A. Pratt. *Spring: An Annual of Archetypal Psychology and Jungian Thought* (1980): 1–20.

Danner, Victor. "Intoxication and Sobriety in Sufism." In *The Inner Journey: Views from the Islamic Tradition*. Edited by William C. Chittick. Sandpoint, ID: Morning Light, 2007.

de Sousa Santos, Boaventura. "Beyond Abyssal Thinking: From Global Lines to Ecologies of Knowledge." *Review* 30, no. 1 (2007): 45–89.

de Sousa Santos, Boaventura. *The End of the Cognitive Empire: The Coming of Age of Epistemologies of the South*. Durham, NC: Duke University Press, 2018.

Deikman, Arthur J. "Bimodal Consciousness." *Archives of General Psychiatry* 25, no. 6 (December 1971): 481–89.

Descartes, René. *Descartes: Meditations on First Philosophy: With Selections from the Objections and Replies*. Translated by John Cottingham. Cambridge: Cambridge University Press, 2003.

Descartes, René. *The Philosophical Writings of Descartes*. Vol. 3, *The Correspondence*. Translated by John Cottingham, Robert Stoothoff, Dugald Murdoch, and Anthony Kenny. Cambridge: Cambridge University Press, 1997.

The Desert Fathers: Sayings of the Early Christian Monks. Translated by Benedicta Ward. New York: Penguin, 2003.

Dikshit, Sudhakar S., ed. *I Am That: Talks with Sri Nisargadatta Maharaj*. Translated by Maurice Frydman. Durham, NC: Acorn, 1999.

Dodds, E. R. *The Greeks and the Irrational*. Berkeley, CA: University of California Press, 1951.

Dōgen. *The Heart of Dōgen's Shōbōgenzō*. Translated by Norman Waddell and Masao Abe. Albany: State University of New York Press, 2002.

Donkin, William. *The Wayfarers*. North Myrtle Beach, SC: Sheriar Foundation, 2000.

Dooling, D. M. "The Wisdom of the Contrary: A Conversation with Joseph Epes Brown." *Parabola: Myth and the Quest for Meaning* 4, no. 1 (February 1979): 54–65.

Dryden, Windy, and Colin Feltham, eds. *Psychotherapy and Its Discontents*. Buckingham, UK: Open University Press, 1998.

Duran, Eduardo, and Bonnie Duran. *Native American Postcolonial Psychology*. Albany: State University of New York Press, 1995.

Dzatrul Ngawang Tenzin Norbu, *A Guide to the Thirty-Seven Practices of a Bodhisattva*. Translated by Christopher Stagg. Boulder, CO: Snow Lion, 2020.

Eaton, Gai. *Islam and the Destiny of Man*. Albany: State University of New York Press, 1985.

Eaton, Gai. *King of the Castle: Choice and Responsibility in the Modern World*. Cambridge: Islamic Texts Society, 1990.

Eckhart, Meister. *The Complete Mystical Works of Meister Eckhart*. Translated and edited by Maurice O'C. Walshe. New York: Crossroad, 2009.

Eckhart, Meister. *Meister Eckhart*. Translated by C. De B. Evans. Edited by Franz Pfeiffer. London: John M. Watkins, 1924.

Eckhart, Meister. *Meister Eckhart: The Essential Sermons, Commentaries, Treatises, and Defense*. Translated by Edmund Colledge and Bernard McGinn. Mahwah, NJ: Paulist, 1981.

Eckhart, Meister. *Meister Eckhart: Teacher and Preacher*. Edited by Bernard McGinn. Mahwah, NJ: Paulist, 1986.

Edwards, Gill. "Does Psychotherapy Need a Soul?" In *Psychotherapy and Its Discontents*. Edited by Windy Dryden and Colin Feltham. Buckingham, UK: Open University Press, 1998.

Elegant Sayings: Nagarjuna's Staff of Wisdom and Sakya Pandit's Treasury of Elegant Sayings. Berkeley, CA: Dharma, 1977.

Eliade, Mircea. *Myths, Dreams, and Mysteries*. Translated by Philip Mairet. New York: Harper & Row, 1960.

Eliade, Mircea. *Patterns in Comparative Religion*. Translated by Rosemary Sheed. Lincoln: University of Nebraska Press, 1996.

Eliade, Mircea. *The Quest: History and Meaning in Religion*. Chicago: University of Chicago Press, 1969.

Eliade, Mircea. *The Sacred and the Profane: The Nature of Religion*. Translated by Willard R. Trask. New York: Harcourt Brace Jovanovich, 1987.

Eliade, Mircea. *Shamanism: Archaic Techniques of Ecstasy*. Translated by Willard R. Trask. Princeton, NJ: Princeton University Press, 1974.

Eliade, Mircea. *Yoga: Immortality and Freedom*. Translated by Willard R. Trask. Princeton, NJ: Princeton University Press, 1973.

Elkins, David N. *The Human Elements of Psychotherapy: A Nonmedical Model of Emotional Healing.* Washington, DC: American Psychological Association, 2016.

Elkins, David N. "The Medical Model in Psychotherapy: Its Limitations and Failures." *Journal of Humanistic Psychology* 49, no. 1 (January 2009): 66–84.

Engel, George L. "The Need for a New Medical Model: A Challenge for Biomedicine." *Science* 196, no. 4286 (April 1977): 129–36.

Epictetus. *The Discourses as Reported by Arrian, the Manual and Fragments.* Vol. 1. Translated by W. A. Oldfather. Cambridge, MA: Harvard University Press, 1956.

Ernst, Carl W. *Words of Ecstasy in Sufism.* Albany: State University of New York Press, 1985.

Evans-Wentz, W. Y. *Tibetan Yoga and Secret Doctrines: Or, Seven Books of Wisdom of the Great Path, According to the Late Lāma Kazi Dawa-Samdup's English Rendering.* London: Oxford University Press, 1967.

Felitti, Vincent J., Robert F. Anda, Dale Nordenberg, David F. Williamson, Alison M. Spitz, Valerie Edwards, Mary P. Koss, and James S. Marks. "Relationship of Childhood Abuse and Household Dysfunction to Many of the Leading Causes of Death in Adults: The Adverse Childhood Experiences (ACE) Study." *American Journal of Preventive Medicine* 14, no. 4 (1998): 245–58.

Feuerstein, Georg. *Tantra: The Path of Ecstasy.* Boston: Shambhala, 1998.

Fitzgerald, Michael Oren. *Yellowtail, Crow Medicine Man and Sun Dance Chief: An Autobiography.* Norman: University of Oklahoma Press, 1994.

Foucault, Michel. *Madness and Civilization: A History of Insanity in the Age of Reason.* Translated by Richard Howard. New York: Vintage, 1988.

Frances, Allen. *Saving Normal: An Insider's Revolt Against Out-of-Control Psychiatric Diagnosis, DSM-5, Big Pharma, and the Medicalization of Ordinary Life.* New York: HarperCollins, 2014.

Francis de Sales, St. *A Selection from the Spiritual Letters of S. Francis de Sales.* London: Rivingtons, 1871.

Frankl, Viktor E. *Man's Search for Meaning.* Translated by Ilse Lasch. New York: Touchstone, 1984.

Freud, Ernst L., ed. *Letters of Sigmund Freud.* Translated by Tania Stern and James Stern. New York: Basic Books, 1975.

Freud, Sigmund. *Character and Culture.* Edited by Philip Rieff. New York: Collier, 1963.

Freud, Sigmund. *Civilization and Its Discontents.* Translated and edited by James Strachey. New York: W. W. Norton, 1989.

Freud, Sigmund. *Collected Papers of Sigmund Freud.* Vol. 2. Translated by Joan Riviere. London: Hogarth Press and the Institute of Psycho-Analysis, 1948.

Freud, Sigmund. *Collected Papers of Sigmund Freud.* Vol. 4. Translated by Joan Riviere. London: Hogarth Press and the Institute of Psycho-Analysis, 1953.

Freud, Sigmund. *The Complete Letters of Sigmund Freud to Wilhelm Fliess, 1887-1904.* Translated and edited by Jeffrey Moussaieff Masson. Cambridge, MA: Belknap, 1985.

Freud, Sigmund. *The Future of an Illusion.* Translated and edited by James Strachey. New York: W. W. Norton, 1989.

Freud, Sigmund. *Introductory Lectures on Psychoanalysis.* Translated and edited by James Strachey. New York: W. W. Norton, 1977.

Freud, Sigmund. *New Introductory Lectures on Psycho-Analysis*. Translated and edited by James Strachey. New York: W. W. Norton, 1989.

Freud, Sigmund. *The Psychopathology of Everyday Life*. Translated and edited by James Strachey. New York: W. W. Norton, 1989.

Fromm, Erich. *The Sane Society*. Greenwich, CT: Fawcett, 1955.

Fromm-Reichmann, Frieda, and Jacob L. Moreno, eds. *Progress in Psychotherapy*. New York: Grune & Stratton, 1956.

Fusar-Poli, Paolo, and Pierluigi Politi. "Paul Eugen Bleuler and the Birth of Schizophrenia (1908)." *American Journal of Psychiatry* 165, no. 11 (November 2008): 1407.

Ghaemi, S. Nassir. "The Rise and Fall of the Biopsychosocial Model." *British Journal of Psychiatry* 195, no. 1 (July 2009): 3–4.

Ghaemi, S. Nassir. *The Rise and Fall of the Biopsychosocial Model: Reconciling Art and Science in Psychiatry*. Baltimore: Johns Hopkins University Press, 2009.

Ghazālī, al-. *The Faith and Practice of Al-Ghazālī*. Translated by W. Montgomery Watt. Oxford: Oneworld, 1994.

Giles, Lionel. *Musings of a Chinese Mystic*. London: John Murray, 1906.

Giorgi, Amedeo. "The Crisis of Humanistic Psychology." *Humanistic Psychologist* 15, no. 1 (1987): 5–20.

Glass, Marty. *Yuga: An Anatomy of Our Fate*. Hillsdale, NY: Sophia Perennis, 2004.

Glassé, Cyril. *The New Encyclopedia of Islam*. Rev. ed. Walnut Creek, CA: AltaMira, 2002.

Glenmullen, Joseph. *Prozac Backlash: Overcoming the Dangers of Prozac, Zoloft, Paxil, and Other Antidepressants with Safe, Effective Alternatives*. New York: Touchstone, 2001.

Goddard, Dwight, ed. *A Buddhist Bible*. Boston: Beacon, 1994.

Godman, David, ed. *Be As You Are: The Teachings of Sri Ramana Maharshi*. New York: Arkana, 1985.

Grof, Stanislav. *Psychology of the Future: Lessons from Modern Consciousness Research*. Albany: State University of New York Press, 2000.

Guénon, René. *The Crisis of the Modern World*. Translated by Arthur Osborne, Marco Pallis, and Richard C. Nicholson. Hillsdale, NY: Sophia Perennis, 2004.

Guénon, René. *The Great Triad*. Translated by Henry D. Fohr. Edited by Samuel D. Fohr. Hillsdale, NY: Sophia Perennis, 2004.

Guénon, René. *Introduction to the Study of the Hindu Doctrines*. Translated by Marco Pallis. Hillsdale, NY: Sophia Perennis, 2004.

Guénon, René. *Man and His Becoming According to the Vedānta*. Translated by Richard C. Nicholson. Hillsdale, NY: Sophia Perennis, 2004.

Guénon, René. *Miscellanea*. Translated by Henry D. Fohr, Cecil Bethell, Patrick Moore, and Hubert Schiff. Hillsdale, NY: Sophia Perennis, 2001.

Guénon, René. *Perspectives on Initiation*. Translated by Henry D. Fohr. Edited by Samuel D. Fohr. Ghent, NY: Sophia Perennis, 2001.

Guénon, René. *The Reign of Quantity and the Signs of the Times*. Translated by Lord Northbourne. Ghent, NY: Sophia Perennis, 2001.

Guénon, René. *The Symbolism of the Cross*. Translated by Angus Macnab. Hillsdale, NY: Sophia Perennis, 2001.

Hahn, Lewis Edwin, Randall E. Auxier, and Lucian W. Stone Jr. *The Philosophy of Seyyed Hossein Nasr.* Chicago: Open Court, 2001.

Hakuin Ekaku. *The Essential Teachings of Zen Master Hakuin.* Translated by Norman Waddell. Boston: Shambhala, 1994.

Hakuin Ekaku. *The Zen Master Hakuin: Selected Writings.* Translated by Philip B. Yampolsky. New York: Columbia University Press, 1971.

Hall, G. Stanley. *The Founders of Modern Psychology.* New York: D. Appleton, 1912.

Hamilton, Edith, and Huntington Cairns, eds. *The Collected Dialogues of Plato.* Princeton, NJ: Princeton University Press, 1980.

Harper, Robert S. "The First Psychological Laboratory." *Isis* 41, no. 2 (July 1950): 158–61.

The Heart of Awareness: A Translation of the Ashtavakra Gita. Translated by Thomas Byrom. Boston: Shambhala, 1990.

Heraclitus. *Heraclitus.* Translated by Philip Wheelwright. Princeton, NJ: Princeton University Press, 1959.

Herlihy, John. *Wisdom of the Senses: The Untold Story of Their Inner Life.* San Rafael, CA: Sophia Perennis, 2011.

Heruka, Tsangnyön. *The Life of Milarepa.* Translated by Andrew Quintman. New York: Penguin, 2010.

Hesiod. *The Homeric Hymns and Homerica.* Translated by Hugh G. Evelyn-White. London: William Heinemann, 1920.

Higgins, Gina O'Connell. *Resilient Adults: Overcoming a Cruel Past.* San Francisco: Jossey-Bass, 1994.

Hippocrates. *Hippocrates.* Vol. 2. Translated by W. H. S. Jones. New York: G. P. Putnam's Sons, 1923.

The Holy Bible, King James Version. Philadelphia: National Bible Press, 1944.

Hopper, Kim, and Joseph Wanderling. "Revisiting the Developed Versus Developing Country Distinction in Course and Outcome in Schizophrenia: Results from ISoS, the WHO Collaborative Followup Project." *Schizophrenia Bulletin* 26, no. 4 (2000): 835–46.

Horner, Isaline B. "Attā and Anattā." *Studies in Comparative Religion* 7, no. 1 (Winter 1973): 31–35.

Hui Neng. *The Platform Scripture: The Basic Classic of Zen Buddhism.* Translated by Wing-tsit Chan. Jamaica, NY: St. John's University Press, 1963.

Hujwīrī, ʿAlī B. ʿUthmān Al-Jullābī al-. *The Kashf al-Maḥjub: The Oldest Persian Treatise on Sufism.* Translated by Reynold A. Nicholson. London: Luzac, 1911.

Hunter, Richard, and Ida Macalpine. *Three Hundred Years of Psychiatry, 1535–1860: A History Presented in Selected English Texts.* New York: Oxford University Press, 1963.

The Hymns of the R̥gveda. Translated by Ralph T. H. Griffith. Edited by J. L. Shastri. Delhi: Motilal Banarsidass, 1999.

Ibn ʿArabī. *The Bezels of Wisdom.* Translated by R. W. J. Austin. New York: Paulist, 1980.

Ibn ʿArabī. *The Wisdom of the Prophets (Fusus al-Hikam).* Translated by Titus Burckhardt and Angela Culme-Seymour. Gloucestershire, UK: Beshara, 1975.

Insel, Thomas. *Healing: Our Path from Mental Illness to Mental Health.* New York: Penguin, 2022.

Institute of Health Metrics and Evaluation (IHME). Global Health Data Exchange (GHDx). Accessed July 7, 2025. https://ghdx.healthdata.org/.

Izutsu, Toshihiko. *Sufism and Taoism: A Comparative Study of Key Philosophical Concepts.* Berkeley: University of California Press, 1984.

Izutsu, Toshihiko, and Toyo Izutsu. *The Theory of Beauty in the Classical Aesthetics of Japan.* Boston: Martinus Nijhoff, 1981.

Jacobi, Jolande, ed. *Paracelsus: Selected Writings.* Translated by Norbert Guterman. Princeton, NJ: Princeton University Press, 1988.

Jagadguru of Kanchi, H. H. the 68th. *Introduction to Hindu Dharma: Illustrated.* Edited by Michael Oren Fitzgerald. Bloomington, IN: World Wisdom, 2008.

James, Henry, ed. *The Letters of William James.* Vol. 2. Boston: Atlantic Monthly, 1920.

James, William. *The Principles of Psychology.* Vol. 1. New York: Henry Holt, 1913.

James, William. *Psychology.* New York: Henry Holt, 1908.

James, William. *The Varieties of Religious Experience: A Study in Human Nature.* New York: Penguin, 1982.

Jamgön Kongtrül. *The Great Path of Awakening: The Classic Guide to Using the Mahayana Buddhist Slogans to Tame the Mind and Awaken the Heart.* Translated by Ken McLeod. Boston: Shambhala, 2000.

John of the Cross, St. *The Collected Works of St. John of the Cross.* Translated by Kieran Kavanaugh and Otilio Rodriguez. Washington, DC: ICS Publications, 2017.

John of the Cross, St. *The Dark Night of the Soul.* Translated by David Lewis. London: Thomas Baker, 1908.

Jones, Ernest. *The Life and Work of Sigmund Freud.* Vol. 3, *The Last Phase, 1919–1939.* New York: Basic, 1957.

Julian of Norwich. *Showings.* Translated by Edmund Colledge, James Walsh, and Jean Leclercq. Mahwah, NJ: Paulist, 1978.

Jung, C. G. *The Collected Works of C. G. Jung.* Vol. 16, *The Practice of Psychotherapy.* Translated by R. F. C. Hull. Princeton, NJ: Princeton University Press, 1985.

Jung, C. G. *The Secret of the Golden Flower.* Translated by Richard Wilhelm. New York: Harcourt, Brace & World, 1962.

Kanamatsu, Kenryo. *Naturalness: A Classic of Shin Buddhism.* Bloomington, IN: World Wisdom, 2002.

Kapleau, Philip. *Zen: Dawn in the West.* Garden City, NY: Anchor, 1980.

Karamustafa, Ahmet T. *God's Unruly Friends: Dervish Groups in the Islamic Later Middle Period 1200–1550.* Oxford: Oneworld, 2006.

Kavanaugh, Kieran, ed. *John of the Cross: Selected Writings.* Mahwah, NJ: Paulist, 1987.

Keene, H. G. "Omar Khayyam." *MacMillan's Magazine* 57 (November 1887): 27–32.

Kendler, Kenneth S. "Toward a Philosophical Structure for Psychiatry." *American Journal of Psychiatry* 162, no. 3 (March 2005): 433–40.

Klein, Jean. *Be Who You Are.* Translated by Mary Mann. Salisbury, UK: Non-Duality Press, 2006.

Koch, Sigmund. *Psychology in Human Context: Essays in Dissidence and Reconstruction.* Chicago: University of Chicago Press, 1999.

Koch, Sigmund, and David E. Leary, eds. *A Century of Psychology as Science.* New York: McGraw-Hill, 1985.

Kraepelin, Emil. *Dementia Praecox and Paraphrenia.* Translated by R. Mary Barclay. Edited by George M. Robertson. Edinburgh: E & S Livingstone, 1919.

Kriegel, Uriah, ed. *The Routledge Handbook of Franz Brentano and the Brentano School.* New York: Routledge, 2017.

Kuhn, Thomas S. *The Structure of Scientific Revolutions.* Chicago: University of Chicago Press, 1996.

Kulhara, Parmanand, and Subho Chakrabarti. "Culture and Schizophrenia and Other Psychotic Disorders." *Psychiatric Clinics of North America* 24, no. 3 (September 2001): 449–64.

Laing, R. D. *The Divided Self: An Existential Study in Sanity and Madness.* New York: Penguin, 1976.

Laing, R. D. *The Politics of Experience.* New York: Ballantine, 1972.

Laing, R. D. *The Politics of the Family and Other Essays.* New York: Routledge, 2001.

Laing, R. D. "Transcendental Experience in Relation to Religion and Psychosis." *Psychedelic Review,* no. 6 (1965): 7–15.

Lakhani, M. Ali. *The Timeless Relevance of Traditional Wisdom.* Bloomington, IN: World Wisdom, 2010.

Landman, Janet Tracy, and Robyn M. Dawes. "Psychotherapy Outcome: Smith and Glass' Conclusions Stand Up Under Scrutiny." *American Psychologist* 37, no. 5 (May 1982): 504–16.

Lange, Frederick Albert. *History of Materialism and Criticism of Its Present Importance.* Translated by Ernest Chester Thomas. London: Trübner, 1881.

Lao Tzu. *Tao Te Ching.* Translated by Arthur Waley. Ware, Hertfordshire: Wordsworth Editions, 1997.

Lao Tzu. *Tao Teh Ching.* Translated by John C. H. Wu. Boston: Shambhala, 2017.

Laplanche, Jean, and Jean-Bertrand Pontalis. *The Language of Psycho-Analysis.* Translated by Donald Nicholson-Smith. New York: W. W. Norton, 1973.

Larchet, Jean-Claude. *Mental Disorders and Spiritual Healing: Teachings from the Early Christian East.* Translated by Rama P. Coomaraswamy and G. John Champoux. Hillsdale, NY: Sophia Perennis, 2005.

Larchet, Jean-Claude. *Therapy of Spiritual Illnesses.* Vol. 1, *An Introduction to the Ascetic Tradition of the Orthodox Church.* Translated by Fr. Kilian Sprecher. Montreal: Alexander Press, 2012.

Larchet, Jean-Claude. *Therapy of Spiritual Illnesses.* Vol. 3, *An Introduction to the Ascetic Tradition of the Orthodox Church.* Translated by Fr. Kilian Sprecher. Montreal: Alexander Press, 2012.

Laude, Patrick. "Humor, Laughter, Trickster and the Ambiguity of Māyā." *Sophia* 4, no. 2 (1998): 142–69.

Law, William. *The Works of the Reverend William Law.* Vol. 6. London: G. Moreton, 1893.

Lawrence, Brother. *The Practice of Presence of God: Conversations and Letters of Brother Lawrence.* Oxford: Oneworld, 1993.

Levine, Peter A. *Trauma and Memory: Brain and Body in a Search for the Living Past.* Berkeley, CA: North Atlantic, 2015.

Lewis, C. S. *The Problem of Pain.* New York: HarperCollins, 2000.

Lewisohn, Leonard, ed. *The Heritage of Sufism.* Vol. 1, *Classical Persian Sufism from Its Origins of Rumi (700–1300).* Oxford: Oneworld, 1999.

Lindbom, Tage. *The Tares and the Good Grain or the Kingdom of Man at the Hour of Reckoning*. Translated by Alvin Moor Jr. Macon, GA: Mercer University Press, 1983.

Lings, Martin. *Enduring Utterance: Collected Lectures (1993-2001)*. Edited by Trevor Banyard. London: Matheson Trust, 2014.

Lings, Martin. *Shakespeare's Window into the Soul: The Mystical Wisdom in Shakespeare's Characters*. Rochester, VT: Inner Traditions, 2006.

Lings, Martin. *A Sufi Saint of the Twentieth Century: Shaikh Ahmad Al-'Alawī, His Spiritual Heritage and Legacy*. Cambridge: Islamic Texts Society, 1993.

Lings, Martin. *Symbol and Archetype: A Study of the Meaning of Existence*. Cambridge: Quinta Essentia, 1991.

Lings, Martin. *What Is Sufism?* Berkeley, CA: University of California Press, 1977.

Lings, Martin, and Clinton Minnaar, eds. *The Underlying Religion: An Introduction to the Perennial Philosophy*. Bloomington, IN: World Wisdom, 2007.

Locke, John. *An Essay Concerning Human Understanding*. London: William Tegg, 1879.

Lopez, Donald S., Jr. *The Heart Sutra Explained: Indian and Tibetan Commentaries*. Albany: State University of New York Press, 1988.

López-Muñoz, Francisco, Cecilio Álamo, Eduardo Cuenca, Winston W. Shen, Patrick Clervoy, and Gabriel Rubio. "History of the Discovery and Clinical Introduction of Chlorpromazine." *Annals of Clinical Psychiatry* 17, no. 3 (2005): 113–35.

Mails, Thomas E. *Fools Crow*. Lincoln: University of Nebraska, 1990.

Mails, Thomas E. *Fools Crow: Wisdom and Power*. San Francisco: Council Oak, 2001.

Majlisī, Muḥammad Bāqir al-. *Biḥār al-anwār*. Beirut: Mu'assasat al-Wafā', 1983.

Malik, Kenan. *Strange Fruit: Why Both Sides Are Wrong in the Race Debate*. Oxford: Oneworld, 2008.

Martin, Jane, and Frank Margison. "The Conversation Model." In *Integrative and Eclectic Counseling and Psychotherapy*. Edited by Stephen Palmer and Ray Woolfe. Thousand Oaks, CA: Sage, 2009.

Massignon, Louis. *The Passion of al-Hallāj, Mystic and Martyr of Islam*. Vol. 2. *The Survival of al-Hallāj*. Translated by Herbert Mason. Princeton, NJ: Princeton University Press, 1982.

Maté, Gabor, and Daniel Maté. *The Myth of Normal: Trauma, Illness and Healing in a Toxic Culture*. New York: Avery, 2022.

May, Gerald G. *Addiction and Grace: Love and Spirituality in the Healing of Addictions*. New York: HarperCollins, 1991.

May, James V. *Mental Diseases: A Public Health Problem*. Boston: Richard G. Badger, 1922.

May, Rollo. "Existential Bases of Psychotherapy." *American Journal of Orthopsychiatry* 30, no. 4 (October 1960): 685–95.

May, Rollo. "On the Phenomenological Bases of Psychotherapy." *Review of Existential Psychology and Psychiatry* 4, no. 2 (1964): 22–36.

May, Rollo. "The Origins and Significance of the Existential Movement in Psychology." In *Existence: A New Dimension in Psychiatry and Psychology*. Edited by Rollo May, Ernest Angel, and Henri F. Ellenberger. New York: Clarion, 1958.

May, Rollo, Ernest Angel, and Henri F. Ellenberger, eds. *Existence: A New Dimension in Psychiatry and Psychology*. New York: Clarion, 1958.

McDaniel, June. *The Madness of the Saints: Ecstatic Religion in Bengal*. Chicago: University of Chicago Press, 1989.

Mencius. *The Book of Mencius*. Translated by Lionel Giles. London: John Murray, 1942.

Mencius. *The Works of Mencius*. Translated by James Legge. New York: Dover, 1970.

Menninger, Karl, with Martin Mayman and Paul Pruyser. *The Vital Balance: The Life Process in Mental Health and Illness*. New York: Viking, 1964.

Metzner, Ralph. *The Unfolding Self: Varieties of Transformative Experiences*. Novato, CA: Origin, 1998.

Milarepa. *Songs of Milarepa*. Mineola, NY: Dover, 2003.

Mīrābāī. *The Devotional Poems of Mīrābāī*. Translated by A. J. Alston. Delhi: Motilal Benarsidass, 1980.

Moncrieff, Joanna, Ruth E. Cooper, Tom Stockmann, Simone Amendola, Michael P. Hengartner, and Mark A. Horowitz. "The Serotonin Theory of Depression: A Systematic Umbrella Review of the Evidence." *Molecular Psychiatry* 28 (2023): 3243–56.

Montaigne, Michel de. *The Essays: A Selection*. Translated by M. A. Screech. New York: Penguin, 2003.

Montaigne, Michel de. *Essays of Montaigne*. Vol. 2. Translated by Charles Cotton. Edited by William Carew Hazlitt. London: Reeves and Turner, 1902.

Moore, Alvin, Jr., and Rama P. Coomaraswamy, eds. *Selected Letters of Ananda K. Coomaraswamy*. Oxford: Oxford University Press, 1988.

Mumford, Lewis. *The Myth of the Machine: Technics and Human Development*. New York: Harcourt Brace Jovanovich, 1967.

Münsterberg, Hugo. *Psychology and Life*. Boston: Houghton, Mifflin, 1901.

Nakken, Craig. *The Addictive Personality: Understanding the Addictive Process and Compulsive Behavior*. Center City, MN: Hazelden, 1996.

Nasr, Seyyed Hossein. *The Encounter of Man and Nature: The Spiritual Crisis of Modern Man*. London: George Allen and Unwin, 1968.

Nasr, Seyyed Hossein. *Knowledge and the Sacred*. Albany: State University of New York Press, 1989.

Nasr, Seyyed Hossein. *The Need for a Sacred Science*. Albany: State University of New York Press, 1993.

Nasr, Seyyed Hossein. *Religion and the Order of Nature*. New York: Oxford University Press, 1996.

Nasr, Seyyed Hossein. "Reply to Wolfgang Smith." In *The Philosophy of Seyyed Hossein Nasr*. Edited by Lewis Edwin Hahn, Randall E. Auxier, and Lucian W. Stone Jr. Chicago: Open Court, 2001.

Nasr, Seyyed Hossein. *Sufi Essays*. Albany: State University of New York Press, 1972.

Nasr, Seyyed Hossein, and Mehdi Aminrazavi, eds. *An Anthology of Philosophy in Persia*. Vol. 1, *From Zoroaster to 'Umar Khayyām*. London: I. B. Tauris in association with the Institute of Ismaili Studies, 2008.

Needleman, Jacob. *A Sense of the Cosmos: The Encounter of Modern Science and Ancient Truth*. New York: E. P. Dutton, 1976.

Neihardt, John G. *Black Elk Speaks: Being the Life Story of a Holy Man of the Oglala Sioux*. Lincoln: University of Nebraska Press, 1988.

Nelson, John E. *Healing the Split, Madness or Transcendence? A New Understanding of the Crisis and Treatment of the Mentally Ill*. Los Angeles: Jeremy P. Tarcher, 1991.

Nicholas of Cusa (Nicholas Cusanus). *Of Learned Ignorance*. Translated by Germain Heron. New Haven, CT: Yale University, 1954.

Noll, Richard. *American Madness: The Rise and Fall of Dementia Praecox*. Cambridge, MA: Harvard University Press, 2011.

Northbourne, Lord. *Looking Back on Progress*. Edited by Christopher James 5th Lord Northbourne. Ghent, NY: Sophia Perennis, 2001.

Oldmeadow, Harry. *Traditionalism: Religion in the Light of the Perennial Philosophy*. San Rafael, CA: Sophia Perennis, 2011.

Osbon, Diane K., ed. *Reflections on the Art of Living: A Joseph Campbell Companion*. New York: HarperCollins, 1991.

Osborn, Eric. *Clement of Alexandria*. Cambridge: Cambridge University Press, 2005.

Osborne, Arthur, ed. *The Collected Works of Ramana Maharshi*. Boston: Weiser, 1997.

Osborne, Arthur. *The Teachings of Ramana Maharshi in His Own Words*. New York: Samuel Weiser, 1978.

Paden, William E. *Religious Worlds: The Comparative Study of Religion*. Boston: Beacon, 1994.

Pallis, Marco. *A Buddhist Spectrum: Contributions to Buddhist-Christian Dialogue*. Bloomington, IN: World Wisdom, 2003.

Pallis, Marco. *Peaks and Lamas*. New York: Alfred A. Knopf, 1949.

Palmer, G. E. H., Philip Sherrard, and Kallistos Ware, eds. *The Philokalia*. Vol. 1, *The Complete Text; Compiled by St. Nikodimos of the Holy Mountain and St. Makarios of Corinth*. London: Faber and Faber, 1983.

Palmer, G. E. H., Philip Sherrard, and Kallistos Ware, eds. *The Philokalia*. Vol. 2, *The Complete Text; Compiled by St. Nikodimos of the Holy Mountain and St. Makarios of Corinth*. London: Faber and Faber, 1984.

Palmer, Stephen, and Ray Woolfe, eds. *Integrative and Eclectic Counseling and Psychotherapy*. Thousand Oaks, CA: Sage, 2009.

Pargeter, William. *Observations on Maniacal Disorders*. Edited by Stanley W. Jackson. London: Routledge, 1988.

Pascal, Blaise. *Pensées*. Translated by W. F. Trotter. Mineola, NY: Dover, 2018.

Patrul Rinpoche. *The Words of My Perfect Teacher: A Complete Translation of a Classic Introduction to Tibetan Buddhism*. Translated by Padmakara Translation Group. Walnut Creek, CA: AltaMira, 1998.

Peck, M. Scott. *People of the Lie: The Hope for Healing Human Evil*. New York: Touchstone, 1985.

Perls, Frederick S. *Gestalt Therapy Verbatim*. Edited by John O. Stevens. Lafayette, CA: Real People Press, 1969.

Perls, Frederick S. "A Life Chronology." *Gestalt Journal* 16, no. 2 (1993): 5–9.

Perry, Mark. *The Mystery of Individuality: Grandeur and Delusion of the Human Condition*. Bloomington, IN: World Wisdom, 2012.

Perry, Whitall N. *Challenges to a Secular Society*. Oakton, VA: Foundation for Traditional Studies, 1996.

Perry, Whitall N., ed. *A Treasury of Traditional Wisdom*. London: Allen and Unwin, 1971.

Pescosolido, Bernice A., Jack K. Martin, Sigrun Olafsdottir, J. Scott Long, Karen Kafadar, and Tait R. Medina. "The Theory of Industrial Society and Cultural Schemata: Does the 'Cultural Myth of Stigma' Underlie the WHO Schizophrenia Paradox?" *American Journal of Sociology* 121, no. 3 (November 2015): 783–825.

Pieper, Josef. *"Divine Madness": Plato's Case Against Secular Humanism*. San Francisco: Ignatius, 1995.

Plato. *The Dialogues of Plato*. New York: Bantam, 1986.

Plato. *The Dialogues of Plato*. Vol. 2. Translated by Benjamin Jowett. New York: Charles Scribner's Sons, 1895.

Plato. *Gorgias and Timaeus*. Translated by Benjamin Jowett. Mineola, NY: Dover, 2003.

Plato. *Plato: Euthyphro, Apology, Crito, Phaedo, Phaedrus*. Translated by Harold North Fowler. Cambridge, MA: Harvard University Press, 2005.

Plutarch. *Moralia*. Vol. 15, *Fragments*. Translated by F. H. Sandbach. Cambridge, MA: Harvard University Press, 1987.

Po-tuan, Chang. *The Inner Teachings of Taoism*. Translated by Thomas Cleary. Boston: Shambhala, 2001.

Porter, Roy. *Madness: A Brief History*. Oxford: Oxford University Press, 2002.

Quine, W. V. *Quintessence: Basic Readings from the Philosophy of W. V. Quine*. Edited by Roger F. Gibson. Cambridge, MA: Harvard University Press, 2004.

Radin, Paul. *The Trickster: A Study in American Indian Mythology*. New York: Schocken, 1972.

Rahula, Walpola. *What the Buddha Taught*. New York: Grove, 1974.

Raine, Kathleen. *Farewell Happy Fields: Memories of Childhood*. London: Hamish Hamilton, 1973.

Rāmakrishna. *The Gospel of Ramakrishna: Originally Recorded in Bengali by M., a Disciple of the Master*. Translated by Swāmi Nikhilānanda. New York: Ramakrishna-Vivekananda Center, 1977.

Ramana Maharshi. *Talks with Sri Ramana Maharshi*. Tiruvannamalai: Sri Ramanasramam, 1996.

Ramdas, Swami. *The Pathless Path*. Kanhangad: Anandashram, 2014.

Rao, T. A. Gopinatha. *Elements of Hindu Iconography*. Vol. 2, pt. 1. Madras: Law Printing House, 1916.

Read, John. "A History of Madness." In *Models of Madness: Psychological, Social and Biological Approaches to Schizophrenia*. Edited by John Read, Loren R. Mosher, and Richard Bentall. New York: Brunner-Routledge, 2004.

Read, John, Loren R. Mosher, and Richard P. Bentall, eds. *Models of Madness: Psychological, Social and Biological Approaches to Schizophrenia*. New York: Brunner-Routledge, 2004.

Reed, Edward S. *From Soul to Mind: The Emergence of Psychology, from Erasmus Darwin to William James*. New Haven, CT: Yale University Press, 1997.

Reichel-Dolmatoff, Gerardo. *Amazonian Cosmos: The Sexual and Religious Symbolism of the Tukano Indians*. Chicago: Chicago University Press, 1974.

Reps, Paul, ed. *Zen Flesh, Zen Bones: A Collection of Zen and Pre-Zen Writings.* New York: Books, 1989.

Ribur Rinpoche. *How to Generate Bodhicitta.* Singapore: Amitabha Buddhist Centre, 2006.

Rosenhan, David L. "On Being Sane in Insane Places." *Science* 179, no. 4070 (January 1973): 250–58.

Roszak, Theodore. *Where the Wasteland Ends: Politics and Transcendence in Postindustrial Society.* Garden City, NY: Doubleday, 1972.

Rūmī. *Discourses of Rumi.* Translated by A. J. Arberry. London: RoutledgeCurzon, 2004.

Rūmī. *The Mathnawī of Jalālu'ddīn Rūmī.* Vol. 2. Translated by Reynold A. Nicholson. London: Luzac, 1925.

Rush, Benjamin. *Medical Inquiries and Observations, upon the Diseases of the Mind.* Philadelphia: Kimber & Richardson, 1812.

Russell, Bertrand. *Religion and Science.* Oxford: Oxford University Press, 1997.

Rustom, Mohammed. *Inrushes of the Heart: The Sufi Philosophy of 'Ayn al-Quḍāt.* Albany, NY: State University of New York Press, 2023.

The Sacred Books of China. Pt. 1, *The Texts of Taoism.* Translated by James Legge. Oxford: Clarendon, 1891.

Śaṅkarācārya. *Vivekachudamani of Sri Sankaracharya: Text with English Translation, Notes and an Index.* Translated by Swāmi Mādhavānanda. Almora: Advaita Ashrama, 1921.

Śāntideva. *A Guide to the Bodhisattva's Way of Life.* Translated by Stephen Batchelor. Dharamsala: Library of Tibetan Works and Archives, 1992.

Śāntideva. *The Path of Light: Rendered from the Bodhicaryāvatāra of Śānti-deva: A Manual of Mahāyāna Buddhism.* Translated by Lionel D. Barnett. New York: E. P. Dutton, 1909.

Sartorius, Norman, Assen Jablensky, and Robert Shapiro. "Cross-Cultural Differences in the Short-Term Prognosis of Schizophrenic Psychoses." *Schizophrenia Bulletin* 4, no. 1 (1978): 102–13.

Sartorius, Norman, Walter Gulbinat, Glynn Harrison, Eugene Laska, and Carole Siegel. "Long-Term Follow-Up of Schizophrenia in 16 Countries." *Social Psychiatry and Psychiatric Epidemiology* 31, no. 5 (September 1996): 249–58.

Sartre, Jean-Paul. *No Exit and Three Other Plays.* New York: Vintage, 1976.

The Sayings of the Desert Fathers: The Alphabetical Collection. Translated by Benedicta Ward. Kalamazoo, MI: Cistercian, 1975.

Schachter-Shalomi, Zalman Meshullam. *Spiritual Intimacy: A Study of Counseling in Hasidism.* Northvale, NJ: Jason Aronson, 1991.

Schaya, Leo. *Universal Aspects of the Kabbalah and Judaism.* Edited by Roger Gaetani. Bloomington, IN: World Wisdom, 2014.

Schaya, Leo. *The Universal Meaning of the Kabbalah.* Translated by Nancy Pearson. Secaucus, NJ: University Books, 1971.

Schimmel, Annemarie. *I Am Wind, You Are Fire: The Life and Work of Rumi.* Boston: Shambhala, 1996.

Schofield, William. *Psychotherapy: The Purchase of Friendship.* Englewood Cliffs, NJ: Prentice-Hall, 1964.

Scholem, Gershom G. *Major Trends in Jewish Mysticism.* New York: Schocken, 1974.

Schumacher, E. F. *A Guide for the Perplexed*. New York: Harper & Row, 1977.

Schuon, Frithjof. *Esoterism as Principle and as Way*. Translated by William Stoddart. Bedfont, Middlesex: Perennial, 1981.

Schuon, Frithjof. *The Eye of the Heart: Metaphysics, Cosmology, Spiritual Life*. Bloomington, IN: World Wisdom, 1997.

Schuon, Frithjof. *The Feathered Sun: Plains Indians in Art and Philosophy*. Bloomington, IN: World Wisdom, 1990.

Schuon, Frithjof. *Gnosis: Divine Wisdom*. Translated by G. E. H. Palmer. Bedfont, Middlesex: Perennial, 1990.

Schuon, Frithjof. *Gnosis: Divine Wisdom, a New Translation with Selected Letters*. Translated by Mark Perry, Jean-Pierre Lafouge, and James S. Cutsinger. Edited by James S. Cutsinger. Bloomington, IN: World Wisdom, 2006.

Schuon, Frithjof. *In the Face of the Absolute*. Bloomington, IN: World Wisdom, 1994.

Schuon, Frithjof. *Light on the Ancient Worlds*. Translated by Lord Northbourne. Bloomington, IN: World Wisdom, 1984.

Schuon, Frithjof. *Logic and Transcendence*. Translated by Peter N. Townsend. London: Perennial, 1984.

Schuon, Frithjof. *Logic and Transcendence: A New Translation with Selected Letters*. Translated by Mark Perry, Jean-Pierre Lafouge, and James S. Cutsinger. Edited by James S. Cutsinger. Bloomington, IN: World Wisdom, 2009.

Schuon, Frithjof. *The Play of Masks*. Bloomington, IN: World Wisdom, 1992.

Schuon, Frithjof. *Prayer Fashions Man: Frithjof Schuon on the Spiritual Life*. Translated by Mark Perry, Jean-Pierre Lafouge, Deborah Casey, and James S. Cutsinger. Edited by James S. Cutsinger. Bloomington, IN: World Wisdom, 2005.

Schuon, Frithjof. *Roots of the Human Condition*. Bloomington, IN: World Wisdom, 1991.

Schuon, Frithjof. *Spiritual Perspectives and Human Facts: A New Translation with Selected Letters*. Translated by Mark Perry, Jean-Pierre Lafouge, and James S. Cutsinger. Edited by James S. Cutsinger. Bloomington, IN: World Wisdom, 2007.

Schuon, Frithjof. *Stations of Wisdom*. Bloomington, IN: World Wisdom, 1995.

Schuon, Frithjof. *Survey of Metaphysics and Esoterism*. Translated by Gustavo Polit. Bloomington, IN: World Wisdom, 1986.

Schuon, Frithjof. *The Transcendent Unity of Religions*. Wheaton, IL: Quest, 1993.

Schuon, Frithjof. *The Transfiguration of Man*. Bloomington, IN: World Wisdom, 1995.

Schuon, Frithjof. *Understanding Islam*. Bloomington, IN: World Wisdom, 1998.

Scull, Andrew. *Madness in Civilization: A Cultural History of Insanity, from the Bible to Freud, from the Madhouse to Modern Medicine*. Princeton, NJ: Princeton University Press, 2015.

Scupoli, Lorenzo. *Unseen Warfare: The Spiritual Combat and Path to Paradise of Lorenzo Scupoli*. Edited by Nicodemus of the Holy Mountain. Revised by Theophan the Recluse. Translated by E. Kadloubovsky and G. E. H. Palmer. Crestwood, NY: St. Vladimir's Seminary Press, 2000.

Seligman, Martin E. P. "The Effectiveness of Psychotherapy: The Consumer Reports Study." *American Psychologist* 50, no. 12 (December 1995): 965–74.

Seneca. *Ad Lucilium Epistulae Morales*. Vol. 1. Translated by Richard M. Gummere. New York: G. P. Putnam's Sons, 1917.

Seneca. *Dialogues and Essays*. Translated by John Davie. Oxford: Oxford University Press, 2007.

Shah-Kazemi, Reza. *Paths to Transcendence: According to Shankara, Ibn Arabi, and Meister Eckhart*. Bloomington, IN: World Wisdom, 2006.

Shakespeare, William. *King Lear*. Mineola, NY: Dover, 1994.

Shakespeare, William. *A New Variorum Edition of Shakespeare*. Vol. 2, *Macbeth*. Edited by Horace Howard Furness. Philadelphia: J. B. Lippincott, 1873.

Shakespeare, William. *A New Variorum Edition of Shakespeare*. Vol. 3, *Hamlet*. Edited by Horace Howard Furness. Philadelphia: J. B. Lippincott, 1877.

Shakespeare, William. *The Works of William Shakespeare*. Vol. 11. Edited by Sir Henry Irving and Frank A. Marshall. London: Gresham, 1907.

Sheldrake, Rupert. *The Science Delusion*. London: Coronet, 2013.

Sherrard, Philip. *The Rape of Man and Nature: An Inquiry into the Origins and Consequences of Modern Science*. Ipswich, UK: Golgonooza, 1991.

Sherrard, Philip. "The Science of Consciousness." In *Psychology and the Perennial Philosophy: Studies in Comparative Religion*. Edited by Samuel Bendeck Sotillos. Bloomington, IN: World Wisdom, 2013.

Shinran. *The Collected Works of Shinran*. Vol. 1. Translated by Dennis Hirota, Hisao Inagaki, Michio Tokunaga, and Ryushin Uryuzu. Kyoto: Jōdo Shinshū Hongwanj-ha, 1997.

Shorter, Edward. *A History of Psychiatry: From the Era of the Asylum to the Age of Prozac*. New York: John Wiley & Sons, 1997.

Silesius, Angelus. *The Cherubinic Wanderer*. Translated by Maria Shrady. Mahwah, NJ: Paulist, 1986.

Silesius, Angelus. *The Cherubinic Wanderer*. Translated by Willard R. Trask. New York: Pantheon, 1953.

Sinha, Jadunath. *Indian Psychology*. Vol. 1, *Cognition*. Delhi: Motilal Banarsidass, 1986.

Smith, Huston. "Foreword." In *The Three Pillars of Zen: Teaching, Practice, and Enlightenment*. Edited by Philip Kapleau. Boston: Beacon, 1967.

Smith, Huston. *Forgotten Truth: The Common Vision of the World's Religions*. New York: HarperCollins, 1992.

Smith, Huston. *Huston Smith: Essays on World Religion*. Edited by M. Darrol Bryant. New York: Paragon House, 1995.

Smith, Huston. "Introduction." In *The Transcendent Unity of Religions*. By Frithjof Schuon. Wheaton, IL: Quest, 1993.

Smith, Mary Lee, and Gene V. Glass. "Meta-Analysis of Psychotherapy Outcome Studies." *American Psychologist* 32, no. 9 (September 1977): 752–60.

Smith, Wolfgang. "Finding the Hidden Key." In *Rediscovering the Integral Cosmos: Physics, Metaphysics, and Vertical Causality*. By Jean Borella and Wolfgang Smith. Brooklyn, NY: Angelico, 2018.

Smith, Wolfgang. *Physics and Vertical Causation: The End of Quantum Reality*. Brooklyn, NY: Angelico, 2019.

Smith, Wolfgang. *Physics: A Science in Quest of an Ontology*. 2nd ed. N.P.: Philos-Sophia Initiative, 2023.

Smith, Wolfgang. *The Wisdom of Ancient Cosmology: Contemporary Science in Light of Tradition*. Oakton, VA: Foundation for Traditional Studies, 2003.

Smoley, Richard, and Jay Kinney. "Tradition and Truth: A Gnosis Interview with Huston Smith." *Gnosis* 37 (1995): 30–36.

Songs of the Bards of Bengal. Translated by Deben Bhattacharya. New York: Grove, 1969.

Sophocles. *Fragments*. Translated and edited by Hugh Lloyd-Jones. Cambridge, MA: Harvard University Press, 1996.

Srimad Bhagavatam: The Wisdom of God. Translated by Swāmi Prabhavānanda. Mylapore: Sri Ramakrishna Math, 2015.

St. Arnaud, Kevin O., and Damien C. Cormier, "Psychosis or Spiritual Emergency: The Potential of Developmental Psychopathology for Differential Diagnosis." *International Journal of Transpersonal Studies* 36, no. 2 (2017): 44–59.

Staveley, Lilian. *A Christian Woman's Secret: A Modern-Day Journey to God*. Edited by Joseph A. Fitzgerald. Bloomington, IN: World Wisdom, 2009.

Styron, William. *Darkness Visible: A Memoir of Madness*. New York: Vintage, 1992.

Suzuki, D. T. *Essays in Zen Buddhism, First Series*. New York: Grove, 1961.

Suzuki, D. T. *Zen and Japanese Culture*. London: Routledge and Kegan Paul, 1959.

Suzuki, Shunryū. *Zen Mind, Beginner's Mind*. Edited by Trudy Dixon. New York: Weatherhill, 1995.

Szasz, Thomas S. *The Age of Madness: The History of Involuntary Mental Hospitalization Presented in Selected Texts*. New York: Jason Aronson, 1974.

Szasz, Thomas S. *Karl Kraus and the Soul-Doctors: A Pioneer Critic and His Criticism of Psychiatry and Psychoanalysis*. Baton Rouge: Louisiana State University Press, 1976.

Szasz, Thomas S. *The Myth of Mental Illness*. New York: Harper & Row, 1974.

Ta Hui. *Swampland Flowers: The Letters and Lectures of Zen Master Ta Hui*. Translated by Christopher Clearly. New York: Grove, 1977.

Taylor, Jeremy. *The Rule and Exercises of Holy Dying*. Oxford: John Henry and James Parker, 1858.

Taylor, Thomas. *The Eleusinian and Bacchic Mysteries*. New York: J. W. Bouton, 1891.

Teresa of Ávila, St. *The Collected Works of Saint Teresa of Avila*. Vol. 2. Translated by Kieran Kavanaugh and Otilio Rodriguez. Washington, DC: ICS Publications, 1980.

Teresa of Ávila, St. *The Interior Castle*. Translated by Kieran Kavanaugh and Otilio Rodriguez. Mahwah, NJ: Paulist, 1979.

Theologia Germanica. Translated by Susanna Winkworth. London: Macmillan, 1874.

Thomas à Kempis. *The Imitation of Christ: Four Books*. Translated by William Benham. London: George Routledge & Sons, 1905.

Three Greek Plays: Prometheus Bound, Agamemnon, the Trojan Women. Translated by Edith Hamilton. New York: W. W. Norton, 1937.

Tompkins, Ptolemy. *This Tree Grows Out of Hell: Mesoamerica and the Search for the Magical Body*. New York: HarperCollins, 1990.

Torrey, E. Fuller. *The Mind Game: Witchdoctors and Psychiatrists*. New York: Jason Aronson, 1983.

Torrey, E. Fuller, and Judy Miller. *The Invisible Plague: The Rise of Mental Illness from 1750 to the Present*. New Brunswick, NJ: Rutgers University Press, 2007.

Toulmin, Stephen, and David E. Leary. "The Cult of Empiricism in Psychology, and Beyond." In *A Century of Psychology as Science*. Edited by Sigmund Koch and David E. Leary. New York: McGraw-Hill, 1985.

Tripura Rahasya: The Secret of the Supreme Goddess. Translated by Swami Sri Ramanananda Saraswathi. Bloomington, IN: World Wisdom, 2002.

Trungpa, Chögyam. "Commentary." In *The Tibetan Book of the Dead: The Great Liberation Through Hearing in the Bardo*. Translated by Francesca Fremantle and Chögyam Trungpa. Boston: Shambhala, 1987.

Trungpa, Chögyam. *The Myth of Freedom and the Way of Meditation*. Edited by John Baker and Marvin Casper. Boston: Shambhala, 1988.

Trungpa, Chögyam. *Transcending Madness: The Experience of the Six Bardos*. Edited by Judith L. Lief. Boston: Shambhala, 1992.

Tsong-Kha-Pa. *The Great Treatise on the Stages of the Path to Enlightenment*. Vol. 1, *Lam Rim Chen Mo*. Ithaca, NY: Snow Lion, 2000.

Uddhava Gita, or The Last Message of Shri Krishna. Translated by Swāmi Mādhavānanda. Calcutta: Advaita Ashrama, 1971.

The Upanishads. Translated by Juan Mascaró. London: Penguin, 1965.

The Upanishads. Vol. 4. Translated by Swāmi Nikhilānanda. New York: Harper & Brothers, 1959.

US Department of Health and Human Services. *Mental Health: A Report of the Surgeon General*. Rockville, MD: US Department of Health and Human Services, Substance Abuse and Mental Health Services Administration, Center for Mental Health Services, National Institutes of Health, National Institute of Mental Health, 1999.

Ustinova, Yulia. *Divine Mania: Alteration of Consciousness in Ancient Greece*. London: Routledge, 2018.

Uždavinys, Algis, ed. *The Heart of Plotinus: The Essential Enneads*. Bloomington, IN: World Wisdom, 2009.

Valenstein, Elliot S. *Blaming the Brain: The Truth About Drugs and Mental Health*. New York: Free Press, 1988.

van der Kolk, Bessel A. *The Body Keeps the Score: Brain, Mind, and Body in the Healing of Trauma*. New York: Penguin, 2014.

van Gennep, Arnold. *The Rites of Passage*. Translated by Monika B. Vizedom and Gabrielle L. Caffee. Chicago: University of Chicago Press, 1975.

Voegelin, Eric. *The New Science of Politics: An Introduction*. Chicago: University of Chicago, 1952.

Wampold, Bruce E. *The Great Psychotherapy Debate: Models, Methods and Findings*. Mahwah, NJ: Erlbaum, 2001.

Wang, Xiao-Jing, and John H. Krystal. "Computational Psychiatry." *Neuron* 84, no. 3 (November 2014): 638–54.

Ware, Timothy (Kallistos). "Foreword." In *Christianity: Lineaments of a Sacred Tradition*. By Philip Sherrard. Brookline, MA: Holy Cross Orthodox Press, 1998.

Waters, Frank. *Book of the Hopi: The First Revelation of the Hopi's Historical and Religious Worldview of Life*. New York: Penguin, 1977.

Watson, John B. *Behaviorism*. New York: W. W. Norton, 1970.

Watson, John B. "Behaviorism—the Modern Note in Psychology." In *The Battle of Behaviorism: An Exposition and an Exposure*. By John B. Watson and William MacDougall. New York: W. W. Norton, 1929.

Watson, John B. *Psychology from the Standpoint of a Behaviorist*. Philadelphia: J. B. Lippincott, 1924.

Watson, John B., and William MacDougall. *The Battle of Behaviorism: An Exposition and an Exposure*. New York: W. W. Norton, 1929.

Weil, Simone. *First and Last Notebooks*. Translated by Richard Rees. London: Oxford University Press, 1970.

Weil, Simone. *Gravity and Grace*. Translated by Emma Crawford and Mario von der Ruhr. New York: Routledge, 2002.

Welwood, John, ed. *Awakening the Heart: East/West Approaches to Psychotherapy and the Healing Relationship*. Boston: New Science Library, 1985.

Westaway, F. W. *Scientific Method: Its Philosophical Basis and Its Modes of Application*. London: Blackie & Son, 1931.

Whorf, Benjamin Lee. *Language, Thought, and Reality: Selected Writings of Benjamin Lee Whorf*. Edited by John B. Carroll. Cambridge, MA: Massachusetts Institute of Technology, 1998.

Williams, D. C. "The New Eclecticism." *Canadian Journal of Psychology* 8, no. 3 (September 1954): 113–24.

World Health Organization (WHO). *World Mental Health Report: Transforming Mental Health for All*. Geneva: World Health Organization, 2022.

Writings from the Philokalia: On Prayer of the Heart. Translated by E. Kadloubovsky and G. E. H. Palmer. London: Faber and Faber, 1977.

Wu, John C. H. *The Golden Age of Zen: Zen Masters of the T'ang Dynasty*. Bloomington, IN: World Wisdom, 2003.

Wundt, Wilhelm. "Psychology's Struggle for Existence: Second Edition, 1913." Translated by J. T. Lamiell. *History of Psychology* 16, no. 3 (August 2013): 197–211.

Yalom, Irvin D. *Existential Psychotherapy*. New York: Basic, 1980.

Yalom, Irvin D. *Love's Executioner: And Other Tales of Psychotherapy*. New York: Basic, 2012.

Yogananda, Paramahansa. *Autobiography of a Yogi*. Los Angeles, CA: Self-Realization Fellowship, 1977.

Yōtaku, Bankei. *Unborn: The Life and Teachings of Zen Master Bankei, 1622-1693*. Translated by Norman Waddell. New York: North Point, 2000.

Zhūangzi (Chuang Tzu). *Chuang Tzu: Basic Writings*. Translated by Burton Watson. New York: Columbia University Press, 1996.

Zilboorg, Gregory. "Rediscovery of the Patient: An Historical Note." In *Progress in Psychotherapy*. Edited by Frieda Fromm-Reichmann and Jacob L. Moreno. New York: Grune & Stratton, 1956.

The Zohar. Vol. 1. Translated by Harry Sperling and Maurice Simon. New York: Soncino, 1984.

Index

Ramdas, Swami, 81
Reality, 3, 8, 16, 23, 25, 28, 38, 43, 49, 63–
 65, 84, 87, 91, 96, 107
rebirth. *See under* birth
Reil, Johann Christian, 61
Renaissance, the, 8–9, 12, 22, 53, 68, 88
Rinpoche, Patrul, 35
Roszak, Theodore, 17
Rūḥ (Spirit), 15, 33
Rūmī, 22, 45, 50, 52, 60, 62, 77, 81–82, 84,
 89, 97
Rush, Benjamin, 67
Russell, Bertrand, 17

sacrifice, 40, 51, 87, 97, 105
sahw (sobriety), 84
samādhi (ecstasy), 63, 85
Samsāra, 34, 37, 63, 74, 79–80, 97
Śāntideva, 35, 81
Sartre, Jean-Paul, 45
Satcher, David, 67
Schimmel, Annemarie, 105
schizophrenia, 58, 68
Schuon, Frithjof, 16, 26, 28, 40, 51, 95
scientia sacra, 8
Scientific Revolution, the, 8, 12, 68
scientism, 2, 6, 9, 17–18, 26
Self (*Ātmā*). See *Ātmā*
Seneca, 93, 100
Shakespeare, William, 49–50, 58
Shamanic tradition, 15, 20, 61, 72, 90,
 99
Shankara, 21, 34
Sherrard, Philip, 14, 21
Shiblī, 63
Shinran, 85, 93
Shiva, 35, 62
Shorter, Edward, 67
Silesius, Angelius, 51, 108
Simeon the New Theologian, St., 106
sin, 36–38, 53, 87, 92
Sinha, Jadunath, 16
ṣirāṭ al-mustaqīm, al-, 93
Skinner, B. F., 10
Smith, Huston, 18, 73
Smith, Wolfgang, 14
Socrates, 59, 77, 100
Sophocles, 102

soul: and birth, 34; and consciousness,
 22, 40; and death, 101, 105; and the
 Great Spirit, 15, 51; human, 23, 31, 33,
 38, 50, 54, 59, 76–77, 79, 87–88, 102;
 phren, 58; and psychology, 2, 5–6, 13,
 61; science of the, 3, 7, 14, 24, 26, 28–
 29, 41, 43, 46, 60–61, 64, 66, 75, 78, 89,
 92, 94–95, 109–10; and suffering, 44,
 47, 49, 91
Soul-theory, 13
Spirit: born of the, 105–6; centrality of,
 10, 28, 76; cutting off from, 45–46, 79;
 and death, 103, 108; and ego, 34; first
 thing created by God, 32–33; Great,
 15, 23, 38–39, 51, 82, 99; Holy, 32;
 indwelling connection to, 53, 66; and
 madness, 77; and modern psychology,
 13; realm of, 22, 31, 75; *Rūḥ*, 33; and
 scientism, 18; synonymous with Intellect, 47; and the temporal cycle, 74;
 tripartite structure, 7, 17, 20, 23, 31,
 33, 46, 50, 54, 59
spiritual domain, 13, 19, 60, 73
Spiritus, 15, 84
Śrīmad Bhāgavatam, 87
Staveley, Lilian, 52
Stobaeus, 101
subject-object cleavage, 18, 46
subsistence (*baqā'*), 107
substance abuse, 79, 83–84, 90, 94
Sufism, 6, 84, 105
suicide, 1, 34, 38–40
sukr (intoxication), 84
Sun Dance, the, 90
Supreme Identity, 7, 21, 28, 97
Suzuki, Shunryū, 96
Syncletica, 52

tabula rasa, 11
tajallī (theophany), 30–31, 33
Taoism, 22, 31–32, 35, 46, 49–50, 97
Tao Te Ching, 50
Tawḥīd (Divine Unity), 36–37
Teresa of Ávila, St., 44, 55, 70, 85
theia mania (Divine Madness), 60–63, 77
theomorphism, 14, 22, 26, 33, 53, 88, 90
theophany, 30–31, 33
therapy, 2, 10, 44, 59, 75, 110